A SPIRITUAL RE-AWAKENING

THE DANCE
of the GOBLINS

1. THE HUMAN CONDITION.

James Alan Conlan

RYEHILL PUBLICATIONS

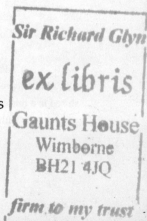

Ryehill Publications
O'Brien's Bridge
Co. Clare
Republic of Ireland

First published in Ireland by
Ryehill Publications 1997
987654321

ISBN 1 902136 00 4

Cover painting by Denise Ryan

Printed and bound in Ireland

EPIGRAPH

'I' am enthroned in the hearts of all; memory, perception and their loss come from 'Me'. 'I' am verily that which has to be known by all the scriptures. 'I', indeed, am the inspirer of their highest wisdom and the knower of their truth.

Bhagavad-Gita, XV, 15.

CONTENTS

How many men and women have looked at their lives, their relationships and their self? How many are able to do so and recognise what is rather than what they want or, perhaps, what they think others see?

It is an intimidating prospect, one that threatens to expose our selfishness and demolish the uneasy truce we have with our fears. It is also a task for which we are poorly equipped. Our usual tools for revealing the truth, our reason and experience, stand in the way offering at best limited description.

Alan Conlan has looked at his life, his relationships and self. As you read his book and judge him ask yourself whether or not you are as willing or better able to undergo such an examination. Then ask yourself if you would be willing to share it with all those you love and hold dear.

Patrick Rooney
Crete

PREFACE

FOREWORD

Welcome ashore from the seas of turbulence, from the incessant confusion of our discursive minds and let us take a reprieve from the ceaseless bashing from our recurring waves of thinking. Let us open our hearts to a clearer understanding so we might come to see our limitations, to see how we seem to be locked up in ourselves in our insular capsules of assumed individuality being endlessly tossed on the oceans of fear and desire with the dark clouds of ignorance perpetually swooping upon us.

We are about to partake on an open excursion into the mystery of our being and of all of us stepping on board this plane of infinite speed there may be but a few who will make it to the journey's end. So be aware my friend of what is about to unfold. We are perched on the pinnacle of time and existence perceived is circling out from where we are at this moment now and spreading its radians beneath us. This is the vortex, so to speak and we all together as one are the eye, like the eye of the tornado as it sweeps through all in the path of its erratic, swirling chaos yet retaining a relative calm in its own heart-centre.

The questions arising as we enter this voyage may be more than disturbing as the psychological image of ourselves vainly battles against the tidal wave of truth. We are about to challenge all that we perceive ourselves to be and to all our beliefs of convenience we adopt to sustain the illusions that we endeavour to uphold. This is transcending the walls of our limitations. We are flickering into another realm of consciousness reflecting through matter that may not have been part of our scene before. For our mental comprehension is nothing other than the collection of thoughts consisted therein, the accumulating past as the vapour of 'now' shooting through time and forever the psychological phantom of the 'has been'. This is where our psychological selves abide in mental congestion endlessly trying to unravel the secrets of life through the intellectual analysis of shadows. These shadows are the mental chattering of thoughts cascading on thoughts as our daily scourge of programmed robotic opinions continuously super-imposing. Each of us think we are individual. Perhaps we are only the fodder for this humanised robotic chain of convulsion forever in the retch outside of itself.

Yet it is only through the individual in the factual 'now' that one can attain to the truth of one's being. This cannot be fully visualised from within the psychological world of rational logic where we live through our minds. The brave-heart who is ready to move into this voyage of discovery, who is ready to step out of this quagmire of thinking, may come to realise the truth through discarding the false thus dissolving the psychological world of the self.

This search for the truth is to take us out of the vortex of spinning and in through the eye of the tornado, to the other side as a manner of expression. It is a journey through the eye of the energy field that is the stillness of the inner 'I' of each of us on this discovery, to a place that is more than familiar yet alien to all our rational assumptions where our walls of ignorance abide. With the speed of consciousness beyond that of light the unidentified objects we are likely to encounter may be seen as little other than our own reflection in the infinite space within. We are likely to discover that outer space is but a reflection of the inner when seen through the sensory body as we look out through the matter of ourselves at the numerous stars of the brilliant night sky. Our history of mankind to date is expressed through our minds of accumulating memory in analytical pursuit of the reflections arising from the spinning of this materialising world of our own rationality. This rationality seems to be endlessly rationalising itself? The Athenian wheel seems to have spun us full circle through all our scientific processing of matter and the proposition being made is that we are now on the threshold of realisation that the stars of the night are but the reflection of the inner realm of ourselves. On our outward haste away from our centre, even when man stepped onto the moon, it was but another footprint of the density of matter expressing the density of self slipping out of the 'I' of our being. Our process of thinking that we take to be truth keeps us avoiding this point. Yet the mind is all that we apparently have, be it the cause of our illusion or not. We must look at the nature of the mind if we are to discover how we can possibly unravel ourselves as we work our way back through the void to that point where it all appears to have found its beginning as the notional flash, the scientific 'Big Bang'.

This perpetual dream of living through the analytical processing of matter should not be other than the cosmic nature we are. Yet 'other' it is in every expression of life we seem to perceive. It is so that we are notionally locked outside of ourselves in our world of beginning and ending. We have fallen away from the truth of our being having created this world of our making where each of us individually fight for our own particular illusory space. This is our place of commencing this voyage that we, you and I, are about to partake in together, this voyage beyond the limitations of mind that keep us impaled on the spikes of recurrence while chasing our illusionary dreams. We are submerged through indulgence in the objectification of truth as being 'other' than whatever is doing the perceiving through these eyes of matter that each of us personally take as our own.

Let us partake in the unfolding of this knowledge that is ours to inherit as you take the key of my lock and make an imprint for yours. For all our locks are one and the same that are made from ignorance re-birthing itself through this mental addiction that we, like our forebears, take to be real. Should we remain endlessly enslaved to this falsehood of self? Must we forever accept this consensual sleep? We need to discover a clearer space where we can impartially look at the conditioned state of our rationally programmed and religious, scientific minds.

Let us stand apart and alert with clear attention and no thoughts arising. If this is to be a journey beyond the velocity of light then must we not travel with nothing as nothing? For even the weight of one thought is all that it takes to bring one crashing again back into the seas of confusion surrounding oneself. So what is about to unfold through the inner side of one's being is the first realisation of clearing the way for this journey to commence.

But let us be aware, for as truth gifts us her secrets out into our place in existence then the truth of the self can never again be denied. What becomes known can never again be unknown and you may suddenly realise that you alone are the 'I', the only 'I' in all the creation and beyond, the only 'I' to this vortex of life. Let us open our hearts with no holding on to the past that is but the contents of limited mind. Let us open our hearts with freedom from our usual barrage of thinking so we may come to a clearer vision as to the truth of ourselves.

Alan

INTRODUCTION

Monday, 22nd July 1996

It is now. From this space, this moment, I am, this condition, this human condition. All that is being revealed to me, through me, I give to you, for mine is an open place, transparent, no hidden agendas, personal secrets, or any other crippling agent that has been my past now dissolved. From this space within I am posing the challenging question, Who am I?

In the enormous haste and spinning of living through life's intellectual confusion have you ever stopped, I mean totally stopped, to a place of absolute stillness within and allowed such a challenging question to be posed from the depth of your being? Well this is exactly what I have done and, as a result, my life and everything I assumed it to be has exploded. How did this come about? Well, only if you are ready to face the truth should you venture further, for this is a journey into the terror of the inner self, the most extraordinary adventure of all.

What is truth? One may ask? We can explore many definitions but the bottom line will inevitably bring us to the realisation that truth can only be understood by demonstration in the moment in one's own experience. Then the questions arise; Who or what is doing the experiencing? Who is this person I consciously take myself to be? Who is it tasting the food I put in my mouth while the mind is lost in some fearful or fanciful thought that has nothing to do with the tasting? Who is it? I ask?

The nearest we can get to the answer of the first question, 'Who am I', is an initial acceptance that I exist. This I, whoever or whatever I am, may be expressed as the sum total of all the programming and conditioning the person in this body has been exposed to, up to this moment in time. In other words, I am the current expression of the human condition. This condition arises through my

10

ignorance. When looking at the past it is easy to accept mankind's limitations in knowledge expressed through ignorance, ignorance meaning the ignoring of the immediate truth in each experience unfolding itself to the fuller understanding, which is the food of consciousness denied, thus causing our repetitive state in weaving and spinning this vortex of time. For example, if it were now the sixteenth century, I would be working and making my assumptions from within the defined parameters of that era. This begs the question when we openly look at our past constraints: Are we yet naive enough to assume that we have really progressed beyond these ongoing restrictions we seem to keep imposing upon ourselves?

In an effort to open this challenge, 'Who am I', further I am making a conscious decision to avoid theoretical argument. Indeed, through the myriad forms outside of ourselves there is, I am sure, more than sufficient literature from varying disciplines relating to the question in terms of theories. My approach is purely practical and taken from my own experience for it is only through this body that life can be truly known to me, as it is with you in your body now reading. All life outside of this body are but forms of life through which I can never experience the earthly truth in taste, touch, sight, hearing or smell but only know it as a reflection of life immediate in me where I am life in this body right now. This is a basic recognizable fact. In other words we are about to enter a journey of participant observation, the object being 'I', as in you, this one universal 'I', as observer, observing and observed. The proposition I pose is that truth is in the moment, and in order to have any real understanding of truth one must first have found the answer to the initial question 'Who am I' as in the wholeness of life, and not as a conceptualisation. This question is other than asking my name, I am man, as in woman or man, or other such notions of answers coming from the programmed, conditioned and limited mind. We need to allow an expansion to happen beyond these limitations before the initial awakening occurs. This is the first great difficulty, particularly if I am the possessor of a highly educated brain in worldly matters and locked firmly in the assumption that I know it all, or at least know more than enough. I can easily check to see if I am in this state by merely paying attention to myself when I speak to others, seeing how I speak, and where I seem to be coming from when I am speaking. This can be done by paying attention, I mean real attention, as an observer from another place, other than my usual rational thinking self.

And who is this 'I' that I continuously use when addressing myself? Let us examine it together, you and I, and not just conceptually, but attentively, in a manner that we may not have used before. Being purely logical when I look at this 'I', I am to discover that there is only one 'I' ever in my own experience where I am in this body right now. Everyone else born or not yet born is a 'you'. This 'I' is the 'I' that is in me writing these words, as it is also the 'I' in you now reading. 'I' am universally alone. Is this not a basic truth? When you check it out in your own experiencing is there anyone else, ever, you call 'I' apart from yourself?

When this first step is allowed to dawn through the intellect and is meditatively held, it may be followed by an emptiness within, a feeling that 'I' am totally alone. Yet this aloneness is not the loneliness usually felt that keeps driving us out in our perpetual hunger for relationship with others. It is an aloneness more like a silence. When one is prepared to enter this silence with this one thought alone of the 'I' within being the only 'I' there is, it will gradually become a door. By remaining in the silence this door inevitably opens and all that needs to be known becomes known, the first dawning of being, the fact that I myself know absolutely nothing. This I have discovered through my own life story unfolding, and observing the devastation of all I had falsely taken as myself. Should yours be other than mine? Let us discover.

All the propositions I make are from my own experience.

The answers that have become known to me I propose that you, the reader, should question. I suggest that you take nothing that I say as true that cannot be tested by you in your own experiencing of life within you. This is not theoretical or intellectual, this is the 'I', your 'I', the observer for now. In other words, true understanding can only come from within, within you, as within me, from the centre of all as being of one. So my experience, my awakening, is yours is it not, in another form, another play in the ongoing story of awakening to life? In our context of speaking what is the meaning of this word 'within'? The answer can only come from you actually experiencing the vastness of the inner realm. If you are an earnest seeker, sincerely courageous, and are openly prepared to meet all that the journey unfolds, then let the adventure begin.

But before we enter the journey let us look at a tale of another expression of life but similar, for it is a mystical place, this existence of earth, when we enter through innocence to experience the delight of its dream. For what is this world but a dream of the goblins, the fairies, the leprechauns, who dance the merriment of life as it unfolds itself to those who can hear and understand the tale that it tells much clearer through the innocence of the child. So let us enter also the story of the infant, your story, my story, the story of all, whether we listen or not.

Charlie, a baby sitting in its cot, wonders at all the confusion of the household at large, and the peculiar change in those enormous adults when they stoop to speak with him, with their 'cooing' and 'geeing' and rattling of things in his face. Charlie yawns, or laughs, or cries at the pain of it, his existential entry now made to perform on the stage of these nappy changers in their eagerness to impose their notions on him. There is no turning back in this forest of living surrounding this river of life. And now little Charlie is caught in its current. Will he skim on its surface, safe and secure in the ways of their world? Or will he submerge to check out the depths? Perhaps it depends on the dream.

Let us follow it through, our quest for the truth, in our search for the 'Holy Grail' so to speak, as one of the Knights of King Arthur's Round Table still searching, through timeless to time to timeless again. And let us travel light, with no baggage of past, no rigid beliefs, but just as we are before nappies were put on our minds!

All that I am

All that you see

Is but a reflection of 'Me'

In your Heart it is known to be true

For all that 'I' am

And all that 'I' be

Is but a mirror of You.

Chapter 1
'SHE' FACES 'ME'

It is a cold wet and dark evening. I find myself attending a funeral of a young man whom I have never met. The sister of his wife is a woman very much in my life and this is the reason I am here, among dark clouds, dark faces, young women dressed in black, blackness everywhere. It is an eerie and foreboding moment. The churchbell rings its ominous single chimes with the silent pause between. The coffin enters in a procession of darkness. The church is packed solid with bodies and I find myself standing alone at the back looking out over this wave of human consciousness, dark in its expression of death.

A 'fire and brimstone' priest rattles off the familiar prayers of prearranged meaningless words, blackness unto blackness flowing into the blackness. Then the dead man's young and beautiful wife arises and faces the people from the alter, and she touches me deeply with the prayers embraced by her heart, she recites from the depths of her pain, in striking contrast to the cold static harshness of the priest who seemed to be frozen in time.

My attention moves to the woman next to her, now rising to speak. There seems to be apprehension in the immediate family, a sense of fear as to what she might say or do. I pick this up from their shifting postures. She rises and walks slowly, yet positively, to the microphone. A silence descends as she turns and faces me and all. She is dressed in black, yet all about her seems to be such light. Her face is shining white, a glow of purity, a gentleness, a beauty yet a fierceness I have never seen before. She pauses. Her stillness permeates the funeral assembly.

She speaks. The body of the man in the coffin is that of her brother. I listen in silence to her quiet yet piercing words until her final quotation from the Holy Book, "Cleanse yourself as you come unto me", causes an explosion within. It is not just the words but the strange energy coming from her voicing the final word 'me', that hits me somewhere below my chest and blows me open, as a dam on a river suddenly exploding.

That is now seven years ago, that awesome experience and I had no idea then that the moment was to change my life completely. Indeed it was not even in my comprehension as to the type of journey I was about to undertake for the gates of heaven were being opened and, before I could enter, I first had to enter hell, this hell of myself, where hell truly is. This is not the place for the weak and the clinging, for the journey to truth is in facing the truth of oneself, as yourself in you, dear reader, whatever the pain, whatever the fear, so be aware.

Four weeks later, as is the custom after a funeral in Ireland, there is a family gathering known as 'the month's mind'. This I find myself unexpectently attending with the sister of the young widow. I am introduced to all the members of the family and sit in their home. It is a most pleasant house of character with many rooms, one with a piano and well-used quality furniture, others with couches, sofas and hard-backed chairs. Photos of family members decorate the walls and sideboards. Unlike most occasions of this nature, there is no gloom but an air of pleasantness instead. The family seem to be celebrating the honour of the presence of the one departed, as the piano is played and his favourite songs are sung in his sweet memory. Tea and food are served and the evening pleasantly winds its way into night. And she is present. There is something awesomely unusual about her as she plays the piano in such a magical way that it brings a shining light into all the faces of the ones who are attentively listening. Yet they seem to hold a nervous respect towards her, from what I perceive, as if some fear is in their hearts. But fear of what, I find myself wondering?

As I am talking with her brothers she introduces herself to me as Mary. My thoughts instantly fly back to a time many years previous when on that one occasion I found myself in the presence of a fortune-teller. She is a woman and she tells me that a woman with the name Mary would change my destiny. My mind is now loaded with this, my own personal baggage of the past loading itself on the moment. I become conscious of the need rising from within me to speak with this woman if only to relate my strange experience in the church. The attraction I am feeling for her is strangely magnetic, beyond anything sexual, as she enters our conversation. It is obvious that she is special and rare by the way she is received by this family, and my desire to understand her I find to be totally consuming.

In Irish folklore there are family members on occasions that are known as 'changelings'. This is said to occur when the fairies carry a baby away and have it replaced by another from some parallel existence. These 'changelings' can be multi-talented and greatly different not only from the immediate family but even from the generation they are born into, so it is said. Yet I am a practical man, and although I enjoy the humour and mystification attached to such tales, I tend to stay with the factual. But this is a challenge. That wild spirit of adventure that has caused me so many times to leap over the edge before looking, resulting in the strangest of consequences, is again triggered within.

I am telling her it is a privilege to meet her as I immediately relate to the experience I had encountered in how her words had reached me from the altar a month previous. I describe the awesomeness of what I heard behind those particular words as she spoke them and how they had pierced right through me as I had stood alone in myself at the back of the church, looking out over the sea of bodies between us. I refer to the calmness in the tone of her voice and her stillness of posture when speaking those words, "Cleanse yourself as you come unto me".

The dialogue opens between us and continues sporadically as she darts to and fro serving all to tea and cakes and attending everyone's needs. I can feel that she is particularly aware of my presence, and the need within me to understand whatever it is I must understand in relation to that strange sensation that had stunned me to silence in her sounding of 'me', and how it seemed as the arrow that she placed in her bow of calmness that evening, then taking aim in her poise, in a split moment immediate pierced open my heart. And the lingering death I found myself entering was that of a wild beast mortally wounded.

All the conversation with the others I am suddenly experiencing as trivial small talk, all rattling along on the surface with much to say about nothing in particular in the light of what I am receiving. As the evening company settles down and the pressure of service eases, Mary approaches my enquiring look. Immediately we are in dialogue about life, about love, about truth, the significance of death, our interpretation of God, in short, the human condition as I would put it. Although she seems to be telling me nothing that I do not already know yet everything she is saying seems amazingly new, and filled

18

with a fresh vitality.

What is truth? Where is truth? "Truth is in the moment, in the now, being true to the situation, and that is only where truth can express itself, in the now, not yesterday, not tomorrow, but only now, right now".

This, she seems to be saying from her exuberance of open heart to give all to me that I am capable of receiving. I try to expand on her wisdom where there is really no expansion in the reality of the dialogue, as she patiently listens to my intellectual rhetoric re-echoing its hollow sound from the insular world of myself.

We are now sitting on the kitchen floor in front of the range as people talk and walk about us. I find myself looking at her beauty, her gentleness, her feet, her fair complexion and fine energy that is radiating to the world so coarse around her. I feel the coarseness in myself, and yet a fineness coming through me that seems to be opening to hers. She seems bursting with enthusiasm to tell me all, to let me know all I must know. I listen and correlate from my own experience and education in this great moment of strange vitality. Then she is asking me about my own importance, and I find myself telling her my immediate story.

I am an Insurance Broker with twelve associates working in my group. In truth I do not know how this came about as it seems to have just happened to me. Here I am in the middle of the life-assurance industry with all these people believing that they are engaged by me, and what a job, selling life-assurance and insurance-related investment products. I entered this field quite by chance after taking a college degree in sociology and European studies as a mature student. The advertisement on the local newspaper read something like, "Are you sports-minded? Would you like a career in sales?" I applied and was suddenly swallowed into the insurance sales mania. The sky is the limit I was told, any desires I may have can be almost instantly fulfiled, this is how it is done. I was swiftly trained in sales techniques, wound up tight like the spring in an alarm clock, and set loose on an unsuspecting public.

The director of the insurance brokerage I had joined, who was then living in Galway, was the proud holder of the European record as having the greatest value of sales in any one month. He had enjoyed this privilege for quite some time, I was told, and his capacity was the shining light, or the carrot, placed in front of all of us. But even to come close to this record did not seem to be in the thinking of anyone in the company. To me it was a personal challenge and at the end of my first full month, I not only broke it, but exceeded it by more than twenty percent. Needless to say the entire insurance industry immediately became aware of my presence.

Now I was their shooting star, and so it continued for the remaining time I was engaged with that company, until I commenced on my own, after being encouraged to do so by the insurance companies competing with one another in their hunger to taste more action. When I succumbed to this, I resigned from the firm and set up as a lone operator. But it was not long before most of the members of the previous brokerage, including the manager of the branch where I had worked, came to join me. Now my situation had all the trappings of Robin Hood and his merry gang. Even 'Friar Tuck' was on the team. The bubble grew from big to bigger and soon we had offices in the city and the provinces. Each month the winding and hype continued with appointed specialists from the insurance companies speaking at our monthly meetings on new products, and new ways of marketing, of forcing ourselves on the public at large.

I had allowed myself to become swallowed, as my mathematical mind showed its agility in a new light creating new formulas as marketing packages. It was excitement and hype, driven on the energy of greed and fear, and more greed. This I was seeing, as I had begun to realise when I was bestowed with trophies at the parties held in honour of my achievements, and when I had been asked to speak to the marketing heads of practically all the insurance companies at a special function given by the brokerage firm in which I had been engaged before I was enticed to go solo.

The head of that firm, from whom I had taken his record, had warned me that knowledge is dangerous, for once the truth becomes known, it can never again be denied, and now it was just beginning to dawn on me that this business I had entered was not all that it seemed. So here I was, a European record holder according to the measure of those about me, in selling life-assurance, and asking myself where was the dignity in this, outside of the supportive hype of all these thousands of people, mostly men dressed up in monkey suits, having given their souls to the insurance industry.

People have held European records in gymnastics, in swimming, in dancing, but me, in life-assurance selling? My God, had my life come to this? Yes, this is what had occurred in my immediate life to date, having been swallowed into this madness directly after leaving college for the second time round. This industry had given me the opportunity to appeasing the ego of this self of myself, by allowing it to shine as the dancing 'King Puck'.

And here I was, sitting on the floor in this country kitchen with this awesomely strange woman called Mary, listening to her oratory of life, of love, of truth, of death, of God and being true to the situation. I was captivated by all she had to say. It was fresh and new in a way that I felt I had always known but never quite seen in the light of her expression as she listened to my story with sympathy rather than elation.

This newness, this richness of truth was exactly what seemed to be missing in my sales group, I was thinking, failing to see it missing in myself. I requested her to be a guest speaker at the next monthly meeting in my world of insurance. She did not say yes or no, but encouraged me to do it myself, pointing out that all I needed was a little guidance to open the channels within. In her enthusiasm she introduced an extract from a magazine written by some wise man, a guru of sorts, and she told me that through him my questions would be answered. I had no immediate interest in that, as I had had my bellyful of marketing gurus, investment gurus, psycho-cybernetic gurus. They all claimed to hold the ultimate answer to their particular ply, but it was Mary, live in the flesh who had become the reality to me now, and not just some other theory of some other self-professed guru to be re-expounded. True, I had listened in awe to all the others, each postulating his wisdom, and swallowed it all. Believing it to be true I put it into practice and discovered that it was not wisdom at all but merely a sham, a cover up for each one's own insecurity. I was in the insurance game, the polished deception, false supported by false, and I was their European champion! No more wise guys for me please! Mary being the breath of freshness, the breath of life itself, the radiance of intellect in the sham existence of the wanton worldliness that I had become and she was telling me to challenge this world myself!

"No Mary, I am not qualified for such a task for I am dealing with the devil in man that I am only beginning to see in my own egotistical nature. It is you who must speak to my group and in turn to the entire financial services industry. With this new dynamic we can get it right. We can be the most exuberant and explosive enigma that ever hit the financial services arena!"

Mary still did not say yes or no as we eventually parted that night but did agree to meet me again. After some abortive attempts we finally met in the city for an early lunch in what seemed to be a vegetarian restaurant. This experience was some distance from the kind of living to which I had become accustomed having been taken out to the most expensive hotels and wined and dined by the marketing managers of insurance companies in competition for my flow of business. Indeed the futility and shallowness of all of it was flooding me now. I had listened to their repetitive stories, themselves convincing themselves of their illusions. Even worse, I myself converted these illusions into a false reality and passed them on to an innocent public. It was as a corridor of mirrors with all of such meetings reflecting the shallow cover being placed over the actual truth of ourselves. In our mutual support of the erroneous world we were thus creating there was scarcely anyone courageous enough to pause and to ponder as to what we were all becoming.

This is what I had become in my life and times as an insurance salesman in the world of money brokerage. I had swallowed the bait as it swallowed me. The industry skillfully trained me into selling myself into greed. Nonetheless, it was no longer able to maintain its mirage in front of my new knowledge. I was now learning faster than the insurance industry could put up its illusions before me. As light is a danger to darkness so I had become, unknowingly, a danger to the sector. Indeed I was a danger to myself, or at least to the image of the super ego I had allowed myself to become.

Mary had ignited something within me that was

DANCE OF THE GOBLINS

evolving an awareness and taking me beyond my apparent limitations. I can only describe it in the exterior as being somewhat like a spacecraft shooting out into space. Now the shallow image of the businessman with manicured nails, neatly pressed suit, shining shoes, matching socks and tie, was fast becoming a diminishing ball of worldly vapour dissolving itself into a ghostly vacuum behind me. The impenitent fat man of elegant dress doing his marketing illustrations was now standing in a transparent suit with naked torso, juggling gut and fleshy roll of obesity. I could not undo what was done, or cease to know what had become known in the light of this new understanding. There could be no turning back now that the grand finale of all that I had mistaken this life to be had finally begun.

The sight of the Holy Grail had flashed in my mind's eye in the darkness of that funeral night when Mary had spoken those words of piercing truth, those words transcending the world of the moving dead and myself being part thereof. This was the beginning of the end for all that I had become in this world of becoming. As this story unfolds, dear reader, the truth may unfold to you, to be heard wherever you are, to your particular hearing. Be aware though, for the truth is the sword of death. And if this time is your time, then enter, my friend. If not, then enjoy the story, and let it be for now, for nothing happens before its time.

Charlie, our friend, was playing in the forest one day. He was not yet seven years old and life was a mystery to him. In one part of the forest three trees made a triangle. Each tree was covered with ivy interlacing together and forming a tepee with just one small opening on the opposite side to the road. No one knew of this place but Charlie. It was his secret domain. He would enter and sit on the soft carpet of dried leaves and converse with his invisible bear. For him this was the teddy bear forest and all the magic of this imaginary world was very real to him, more real than the other world being forced upon him by adults. Here there was no striving, no calling from parents to do this or that. Here all was at ease. Charlie could sit as he pleased listening to the sounds of the silence about him. All the little wild creatures were part of this world where everything seemed to be in a natural harmony, a natural rhythm of life apparently unseen by others.

It had been misting that day and some of the mist was glistening in cobwebs around, on the branches and shrubs that were close to the ground. Suddenly he was stricken in awe, for it was the end of the rainbow he saw. It was rising from the earth beyond the clearing and sending its rays of delight through the most gigantic cobweb he ever had seen, and illumined what looked like a Goddess, a Queen. She beckoned to Charlie through the glistening haze, beyond gorsewood and maize. Such beauty, such magic, never before had he seen, or felt what he felt shimmering through his being. Time entered stillness, as he, for that moment, escaped from its clutches. Charlie was enraptured to the wonderment of this, his first known experience of the unbounded timeless. He sat, frozen to the moment endeared. And then a dark cloud swept over the sun and, suddenly, all disappeared.

Chapter 2

KINGS OF THE DANCE

We were gathered together in immaculate attire for the monthly meeting. The creases in our suit trousers were razor edged, and the ladies in the group were glistening in their layers of facial make-up. Egos reflecting from egos were on an all-time high. The spectacle of dancing through the shadows of reality was about to be performed.

It was a momentous occasion. I was about to be crowned king of the illusive play, the new European champion of all these life-assurance sales-people present. Anticipation of the honour to be passed from the previous holder, my boss and my employer, was high, although the real passing over had happened some weeks previous when I attended his father's funeral in a remote but beautiful part of Donegal.

When I entered the home on that sad occasion and offered him sympathy for his bereavement, I could sense his displeasure with me for taking his record away. It was a double sadness for him even though I had earned a substantial amount of money for his business. It was obvious that sales was his life, and his success the shell built around his own insecurity. Now this shell had been audaciously cracked open, and all of his team, as his mirrors at hand, were reflecting his discomfort within. As for me, I was on my own wild horse and travelling too fast to even notice his pain. I had now been spawned as an insurance salesperson and perched on the highest pinnacle. Through the ego expanding into this new world of

26

becoming I had gone beyond my own self-recognition. Indeed, I was walking on air instead of the ground, through the faces of the many cheering and laughing.

The funeral of my employer's father was held in November of 1987 and October had just been my time of achieving. I had spent September warming myself to the nature of selling life-assurance products and with the arrival of October I was on high speed. This was to be my month of months. By the end of the first week I had nine new cases of business on the books when the average was one per week. My manager was not quite expecting it. He would have been more than content if I merely achieved the honour of salesperson of the month but this first week's business had surpassed the best monthly return ever achieved by that company.

The best, that is, apart from the Managing Director himself who was the European record holder. His team operated in Galway and he and his team were in fierce competition with my immediate manager who was his second contender.

By the end of the second week's business I had surpassed the highest monthly achievement of the manager himself and the insurance world was buzzing with the wild excitement of it all. I was now just two weeks into the month and already over half way to taking the record. Even more exciting was the fact that all of the business I was pulling in for the industry was fresh and new with none of it pre-arranged. My work was in cold calling and immediately following up on any referrals received. Everything was speed. Days were commenced at six in the morning and usually finished at midnight or later. My nights were kept sleepless by planning.

At the time the world markets were at an all-time high. Some of the investment related life-assurance funds were growing at the incredible rate of ten per cent per month. I was right there in the middle of it all, riding on the crest of the highest wave splashing enthusiasm over the exuberant faces of the insurance industry. Then, suddenly, the unexpected happened. It was a Friday morning, and the strong winds blowing in over the east coast of Kent increased in volume, being a response from nature, perhaps, to the apathy of man. By mid-afternoon it was a raging tempest.

Giant trees on the south east coast of England and even in London were uprooted as the wind blew ferociously over people and land. Power lines came crashing to the ground and telephone communications were severed. Even the London Stock Exchange was totally blacked out. This meant that the usual readings were not placed on the lines of frantic financial communications then spinning the global expression of the over-inflated world stock markets.

There was darkness and silence on that Friday afternoon in the City of London as Wall Street, on the other side of the great ocean of confusion, drew back its curtains to welcome its morning sun. The Wall Street computers did not receive their message of assurance from London, as they usually did for each day's trading, and automatically assumed she had sunk. In response the computers, programmed by man, hastily issued the command to sell. Thirty per cent or more disappeared on the values blown up by the frenzy then running at high speed round the world of man's greed from London to New York to Tokyo and back. It was this stage of activity that had been going on for some years that I had just entered to suddenly meet with its final convulsion. I was the seller of the life-assurance products strung to these fields of investment and experienced first-hand the panic driven by fear then circling the globe. When Monday in London arrived and the Stock Exchange opened its doors and switched on its lights the speed of computerised selling was more than bizarre. There are analytical volumes explaining the causes of the stock market crash and indeed the causes are many. But this is how it occurred.

It was if the storm that had uprooted trees and brought the lines of communication crashing to the earth had now entered the system. All were at the mercy of the elements of man's making, triggered by the elements of nature in her service to the equilibrium. Everything is inter-linked it seems, a state blindly overlooked by the financial gurus of mathematical equations. Now on the screens of world trading everything was crashing to the ground. And every ten thousand pounds my eager clients had placed on the markets, through me and my life-assurance products, was now suddenly devalued to seven or less. So what could I do with the situation? I was thinking to myself. I considered the experience I once had when working for a banking institution in London in the late sixties. Here I was an assistant to a currency dealer who had trained us to take advantage of issues. This was how the bank made its profit. We would jump on a currency at its weakest point, in accordance with our training, and then sell it when it would appear to recover.

All that play was closely linked to reading political and economic positions of the time, and even the effects of the weather. Now I was looking at a position of panic selling on the world markets with no one wishing to be buyers. The appropriate response was clear in my vision.

I had to do an about-turn and with this in mind re-visited all the clients of the month to date. These people had placed their nesteggs into the froth of the investment funds through me and my life-assurance products and I sought to re-assure them. The news reports coming at me from the industry advised that the downward spiral would be short-lived and that all would be back to normal in a matter of months. I wrote my first article on the subject in a local newspaper telling people that now was the time to invest, unit prices were at an all-time low and great profits were likely to be made on the return.

This pause and re-assessment took a week out of the month of selling. The previous excitement in the sales office had by now cooled down. There was gloom on everyone's face as all felt that sales would collapse following this terrible turn of the tide. Still, each week a particular insurance company visited our sales office with an on-going video-tape of an Australian marketing guru. This guy was really unique and through the dynamic force of his presentations even the nomads of the deserts would be flocking to buy sand with the last of their life-savings. I listened and absorbed the contents in blind and ambitious enthusiasm. I applied his philosophy to our bewildered situation and I discovered a silver lining in the cloud of despair that had descended upon us. Soon we were back. The show was on the road with even greater hype than before, the new message broadcast the opportunity to catch the markets return, "be on hand for quick profits". We refuelled the deflated egos with this resurgent tempo of greed.

Again, I was on the pig's back and galloping at speed towards the Managing Director's European record. With a few days to spare before the close of business that month I blazed through the psychological barrier it posed and continued in haste to swiftly exceed it by more than twenty per cent. Only at the end of the month when I stopped for a moment to pause, I realised what had been done. I was being hailed the new champion of all and was placed on the shoulders of the industry now possessed by the demon of hunger. But there is more to this than meets the eye. The fading words of the champion dethroned echoed in my ears, "Be nice to them on the way up, you may have to meet them again on the way down". And my answer to this at the time, "Come what may, I will deal with it as it comes". This was the challenge I unwittingly sent out to the Cosmos.

Then the Managing Director played his final card with the financial industry by attempting to sell us all, lock, stock and barrel, to an insurance company that had become acutely addicted to the extraordinary flood of business from his brokerage firm. Here we were, quite saleable indeed, as one of the top performing sales teams in the country. The insurance company, however, fumbled through the clashing of vested interests of roosters within. In spite of its high profile to the public at large the insurance company was unable to make a decision. It may have been the question of the acquisition not being in its immediate budget. Or, perhaps, the decision makers were over cautious as to what they could or could not spend. These are the dilemmas when faced with the marketing of concepts. Indeed, such are the illusions that our conditioning leads us to perceive as wealth. But then, is it not all an illusion dressed up with figures, formulas and equations? Please do not turn on the lights!

In anticipation of the sale we were all given a party and royal stay in a top hotel and sports complex at the foot of the Dublin mountains. Everything was top secret, of course, and the insurance company sponsoring the elaborate spread was obviously trying to measure the cohesion between the members of our group. They knew the game. The strokers themselves were nervous of being stroked.

My friend John, who was at that time doing a masters in political science, happened to be on vacation, and I invited him along. This caused great anxiety as he was a stranger among all the players on the stage of pretence and he oddly appeared to be free of its programming. Thus he was deemed by the insurance company feeding us the alcohol of illusion to be a plant from another company, or a reporter perhaps! Really he was merely there to enjoy the food, the wine and the crack, in short to enjoy the party. Such simple truth, however would not find acceptance in this sweetly sinister dance of deception. The deceivers of all were now turning inward in the game of deceiving themselves. I was their reigning champion.

I forewarned John not to speak or pose questions at the meetings and to keep a low profile lest he be discovered as not being an appointed member of our team. But one cannot hide a lighted candle under a sheet of newspaper and not expect a blaze! He sat still for as long as he could manage yet his mere presence was intimidating. It was obvious even from his appearance that his mind and everything about him was totally free of the directed way of thinking of everyone else in the conference room. When the insurance company's key representative was in the middle of an elaborate illustration, deliberately pausing for a moment for a penetrating effect according to his training, John posed his first question. The question came straight from the intellect. Pure and precise, like a torpedo or scud missile, it blew the presentation to pieces. The presenter floundered. His balloon had been burst. A flash of light entered all of us and revealed the ridiculous nature of the dance. The shutters were off the windows and light was flooding in. It was a direct hit that exposed the hidden agenda of the game. The meeting was hastily closed and strategy two was brought forward. We were all invited to the bar. The real party was about to begin. John had no understanding of what he had innocently succeeded in doing in getting us moving to the lounge, as he asked with his usual enquiring look, "Hey guys, what's cookin"?

My boss and his business partner were sitting aloof, obviously discussing the strategies of the sale, so I approached them and advised that they do it now. As I was not supposed to know their plan, I could not brief them further. A rival insurance company had already offered me an independent agency and I knew I was about to go solo if my achievement was not to be financially acknowledged in their deal. But they had their own plans and were trying to sell the sales-team without our knowledge, or so it seemed. I, their star player, was sitting it out and frantically polishing my diminutive halo feeling excluded from the dealing at hand. And why should I not have been excluded, having been gullible enough to have swallowed everything they had fed me to date?

The Guinness flowed freely into bellies born to take it and even the tightest lips of the bizarre assembly began to open. As the darkness of the night approached the feasting commenced with tantalising tastes and succulent wines. John was enjoying it all and had become a centre of attention at his own end of the table, seemingly oblivious of what he had done. Certainly many tongues were loosened and the entire affray was fast becoming a mid-summers nights dream of sorts. Drunkenness was in abundance but the show was only beginning. John, still a young man in his twenties, fell madly in love with a mature member of the group and spent the rest of the night reciting loving ballads to her bewildered eyebrow.

Many hours passed for others endeavouring to get past the first sentence of profoundly meaningful dialogue. The perpendicular was fast becoming the horizontal as previously elegantly dressed bodies slouched in the most peculiar positions amazingly balanced, even in defiance of Newton. And so it continued, as the thief had stolen the night, until daybreak dawned exposing some of the team scrambling on all fours in search of invisible balls on the adjoining golf course.

Day two commenced. Strong black coffees were the order of the morning. The party members began to resurrect in ones and twos dressed in auxiliary suits, with fresh shirts, socks and ties, and their night's baggage beneath their eyes. As quietly as humanly possible I edged to my seat with the staleness of wine still spinning my head like a buckle in the washing going round and round. The ladies arrived a little later, some looking amazingly fresh while others had put on extra layers of make-up to cover their faces now falling asleep. We were foolishly assuming, it seemed, that a few hours slumber would have been sufficient to patch over a whole night of ravishing our wretched bodies with excessive feasting and drinking. We had gluttonously partaken as the dancing goblins on speed, using our bloated egos for our halos of self approval. Nonetheless, we were all in the one boat, the presenters of the spectacle had also feasted to excess at their company's expense, along with ourselves, the recipients providing acceptable purpose, it appeared, for that wild abandonment of reason.

The conference room was prepared with the tables of plain plywood covered in elegant cloth and joined together to form a semi-circle with corners around the presenter's forum. We were all assigned our places. There was even an emergency nameplate for John who was by now officially acknowledged. Eventually most of us found our arranged positions appearing through the haze of weary eyes. The first presentation began somewhat later than scheduled. Water was in great demand and the waiters in attendance were kept extremely busy refilling the jugs.

Two people were missing. John's seat was ominously

vacant and the lady, the subject his ballads, was nowhere to be found. Few were paying any attention to the presenter as eyes seemed to be focused on John's empty chair. It was obvious from where I was seated that his lack of presence was causing even more anxiety than his actual presence on the previous day. The air of wondering seemed to be in everyone's minds. Even their thoughts were dancing through faces vacated and numbed into frozen assertion.

We were sitting at the edge of a volcano. The presenter bravely continued and included some light-hearted jokes to get the attention of the room moving in his eager direction. Gradually his new illustrations became interesting as he seemed to be playing into the economic field of causal analysis of sorts. Ears picked up and even some questions that would be expected came from the floor, or so it seemed. Most of the questions would have been pre suggested by the presenter to the minds of ourselves too sluggish to know. At last he had us moving along with his opinions, or the opinions of the insurance company he represented.

All was well again and we were merrily being carried along by the current as the pulse of the presenter's world was re-entering our bodies. This insurance man was certainly doing a better job than the presenter on the previous afternoon. We were back on the rails, so to speak. The morning was slowly conjecturing an air of seriousness, of assumed importance, as we were being re-swallowed back into the belief that it was the reality of life we were being offered.

The few who had been totally absorbed, those who had made the insurance industry their one credible god, were beginning to thaw out from the frozen shock of the previous night. Their god, it seemed, was again in control after loosing itself to a night of debauchery. Straight ties were being re-straightened, pens of rolled gold made marks of postulated importance on blank sheets of paper, and wigs were checked for position by the nonchalant touch of fingers, as though gently scratching the bite from an imaginary flea in obliging attendance.

The presentation was now focusing on Japan and the Middle Eastern markets, somewhat outside the league of the assembly but very much in the arena of impressionism being put out by the insurance company. There was no one there to contradict or even challenge the vain of economic interpretation being presented, or the vanity of the presenter presenting.

The entire team were gliding up the marriage aisle until suddenly the doors flew open, and in walked John, unshaven, in the same suit as the previous day but now totally bedraggled, with missing tie and grass on his shoulders. He apologised for his late arrival and hastened to add that he had slept out. From his appearance it looked as if he had been awakened by the mid-morning golfers, he, having mistaken the fairway for his bed. He seated himself on the presenter's vacant chair, which was closest at hand, oblivious to the fact that a special place had been allotted for him with his name-tag on it. No one moved to bring his attention to this as he swiftly devoured two jugs of water before coming to attention. Then focusing hazily on the frozen countenances of all of us present I could feel he was endeavouring to re-enter his senses.

After a long pause of shuffling by the group, the investment analyst continued the presentation. Now he was talking about political influences on the stock markets, a subject directly in the field of John's own course of intensive study. John must have thought he was back among his university peers as he suddenly went into attack with a barrage of challenging questions. The presenter was struck dumb. All eyes were on John as he proceeded to clarify where he considered clarification was needed. Eventually I caught his eye with a 'keep a low profile' look and he suddenly paused in mid-sentence handing the attention back to the deflated presenter with a sheepish grin on his unshaven face. The boss and his business partner of our team smiled amusingly, silently delighted at having their very own analytical guru on the team in the name of John, from wherever he had come. They were probably now considering raising their price, or wondering if they should sell us at all!

There had been much talk about an international sales team of nine having been bought out for nine million pounds. We were all believing it and everyone was up there floating in the clouds. We had the weaponry, even the economic vocabulary; market penetration, exploitation, comparative advantage over the weak. This was the psychology of persuasion disguised as marketing techniques, the indulgence of greed, all creating and feeding the public hunger, fuelled by the excitement of immediate gain or the fear of missing out. We were the puppets of the insurance industry, their ready-made instruments at hand.

Were we to be the mega rich team should this takeover occur, as some of us wishfully believed? But our boss was keeping his cards close to his chest, as he obviously felt he could conclude such a move without open discussion with all of us concerned. And why should it have been any different? Were we not eating his grass as sheep on his Donegal mountains? Was it not his road-show of wild expression that had brought us all to this particular stage of bizarre amusement? Had I myself not given over my integrity in becoming the new European champion of this weird assembly of people perpetually outside of ourselves?

The meeting concluded as it had begun with nobody making a decision. But we did have two days of revelry that undoubtedly boosted the profits of the hotel. Indeed it was the innocence of John, his openness and extraordinary sense of honesty that eventually proved to be the enlightenment of this experience long after I had passed through this suit and briefcase brigade, or should I say, it had passed through me. In crossing this precarious bridge of human utterance amid the rapids of insecurity the clarity of life portrayed through his innocence of expression was at that time a solid stepping-stone that allowed me to pause and ponder in the midst of the human greed then convulsing itself both about and within me. It was an anchor point, perhaps, that was eventually to guide me in the direction of Mary.

Yet here I was to remain for some time, my ego inflated by all the participants of this play and being totally lost to it wantonness. Even the beautiful woman in my life, present before I had entered this circus, had long since departed after I had handed myself over to the glory of its insanity. Somewhere within I was hoping to win her back, thinking it could happen when I eventually decided to go it alone as a solitary broker in what I assumed would be a gentler expression. But her wisdom was purer than that. This was not her realm of acceptance, for hers was the world of a natural honesty ignored in the world of insurance that seemed to have had a peculiar way of instituting its own.

When I opened my first office as an independent broker my intention at that time was to give it a maximum of three years working alone. After that I planned to return to college for post-graduate study. Surprisingly, however, most of the team I had left now came knocking on my door. I opened it and said yes and before I realised what had happened I had won the deal of the moment by apparently walking away with the sales-team of my previous employer at the drop of my hat. The industry saw it as a coup d'etat and my former boss was left with little more than his memories.

And I had no intention of doing any of it! Yet such is how the ongoing play had taken its course. I foolishly considered myself the Director, as we all do perhaps, in our own particular play of life until something occurs to wake us up. If we are lucky, that is, before we are suddenly awakened by the call of death. For this is how it usually is, is it not, when we are so busy dealing with living our lives, that we actually miss life itself.

How wonderful it would have been to sit by the river again with my love by my side, in natural simplicity, sharing a take-away pizza. I suddenly realised that I had abandoned love in itself that is life for this living confusion. And there was no turning back. I had entered the very heart of the world created by man, this world of money and money management. But at least it was becoming my immediate teacher, in showing me first-hand how we are all enslaved in service to it. I had openly allowed myself to be carried away by the undercurrents of its persuasion having believed in its alluring promise of delivering eventual contentment. Yes, I had unwittingly tested it and while others rested I danced to its continuous tune. But was I free as I thought when tasting its lure as it was winding me tighter and tighter into its web and I like the frantic fly about to be devoured by the spider? But then again even hell itself must have its day, and am I not here to be part in all of it? If not, pray tell, then what is it all about? Such questions of personal challenge, such bewilderment was beginning to dance in my mind now spinning at such extraordinary speed that it seemed to be spinning itself right out of existence. And this is the new captain of your ship calling full steam ahead!

Now I had found myself surfing on the tidal wave of other people's dreams, arousing them to live out their fantasies, the sky being the limit. The wizardly financial packages I created were enough to get even the dullest entrepreneurs into exciting and dare-devil action. This was new ground for the insurance industry, a new and expanding market space not previously recognised, or so I naively thought. Here I was leading them in as one of their top performers with a ready-made sales-team on the tail of my coat and without having the personal time to tie my shoe-laces to prevent me from tripping over the speed of myself!

Charlie was chasing a butterfly at the edge of the forest when he tripped over some stones and fell into the stream. He felt the pain as his knee grazed a sharp edge and then suddenly he was eyeball to eyeball with a giant bubble on the waters lapping a stone. It was blue and purple with a whole world inside as it grew bigger and bigger. Charlie was dazed as he gazed at the wondrous sight, as if he was there forever. The bubble grew and grew in its purple and blue until Charlie was moved to touch it.

Chapter 3
'A JOLT FROM THE COSMOS'

It was late afternoon and I was stuck in a traffic jam on the western route through Leixlip. With no movement of wheels I was still anxiously pushing my way to Galway, a city which seemed to keep calling me back. As I busied my mind in reflecting on my situation I wondered what kept calling me to this place in the west coast of Ireland through the different stages of my life.

It was five weeks before my eighteenth birthday when I first entered Galway city as a young student at its university. his was my first taste of its hard stone face and its burning heart of strange energetic fire. The professors and lecturers in the fields of commerce and Irish literature presented a similar rigid appearance, protruding from a channel of thought that was frozen in time. This was the era of the sixties. Nothing had changed since the turn of the century. Intellectual ignorance as expressed through the old school of sophisticated assertion still seemed to be in abundance as the world awaited the student revolution and the dawn of an opening awareness.

To a young man opening into this world the raw energy on the narrow Galway streets appeared explosive and uncontrollably wild yet it held a strange sophistication with an untapped mystery prevailing. The deep historic imprint carved into its rocks was in contrasting harshness to the soft rolling hills of East Clare where I had spent my childhood in harmony with nature. This harmony was expressed in childhood verse that I could still recall at will.

Memories of those early years of innocence flooded into my mind as I impatiently sat in the build-up of traffic in front of me. It seemed that I was still being beckoned by the call of that city even though it had exploded me into sudden adolescence those many years previous. It was apparent to me now that the city was not quite finished with me yet. The monster let loose when relinquishing my innocence was still driving me forward it appeared.

But what was the innocence of heart, my childhood harmony, before it was exploded on those Galway streets? Although I can recall through memory, yet we must not rely on this, for the images coming through memory may be distorted by my current conditioning in mind and body. Is this not the usual case, when we look and assess through our shifting opinions? Is it not so that the message in whatever data we may have at our disposal is tarnished by this conditioned impasse as again and again we fail to meet with the truth of the situation at hand? Perhaps this is how we are forced by ourselves to re-enter our own wheels of anguish, re-living a repetitive past?

In this journey of observation of my own particular adolescence, in our examination of the actual state of the human condition as reflecting through you and I, we are fortunate to have more relevant data than the interpretation of memory recall. Let us look at it through some of my earlier poems. Here we have a window to clearly look through as poetry is the reflection of the state, the inner truth inherent, and the state is our field of enquiry. The state in one's being is all that is permanent, but rarely recognisable through the condition where unfortunately, it seems, most of our psychoanalysis is preoccupied. Within the confines of a conditional world of cause and effect, where we seem to be spending all of our time re-asserting our positions, can we ever hope to see beyond the reactionary robotic nature of ourselves? So let us together unravel our reactionary minds so we can enter this state of being, that we seem to be wilfully burying beneath the human calamity at large in abdication of our true nature.

The following poem passed through me at the ending of my childhood years, before I was absorbed by the wildness:

The silent shadow of the trees
In the early month of June,
Shows solitude in nature's ways
Beneath a glistening moon.
This gentle magic to be felt
From nature in a slumber
Tells how it is supreme to man
In June or in November.
The sight of every bush and tree
And the midnight star above
Bring back the sweetest sounds to me
And tells of every mystery,
Now cherished by my love.

Galway entered me with its wild exuberant expression. There everyone moved at great speed. From my previous place of relative stillness I was suddenly spinning in wild bewilderment. The trees were left un-noticed and people about me were racing through themselves by the sea. So few seemed to be connected with its majestic presence as the insatiable lust for wild living flooded into every space in its perpetual panic to consume.

Even during those rare nights when I decided to sit quietly in my room reading or studying for exams the continuous flow of footsteps passing the window inevitably sucked me out onto the streets and into the crowded pubs of searching souls in omnivorous hunger. There was no escaping it and I eventually became as one with it.

What I seemed to be entering in the outside world was calling to the seed of itself within me. Fighting against it was a battle in vain, like fighting my shadow. My poetry took a different flavour in my asking the reason why:

> Arise my friend from wasted grief
> From suits of solemn black
> Arise my friend from such belief
> Of threading mankind's track.
> To live a life wrapped up within
> Dejecting to the eye
> Leaves you a prisoner to routine
> As youthful years pass by.
> This life it can be sadly spent
> By some as just a show
> While deep within their hearts are bent
> And trapped in suits of woe.
> It is a grief how mortal man
> Sets fruitless flame alight
> For passing pleasures which he finds
> When wrong wrings round to right.

Yes, even at the age of eighteen the human condition in the city of Galway was expressing itself to me then as it still is today, these many years later, like the cities of confusion that are universally harboured within all of us, perhaps. Now its concrete promenade must be over three miles long with people of all ages furiously walking upon it. Few of these people, I notice when I am there observing, actually connect with the sound and smell and sight and touch and the taste of the ocean. Perhaps we are still too busy with our intake of food and stress and the speedwalks to keep our spacesuits in working condition to take time out just to be in

DANCE OF THE GOBLINS

the joy of life. Perhaps we over-consumed in our condition of becoming to even consider who or what we really are.

What is it with Galway city in particular, I ask, that drives people into this speed of urgency? I was swallowed as a youth into its lair of perpetual hunger, but also into its beauty on those odd moments when I paused to savour it. One particular night during a storm I sat by the sea as the great waves washed over me out onto the streets and the rocks by the seashore rolled and laughed. I could feel myself calling it up. I entered the storm that night and sang with its turbulence to the people still sleeping. It was time to wake up and to be at one with this great upheaval of nature in her fiercest beauty. That night when back in my room I wrote in her praise, for she had again connected with me, but in a way not presented to me before, for now she was showing me her fury:

Softly glide Oh Mighty Ocean
From shore to shore spread out thy wings
Show your powers to every nation
To humankind and earthly things.
Raging torrents clashing fiercely
The clouds of darkness soaring nigh
Wives of seamen in anxiety
A mocking sun laughs from the sky.

Rocks and stones on beaches shattered
As rippling waters turn to fury
Screaming winds 'midst seagulls scattered
Survivors with a grieving story.

Down beneath the torrents growling
With rage upheaves each rippling sight
Souls within begin their howling

As grasping wings reach out in might.
Gentle sights their haunches shaking
Lie cold and naked waiting for it
Dogs amazed with aimless barking
At souls they see upheaved upon it.
Mountains raise then they diminish
As swallowed in a gaping valley
Fluxing foam boils to extinguish
The hope of sea-men lost in folly.
Swooping black winds whirling lowly
With shaving sharpness of shark's fins
Waves extruding flung in fury
Then suddenly it ends.

The following morning when making my way through the uprooted pavements to the college I listened with an inner glee to the people moaning at the inconvenience caused to the sullen movement of flesh and bones on feet. And it was me, it had been my night of nights as I had been one with the storm. I was every wave from the fiercely surging sea tearing up these concrete barricades of ignorance, man's monumental blindness to the omnipresence in nature's beauty, even when she is so fiercely expressing herself.

Now many years later I was still being drawn back to this place to deal with the situation of this ongoing recurrence in my life, whatever it was. As I sat there in the traffic-jam in Leixlip, tense in my body and again rushing my way through to Galway,

I asked myself, "has anything really changed?" Then suddenly I was jolted from such thinking when the car-phone rang. Another disgruntled client, was my first reactionary thought, demanding news of a mortgage, or faltering insurance investments. But no, to my great surprise, it was Mary.

"Mary, how wonderful to hear your voice".

"Where are you?" she was inquiring.

"Where am I? I am on my way to appointments in Galway, in a traffic build-up and way behind schedule".

Then she was telling me to place my attention on my hands and to relax my grip on the steering wheel. I was utterly amazed. It was like letting go of a ton of cement. Now she was bringing my attention to my feet and she was telling me to connect with my toes.

"Release the tension by consciously stretching them", she was saying.

Wow! What a relief. Up to that moment I had been out on the front bumper of the car pushing my way through the traffic.

"It is much easier on the body driving the car from where you are sitting," she was telling me "and being fully conscious of where the body actually is, in the moment, every moment, in staying with the body, where you really are and being aware of how good it is in there. You will still get to Galway just as fast and you will be in much better shape when you arrive. Come into life, into your body, exactly where it is, right now".

This was like a jolt from the cosmos as I was suddenly jerked back into alignment. Mary was going to meet me the following day back in Dublin and for the rest of the journey I found myself thinking about her. Were we going to be lovers? No. At that moment there was nothing like that arising, even though the sensation within me was even greater than such expectation.

My first two meetings in Galway that evening were efficient and swift. But the third and last meeting was with a widow who had become obsessed with the idea of me as the man in her life, regardless of how I personally felt about such a situation occurring. As she was considerably wealthy and classed as good potential for the firm by the lady associate who had initially introduced her to me, I felt obliged to continue with these meetings in the loose form of business they seemed to be taking. The relationship had now advanced considerably to a point where she was drawing me more and more into her personal affairs. Because I had not succumbed to her amorous advances and avoided sexual contact, I assumed we were on mutually understood platonic ground. Indeed I felt we had firmly put behind that one occasion when after a dinner dance she had almost managed to seduce me to her personal demands. In my naivety, I was to discover that there are more ways of determining an affair than one. Nonetheless, this particular evening was short and sweet, and I was out of Galway before midnight.

What a beautiful night it was. A cloudless sky and full moon to my right casting magnificent shadows across the open countryside. Some fields were blanketed with low white mists which the bodies of animals appeared to be floating upon with legs invisible. It was mystical indeed with castle ruins and the remnants of ancient monasteries periodically presenting themselves. Apart from the hum of the engine there was little or no traffic out and a hushed silence was on the land. I drove with the car-roof open, taking in the rays of the moon. This was my time, my personal space, driving unperturbed through the beautiful moonlight in its silent splendour, and the urgent madness of the world lost in its sleep to the moment. Here nothing disturbed the awesomeness of the night as I journeyed along, at one with myself.

Dublin appeared too soon and after a few hours sleep in my single couch bed I was in the office at six in the morning ploughing through my days work before the others would start arriving at nine. These were my usual disturbance-free hours of productive work, if one could class any of it as productive. But this was a special day. By mid-morning I was finished and on my way to my meeting with Mary.

She was so naturally beautiful, her clear skin with no facial make-up whatsoever, her hair fair and loose and her dress colourfully gentle. She was sitting facing me and sipping her herbal tea. There was stillness, absolute stillness, the exquisite wildness of the moonlit night dissolved, the problems of tomorrow forgotten, that moment so special, that glimpse of eternity that always is and I was in it with her. It was as if she had brought me to the centre of my being.

Describing the undescribable one cannot. We paused and sat in silent wonder, with no words, no foolish chatter, until my mind slipped back into my world of turmoil, being unaccustomed to the depths of such stillness. Now I was telling her of the beauty of the night before, back in yesterday, in the past, where I had, until that moment, been spending my precious time living. I was aware of the courseness in my voice as if I was out of tune with the unusual ease in the awesomeness of the actual moment being experienced. She smiled at me as she gently yet firmly spoke.

"It is good now. Stay with this moment. Last night has passed. It is now but a memory. This is a lovely day. Let us truly be in this moment, with the taste of the tea".

"What is the secret? What is it?", I asked.

Then she was telling me about him, this man of master consciousness who had brought her light to life. She also said that she would love to speak with my team but did not have the free time. "You can do it yourself", she was saying, "I will introduce you to his books and tapes, these will surely help you to understand more clearly for yourself".

It was a beautiful afternoon walking with Mary on the streets of Dublin down narrow alleyways, over cobblestones

I had not noticed before. We paused to acknowledge a mother with child in shawl begging on the footpath and leisurely onward again until we reached our destination, a book and oddments shop known as 'The Source'. The happy pair behind the counter were introduced to me as Liz and Rohit, and both were eager to assist us.

"With such an unusual name as Rohit, where are you from", I inquired.

"From County Clare", he replied.

"Well so am I from Clare, and I have never heard such a name before".

"It's really James", he said with a smile, and James it has been since.

Mary introduced me to the tapes she had in mind, tapes on 'Making Love' by the Australian master whom she had personally acknowledged as being of master consciousness. She advised me that these would help me understand more clearly all that she had been trying to say relative to living the truth. Time was running out. She had to leave as her mission for now was accomplished but she told me we would meet again. Once more I was on my own, walking back to my mad world of hollow sound with that strange bundle in my suit pocket.

By the edge of Charlie's secret place at the lower end of the forest there is a small opening in a fence. The opening leads out into a large field owned by a wild old man. He lives on a mountain with his sister who has a peculiar stare. At the other side of the field there is the stone shell of what was once a house, now covered with ivy. This day the bull is gone from the field and with pounding heart Charlie decides to explore the ruins for there are many bird sounds coming from there.

After squeezing his body through the narrow gap in the fence he dashes across the field as quick as he can, lest he should be spotted. He enters the ruins through a hole in the wall that would have once been a window. The pigeons disturbed fly from their nests in a terrible flutter of sound and then, before him, he sees one of their eggs rolling along the ground. He picks it up and swiftly puts it into his pocket, for this is his discovery, and this is what pockets are for.

Then he hears a roar from the adjoining field at the other side of the ruin. It is the man from the mountain with his bull and his cattle now approaching. Charlie runs for his life as he hears in his ears the hoof-beats of the bull and the roar of the wild man shouting the words, "Get out of my field".

He dives for his life through the hole in the fence that leads him back into his forest. Charlie does not stop running until he reaches and enters his secret domain. Then he takes from his pocket his find but the shell has cracked open and what looks like the shape of a bird is moving inside. He peels off the shell surrounding this life that wriggles a while, then stops. It has died. Charlie has carried many strange objects in his pockets before but nothing as immediately mysterious as this.

Chapter 4
BUSINESS SUITS IN A MYSTICAL LAND

It was a pleasant morning with a light and fresh wind blowing from the west as I arrived at Dublin airport for my appointment with the marketing manager of a particular life-assurance company. He was waiting by the check-in counter with air tickets in hand and we were soon boarded on a small aircraft, shaped something like a bus with wings, and on our way to the Isle of Man.

This little island, approximately thirty four miles long and twelve miles wide, is located on the Irish sea between the two larger islands of Ireland and Great Britain. The Isle of Man enjoys international financial status apparently accorded to it through the vested interests of the Banking City of London sometime in the distant past. Its government, known as 'The House of Keys', is one of the oldest established systems of governing in the world having sustained over a thousand years of peaceful stability. It stands in vivid contrast to the external heritage of political quandary as experienced by the larger democracies surrounding it. Indeed, through all the changing faces of the climacterics that others seem to be creating, this little island may be classed as a pristine microcosm of balanced perpetuity in the midst of the macroeconomic fiscal uncertainties of the exterior world, a world stumbling from one confusion to the next outside of its shores.

Here sits the Isle of Man, in the magical bubble of its own illusion, geographically positioned between two islands at war for over nine hundred years, yet it in itself seemingly unchanging. Now its inner mystery and beauty were about to be presented to me. I felt like a bird in the sky as the little plane descended through the few white clouds on that clear morning and the island gently appeared, in its unassuming fragility, peeping through the gentle mists caressing its peaks. It was a rare moment of occurrence, as this was another adventure into the unknown. I had heard of the existence of this place before and indeed I was aware of its significance as an international financial zone enjoying the tax free status afforded to it. Yet its meaning was much more than this to me. I was sensing that the freedom it was actually offering to the world of finance and business was but the outer cloak of the greater freedom it was laughingly enjoying within itself.

Our little plane broke through the clouds and touched its wheels on the runway. We were expected and welcomed by the financial house who had arranged our meeting. The man accompanying me on the trip, who was head of the marketing division of their sister company in Ireland, was their Irish connection in this instance. This was the first international agency being offered to me. I knew the play, or so I assumed. I was aware of my potential and so were they, being fully briefed on my background and success in taking the prized European marketing record in the life-assurance industry from my previous employer.

But apparently more important than that, I was just beginning to see, was the fact of having his marketing team in my court as well although I had personally little or nothing to do with this acquisition. This coup was seen by them as my most remarkable feat. The team had previously been offered for sale with a price tag in excess of a million pounds, and they had followed me out of the sales-ring and knocked on my door free for the taking!

This was the dance of the of the fairies, was it not? Why, there is even a place on the island, I discovered, called Fairies Bridge. "Am I here to be acknowledged by them" I was asking myself as the magical carpet was rolled out for my arrival. Indeed it was all becoming a dancing anomaly! Was I arriving as honorary guest to the magical folk of imaginary wonder? Was I there to be acknowledged by them? I was silently bemusing myself with such questions. Well what is real if the magic is not? Certainly this world of insurance and finance cannot be real, outside of its own make-believe reality. For those of us who serve it in our assumed importance it conveniently serves us through our battered and porous egos! We were doing little more than fooling ourselves, I was to discover.

Here I was being whisked through the royal presentation from the insurance company now biting the cherry they perceived me to be. After the usual exchange of courtesies I found myself being wined and dined in an extended mid-day dinner in rare Victorian style. There were five of us seated at the round table and when the main course of five large dishes arrived for consuming they were covered with five excessively large solid silver domes. This was somewhat confusing for me, as I had not experienced anything like it before, while the others were taking it all for granted. How was I to remove this awesome sculpture from my plate when there appeared to be no place to put it down and my stomach aching with hunger? Every square inch of the table was preoccupied with the wines and all the extravagant additional decor as indeed were our minds with all our factual knowledge and opinions.

I sat listening and observing in stillness, a good motto in life as in this state usually what needs to be known will eventually present itself to those who have patience to wait. Sure enough three waiters arrived, surrounded us, and in ascended upwards, over our heads and out of sight. This occurred as the company at hand continued their discussion about the extent of their markets, rolling their tongues as far away as the markets of China. Amazing it was, how our gushing discussions in our cross-correlation of financial importance encircled the globe, as we jostled each other in our world of impressions.

Yet of all the matters of financial importance we spoke about, myself being as maniac as them, the image of the silver domes is the only thing of that day that still remains in my mind.

Following our dining and warming to the sight of each other, the afternoon at the company headquarters was pleasantly light. It was just showing me sufficient to state, "Here we are, the international players, you are welcome to join our exclusive club". For all that was really said throughout the day was little more than that. Then the rich gravy of the excessive midday feasting began to take movement in the intestinal gut of the assembly as the effect of the wine was flooding each head. All that had to be said they had said, and said, then said it all over again. I had bitten the apple, it seemed, and their mission of the day was sweetly accomplished. Gestures were made to the chauffeur at hand, and soon we were being whisked back to the airport to catch the evening flight to return us to Dublin.

But there was something more awesome that touched me that day. Behind the scenes of human physical indulgence there was a hidden scene of mystical delight showing itself to me. It was not only in the hedgerows and the unusual shapes of the trees but also in the vocabulary used by the polished financial men who seemed to have unknowingly been swallowed into it themselves. I felt acutely aware of my presence as being from the land of Eireann with all its mythology alive to the truer reality present before me. It seemed as though I was being given a special welcome by seemed as though I was being given a special welcome by the polished men who were unknowingly the puppets of the mystical show. I could almost visibly see the invisible masters of the dance bow farewell to me as the little plane raced down the runway to join its predestined ascent out over the sea.

Soon the little island dissolved itself back into the mists of nothingness from whence it had made itself known. The nose of the plane aligned towards the western sun and the Irish shoreline soon appeared. It was as a clumsy giant in comparison to the little pearl now but a mental image, like in a dream, lost to the waves of unpredictability behind me.

Back in Dublin nothing had changed, yet everything was changing within. The illusive nature of the financial dance was growing more apparent. In wild enthusiasm I related the experience to some of my clients of it all being a dream outside the constraints of the norm. And I was surprised to discover how so many of them wished to place their deposits offshore. But it was not that simple to effectuate as there were still regulatory restrictions in place to prevent money leaving the country. This business was meant for international players and not aimed at nationals in their own domiciles. Nonetheless, this was not to deter the bolder ones and their business was arriving our way through the ostensible channels of the banking system even before the regulations were relaxed. This is the Irishness of business it seems. Although legal definitions may be quite clear the action of the play does not always fall between defined parameters. This was to become a dance at the edge of the cliff where it would take no more than a sudden breeze to topple us over, back into oblivion from where we had come. Life is in the minute, the second, today. What will happen in a few minutes can anyone know? You ate yesterday but today you are hungry. All you can see is that you are hungry. You forget that you ate yesterday. In all our apparent knowledge yet how limited we really are.

Something within seemed to be saying that I would not be in this situation if I was not meant to fly. Is this not the spirit of adventure in all of us that can be deeply buried under our personal clouds of fear? My inherent problem, it appears, is the fact that I have the compelling urge to dive head first into any challenge that presents itself, and do the assessments later. On this particular platform, standing on unsecured bridges between the raging torrents of greed and fear wildly flooding the investment markets,

I was faced with the reality of man's mis-adventures. It was not a place for the timid approach. I had allowed it to enter me and now I was becoming as one with all of it and testing its limitations. I was at war, for war had been declared between this self of myself in its becoming and the truth of that, that I am. My faculty of reason was the sword of challenge as to the unreality of what all this world was assuming in itself to be real. In mental terms it appeared as if my better judgement was declaring a war on myself.

The other front of battle were the fluctuating markets. When I won I was awarded gentle applause, but when I lost, the greeting was a roaring rage. Indeed it was not long before the cliff-top of assumed adventure dropped its masquerade and exposed itself as the gaping gates of hell. I had entered, going deeper and deeper in, alas, to discover the truth behind its mask of dazzling lure. It had handed me a polished mask for myself to put upon my face. I eagerly took it for I had given myself no other choice. Try as I would, however, I could not get it to fit. This is the world, the world of man's madness, with crazed frenzied souls dressed up in suits, armed with calculators and personal computers cursing in dismay at the unexpected inevitable and the other brigades, the technicians and computer programmers, researchers and discoverer's spilling their essence upon it. In this is man's excellence wasted and where, pray tell, is love in all of it?

There seemed to be no one awake as I was spun to and fro, from one situation to the next, all holding the same likeness, the same mass expression of the human condition in its acute ignorance and appaling pain. It was as if the entire story of humankind was flashing before me, from prehistoric man battling with flesh and bone to current man battling with his mind, both seeking an extra cushion for their transient chair! And this was my world of becoming, in what had become of myself. Now I was asking; Is this what all of it is about? Are we enslaved as such with all energy exhausted for temporary creature comforts as we blindly cling to this false notion of immortality that passes in an instant pace? Are we thus deluding ourselves? Yes, we are as foolish as that, it appears, from all that I had begun to see when looking through the thin skin of myself, as it is with most of us blindly believing this make-belief world to be real.

Soon more challenging questions posing to the madness of it all began to arise from somewhere within me. Is this the grand finale of this human patriarchal expression of man's world, the world of outward projections, with skyscrapers obscenely protruding upwards, as the current phallic statement of those ancient monastic turrets in another holy disguise? Is this another mask of the past folly of man again repeating itself? Are these city skyscrapers, filling up more and more with the money equations of this illusive trance, now coming to the point of final ejaculation?

Woman, where are you now? Have you too become one of these shallow equations? 'She', the Goddess, as in Florence Nightingale, where is this essence of 'She'? Is there any real purpose in it all? And what am I doing here? Who am I anyway? Perhaps Shakespeare's wisdom is truer than true when he tells us through one of his plays;

> *"All the world's a stage,*
> *And all the men and women merely players*
> *They have their exits and their entrances*
> *And one man in his time plays many parts".*

And my part now had become the part of experiencing hell as my eyes were just then clearing to see what was really happening in the fathomless depths of this hell of man's making, that is the hell of myself. I was being swallowed up in this descending darkness until my torch of life was re-ignited by a spark of chance encounter with the essence of truth through Mary. That chance encounter was to cause me three years of a burning tormental death to all that I had blindly become in this world of becoming. How awesome it is, having descended into its fires, to ascend again to this place of now, beyond the ashes of that dark prison of hell where I had spent most of my life. How awesome, this truth of immortality.

But still the shell hung on in the bodies of all the others in the play who were committed to their perpetuating grief. My commitment now was to find some honour in my own fading corpse to fulfil my part. Where I had played and won all was well, yet where I had played and lost I felt I must make amends. But it was quicksand and the more effort I was making to amicably conclude my part in the play the deeper I seemed to be sinking.

I was still dressed in a business suit with matching tie and scarf, driving through the magical mists of Eireann with briefcase in hand, selling these concepts called life-assurance and money-assurance to people of all walks far and wide. I was listening to their stories and telling them mine in the spinning excitement of this merry-go-round world of business and fun, yet always ending in grief, sooner or later for every player attached to a particular outcome. Then more business and more blind belief gushing in through the doors of our minds that this time it should be different.

Even the insurance industry itself was on this high in its own self-denial of the truth. Indeed it was all an amazing discovery to me to see first-hand this play of life with so many players telling different yet similar tales. When people invested in life-assurance products all was well when the markets were able to cover all of the costs involved, even at times giving a profit. But when the markets went bad then all the demons were loosened as everyone, including the clients, abdicated responsibility. So it continued, with more selling, more costs and more accountability as I placed myself captive to the insurance world's image of being their sales champion. Even so I knew deep within that it was nothing more than a bubble.

I was at the pinnacle of this worldly glory when Mary arrived, gentle as a dove, yet fierce as an army set in battle array, with those words she softly spoke at her brother's funeral, "cleanse yourself as you come unto me". Was this the cleansing, I asked. Was this the message being given, as I was being scorched to death in facing the truth of myself?

The business of the day continued in its role from debit to credit and then back to debit again, more serious than before, on its precarious imbalance of promises that illusive options would bring the awaited salvation. Thus blindfolded on a tightrope we were dancing, and without a safety net, towards another promise, another hope, awaiting the final accounting.

Charlie was at school one day trying to come to grips with a sum of ten divided by three. He is doing decimals now and even three point three, three, three is not the full answer for him. If he should live forever he feels he would not get to the end of it. How strange it all seems, he thinks. Yet the teacher is so sure and precise as she closes the books and finishes the class. "But Miss, we have not yet finished the sum".

His friends on the road lazing their way back home refuse him attention relating to it as they fight over marbles and sweets. His mother or father won't talk to him either about where the sum should end. Nobody cares. But where does it go, this three point three, three, three? It has to go somewhere. The swallows swooping on the May fly, do they add and subtract and divide as well? But there is something strange about this particular sum, and that odd word the teacher had used: Infinity?

Let us pause for a moment and ponder
In the midst of our reaching out yonder
To the next encounter arising
It may be the one from whence we begun
Before loosing the Sight through mental surmising.
For all that is seen in our moments depleting
May be each day again repeating
And telling us how we are lost in a trance
And foolishly out of step with the dance.

Chapter 5

MY FIRST MEETING
WITH THE MASTER OF THE WEST

The time arrived. Mary's guru was to visit Dublin and she asked me to bring it to the notice of as many people as possible so there would be a good attendance. To my amazement no one I spoke to seemed interested, except my widow friend who was eager to avail of any opportunity of the two spending time together and she was curious to discover where my attention was focusing.

Personally, I had an open approach to it all although I considered myself to be acutely aware how easily religious sects and particular cults can captivate receptive minds. I was eager to attend as a participant observer for what I had read and heard of this man to date had been a challenge to all that was false to the truth. Indeed all of this world that I had fervently believed in was now showing its insidious nature whenever it was put to the test to validate my own misconceptions. Such testing occurred at those odd moments in time when the circumstances of a critical situation would cause me to stand apart from the rational and opinionated side of myself in order to truly observe. And what is participant observation?

In the field of the social sciences of anthropology or sociology, participant observation is a method of research that involves immersing oneself into the 'consciousness' of the social group being examined and directly and impartially getting first hand experience in the area of study. For the research to be pure participant observation demands that the observer remains unbiased and detached and not to go 'native' to the group being observed.. It also demands that all the preconditioning previously absorbed by the observer must be put aside, including the programmed analytical mind. How else could the observing be pure? These are the tasks that are consciously or unconsciously incurred by the social scientist in the role of research in the perceivable world of objectivity as in 'cause and effect'. Even the notion of objectivity depends on conceptual dichotomy so surely this basic concept must also be put aside if the research is to be pure. I knew I needed to cleanse myself of all my opinions and all my beliefs, of everything that was either for or against. In other words I needed to cleanse myself of all my conditioning to date, before I would qualify as a warrior of the truth.

The subject of study being the self, we are now moving our observation into the realm of the singular 'I'. In my reference to being a participant observer I am the one who is being observed. This is most important. I do not wish to engage in argument justifying the possibility of 'objective' research or indeed the existence of an objective 'truth'. I am the examiner of 'me', this one 'me' in all of existence as in you and I where everything begins and ends. This journey of participant observation is about rediscovering the subject. It brings us back to the initial question, 'Who am I?' This is not objectivity, nor is it denying the object. It may show that the object can only have existence in relationship, in relating to 'me', the subjective observer. Can there be an object without a subject? This raises the proposition that the subject and object may be ultimately one and the same when we look from a silent mind.

As I am the writer in this instance let us continue in my own field of experience. But let there be caution against going 'native', for the truth can only be known to you in your own particular experience that is your own special road to enlightenment. By enlightenment I mean the letting go of all the baggage we seem to carry around in our heads, an enlightening of the load so to speak, so we can stand empty and naked, enriched by the acknowledgement that I myself know nothing.

When, through a rising awareness we can truly see the chronic human condition we are in, as in one's own personal condition, then we are ready to eagerly seek our deliverance. Other than that seems to be an ongoing doctoring of the false, where we seem to be endlessly trapped in the chasing of our illusive dreams when we are unwilling to look beyond the next arising moment of short-lived satisfaction for our never-ending stream of desires. Our journey of seeking takes us into the personal state, where each of us must individually go to discover the inner truth of ourselves. This is the journey into the question, 'Who am I?'

Nonetheless, as there is only one 'I' in all of the creation, the 'I' that is me as the 'I' that is you, let this be the seat of the participant observer, where you and I are synonymous. This is the true participant observer, this witness within that is free from all societal conditioning and from the scientific world of objectivity. In order to recognise or experience this, one must let go of absolutely everything one has received from the moment of leaving the womb. Is this a possible quest? Well, let us examine and see.

It may be argued that first we need to understand the nature of our conditioning before we can truly transcend it. And this I agree when we impartially look at the story of ourselves from a silence within. So what has been the moulding of this person that I have become, having entered this conditional world of becoming? I was born into rural

Ireland and entered my childhood school days in the early fifties. The predominant colour to all that I received through the minds of the time was black. This is the colour expressed by Catholicism and Nationalism, extraordinarily dark and sinister to my childhood innocence. It was an experience in contrast to the inner warmth of my home built on a foundation of love, a foundation outwardly expressed with open fires and lanterns for night lighting. My immediate family was as the womb in the oneness unto itself.

Neither were there specific roles in the family unit. We all shared according to our measure in the outside work of subsistence farming, both males and females alike, as we did within the household in preparing the food, cooking, mending and cleaning. Both my parents worked within the home and in the farmyard without question except for the heavier manual work such as ploughing with horses that was usually done by my father. Apart from that, most everything else was shared. Although it had its joys and its hardships, yet it was a group expression of love in abundance.

In contrast, my schooling in the national school system can only be described as below the level of the worst concentration camp imaginable. There was no warmth, no sanitation whatsoever and rat-infested playgrounds of mud. Worse still, that was the acceptable part. Although these schools were state run they were under the rule of the priests of that time. These priestly men of black cloth, in particular the arch-deacons and bishops, believed themselves to be the Princes of God. They expounded their status with the solid gold bracelets and rings that they wore and the mansions, housekeepers and bathrooms of brass they demanded as fitting. Through the imprisonment of human consciousness they placed levies on their captives to support their black godly reign and, in their ignorance, most of them blindly believed that they represented the good.

Within the consciousness these priests imposed the woman was classed as a childbearer only and the greatest avenue of recognition open to her was in being the mother of one of them. Even the act of childbirth was silently damned as the new mother was obligated to go to church for ritual cleansing under the weight of the priestly superstition placed upon her. As a young child I looked with question at this when I noticed a woman patiently waiting by the alter-rails after mass one cold Sunday morning. She was weak and pale after giving birth just a short while before. There, on her knees, in her wretched condition of guilt she submissively waited for the priest to emerge from the sacristy. After eating his hearty breakfast he emerged in his own good time to perform the ceremony and she still bleeding from childbirth.

This is exactly how it was in my own experience, looking out at it all through these eyes as an altar-boy in rural Ireland and seeing first-hand the round belly of priestly expression. When my mother one day, in rebellious distress, ordered one of them to be gone from our home following his attempts to impose his importance upon her, she plucked a daisy from the ground and after silently looking at it for some time said to me calmly, "Look into this daisy, look into its beauty and its natural perfection, this is from God, but not these black demons from hell".

There were good men who came among these priests with wisdom of life and of love and these ones were precious, but few. Nonetheless, let us not judge for if I had been born within their confines, would I have been any different? In the years that have passed since then, this priestly dominance has become more refined in its expression. The sinister blackness is being driven back by the grace of God, that is, the enlightenment now entering us all through the evolution of human consciousness now moving out from the shadow of this dark patriarchal cloak.

And now this man from Australia who calls himself 'Master of the West' has come to Ireland to expound his own particular notions of love, of life, of truth, of death and of God as accordingly explained to me by Mary. Could I still be the impartial observer? On the morning of the first day, having made sure I was sitting alone so that I would not be distracted by a running commentary from the widow who had accompanied me there, I was fully prepared, I thought, to take this guru guy on head to head. Darn it, I had already taken on the false credibility of the insurance industry, the false piety of the priestly world, this Australian guru I would easily dispense. Not so I discovered, this was to be a strange experience.

I felt stillness in the silence of the room among the eighty or so present before he entered. When he started to speak his words had such burning directness that everything within me became exposed to his piercing eyes. This was the first time in my memory that I had met someone out there whom I could not look at directly. Now Mary's words were echoing in my ears. I immediately knew that I would have to be cleansed beyond the slightest blemish before I could pass through this guy, now having seated himself bang in the middle of my road in life. I knew this was to be a big one as the seminar got under way and for the second part of the day, and the following day, I found myself sheltering behind whoever was seated in front of me rather than directly connecting with his eyes.

Mary was there and she looked awesomely beautiful as she attended to the flowers and played the role of hostess to the occasion. But I was given no opportunity to speak with her as in the intervals my ear was consumed by the widow's comments. She had me snared in her financial web and here I was in this fair gathering of gentle people with this woman, the black widow spider asserting ownership on her prey. She would not loose it to anything, not even to the master himself. She challenged him on the subject matter of death, where he transformed it to love, but she held to her own story and took it back to Galway still clinging tightly to the sackful of beliefs and opinions she had brought with her, or so it appeared. No one is to know the workings of the inner self when exposed to the presence of a spiritual master.

The real battle in myself had begun. This man of master consciousness left a deep impression in me that weekend, so much so that on the following week I travelled to London to attend a full days seminar he gave in Commonwealth House. This time I was alone and crying for freedom in my innermost heart. I had managed to escape from the business world for this day of grace and the widow had decided not to come. This was a day of serenity with nothing false and no manoeuvring deceptions sticking to me. I was breathing my own air into my parched lungs in the clarity of this gentle light emanating from the stillness of everyone present.

I could hear him clearly now and I could look him in the eye but there was a fear in me, a fear I had not been aware of before. I was scared of having my very essence exposed with all the sham pretence that I myself had imposed upon it in my relentless pursuit of worldly impressions. Even in silence this man could not be deceived. Everything seemed clear to him as he looked straight at me. I could see myself exactly as he was seeing me, naked to the world, transparent for to witness what I had become in my service to the impostor within.

A silent dialogue had begun within. I had no questions

to ask or actions to take, I just allowed the process to commence. This was the process of letting go, letting go of everything, starting with the image of all that I perceived myself to be. Nor was it going to be quite as easy as it seemed as more than just me was involved. All of those building their own importance to their own particular images about me in the insurance industry, where I had been placed through my wild pursuit of worldly glory, had become dependent on this image of mine. This is what I had cultivated. If I were to abdicate now they would surely fall on their faces. I was beginning to see more clearly what Mary had been saying, that I would have to bring them the message myself and it could only be done by example.

As I faced this situation I recognised that there was no turning back for once the truth becomes known it cannot be denied. By the light coming through this Australian guru I had been opened to see it exactly as it had become. Even in the world of insurance, when I was its novice I recalled some of the older roosters warning me not to be too eager for knowledge. They promoted from accountability through sheltering in ignorance. But ignorance itself is the damnation of man and a demon to be slain.

Now the sword had been placed in my hand and the light that Mary ignited on that cold dark evening was exploding] into a raging inferno within me.

Charlie is back in his secret domain in the forest. The afternoon sun is casting its rays through the ivy loosely hanging about him. He blissfully sits in the joy of the moment, until the decimal equation enters his mind. This sum of ten divided by three is his greatest confusion to date. He is thinking that if nobody can answer it fully, and they all pretend that it does not matter as they carry on with their adding and subtracting like they do when counting their money, then they must all be fooling themselves. Ten divided by three does not give a true answer to him. And this word 'infinity', if it really means what it means, then who can finish this sum? He can only conclude there has to be something seriously missing in the way of our thinking. Still nobody seems to be bothered but him.

Chapter 6

THE MERRY WIDOW'S MOUNTAIN

PAGEANT

Back on the witness trail and between the bouts of pressure I endeavoured to hold to the seat of participant observer. This became more and more awkward as I began to experience friendship and love as if from another dimension in the varying play of life unfolding itself before me.

I found that people were using me as mediator in their legal battles with one another, in problem solving, and on the odd occasion as a facilitator in dealing with broken relationships. The emphasis of my play was shifting from the fear and greed brigade to a clearer place of mending by the use of practical logic and common sense. Things were beginning to change as I set about bringing this new vision into the consciousness of the twelve members of my team. I still expected Mary to speak to us but her life was taking its own direction. At least her outward journey was in a different direction to mine. Yet on the inner, deeper reality we seemed to be hand in hand. She was showing me how to recognise that angry void that is the living confusion of the human condition and this recognition pointed the way through it.

But the widow was competing with this. She sent me several invitations to various events and finally succeeded in having me attend a religious pageant organised by an exuberant priest on a mountain in Connemara. This was an overnight occasion centred about a little chapel close to the base of the mountain. The chapel was ablaze in candlelight when I entered and the prayers and hymns of glorious praise commenced in what I can only describe as a tidal wave of fervent devotion. It was a momentous occasion of Christianity at its best and lasted throughout the night with the later hours being given over to silent vigil.

The widow had a captive audience in the palm of her hand and was on a high. She exuberantly showed me her colours, having succeeded in getting me there by her side as her man, her partner in appearance to the others. We sang and prayed in the emotional parade until eventually we all went to supper. Later, after getting a few hours sleep in a local bungalow, I was up before the dawn to join the ones on my rota for the candlelight vigil. On entering the little church from the blackness of the final hour of night before sunrise, I found an awesome stillness within. Candles flickered their light in a warm red glow and it was as if I was entering the womb of life on that special moment, this rarest of rare. I felt I had been in that space before, in that space of utter serenity within the womb of all existence. For an hour I was one with it, until the next group entered. I sat and extended my peace becoming a part of their hour as well.

The dawn arrived pushing its light through the black and pregnant clouds sweeping in from the Atlantic. Bursts of rain came, sudden and sharp. I returned to the bungalow and sat in stillness in the glass porch as the house was still in slumber. The silence was occasionally disturbed by the rain being blown horizontally against the windows. My only disturbance within was the knowledge of the widow's acute obsession on me. Was I ever going to get this woman to heal herself of this? I had become her mentor and counsellor by her appointment to help her solve her problem, and I being it! Could there be anything more absurd.

There was movement in the kitchen. Sounds of cups and saucers being placed on the table came to my ears. Breakfast was on the way. The new day had begun. After all had eaten we faced the morning weather on the short trip back to the chapel for mass. At the end of prayers the priest confirmed that the weather was clearing up and, to the excitement of all, the mountain ascent would go as scheduled. It looked like I would be there for the day as there was no escaping from it now.

We all made our way by car to the mountain base. There must have been over fifty of us present. A statue of the Virgin Mary was fixed on a special stand carried by four persons leading the procession. The whole group recited the rosary continuously throughout the climb.

The views from the mountainside were breathtaking and I had plenty of time to enjoy it as there was a considerable amount of older people in the group and we moved at their slower pace. I enquired from a local, now making conversation with me, if this procession to the top of the mountain was done on a regular basis. He informed me that it used to be in the distant past but had been stopped by the bishop some forty years previous. It seemed that too much poteen was being drunk on the day and on one occasion a fight broke out and a man was killed. When the new priest was appointed to the parish he decided to start it up again. So here I was climbing up the steep slope in this ritual of ancient expression feeling somewhat like a man from Mars, more at odds with it all than the drunkenness of forty years previous.

At last the summit was reached. We could see a little chapel of less than forty square feet and, to its eastern side, a magic ring of stones. One structure represented the Christian church, the other was a surviving relic of a pre-Christian mythological world of ancient mystery, oozing its stillness up through the feet of moving flesh on the mountain.

Everyone gathered around the priest in the recitation of prayers while I rested on a stone ledge by the little chapel. As I gazed over the peaceful landscape I decided within myself that there I was going to remain for the rest of that day. I would allow this group, with this woman, to descend from me back down the mountain in their ritual of pageant. They would surely not miss me. The beauty of that place was all the God I needed and I was then on it and there I intended to stay.

A nun, who had become a hermit by choice in County Mayo, came and joined me for a while. She remarked on the loveliness of the flagstones that had been placed in front of the chapel and how she wished to have similar work done in her place of refuge. I explained to her the simplicity of the skill, as I had been involved in the placing of similar stonework in one of my past activities. She hinted at offering me the job but I was not taking on any new commitments for my hands were already filled in my current dilemma and I could see the widow questioningly glancing my way.

I needed to be left on this mountain alone, away from the pressure of woman's desires, even this gentle desire that was innocently spoken in the placing of flagstones for a beautiful hermit nun. If I had the freedom I would have loved to have performed the task but such freedom was not available to me as the widow, in her astute agility, danced through the psyche of everyone present, even the priest's, in keeping his focus upon me.

The time of descent had arrived and the priest seemed to be reading my mind through the force of the widow's attention. He told me he was not allowing me to stay behind and appointed me as one of the four bearers of the Virgin Mary's statue for the journey back down. It appeared

74

there was no escaping, so I took up my allotted position being hand-cuffed as such to the descending procession. All was well on the way until one of the older ladies fell and fractured her ankle. She was seated as comfortably as possible and some of the members remained with her to await for a stretcher and ambulance crew to arrive from Galway. The rest of us continued downwards and on to the local schoolhouse where the concluding ceremonies were performed. The priest, I assume, went back up the mountain to be a comfort to the injured lady. Eventually afternoon tea was served and the young priest, flushed with excitement, arrived in the door praising the Lord and filled with exuberance. He relayed to us news of the most extraordinary occurrence that the remaining few had bore witness to on the side of the mountain.

"While we were waiting up there", he said, "and keeping the good lady company until the ambulance crew arrive, we heard the most unmerciful roaring coming from the other side, 'twas as if hell itself had been let loose. We were shivering in fear. Was it an aircraft crashing? It seemed as if the whole mountain was about to explode. The noise got louder and louder and it became obvious that it was coming in our direction. We began praying like we never prayed before and then, suddenly, they appeared, a whole battalion of them, with paintings of skulls and bones on their helmets, a dozen or more hell's angels on scrambler motor-bikes. They circled us in amazement at our shivering sight, as we clung to the side of the mountain in fear of losing our lives. One of them dismounted and curiously approached us. Then to our surprise they all dismounted when they became aware of our dilemma. They had splinters and bandages in their kits and proceeded to secure the lady's fracture, then helped her up on the back of one of the bikes and roared off out of sight down the mountainside to meet the ambulance crew on its way out from Galway. The Lord he works in mysterious ways".

After this news had been tossed around amongst the group the final prayers commenced. These were followed by a workshop which was really an exchange of sad stories. The priest called silence for the widow's, which exceeded by far all the others put together, and she delivered it so very well, with tears and sighs thrown in. This was her place of glory, her religious balance for her worldly endowments that exceeded most of the others by far. But she had exposed the truth behind this mask to me and sooner or later she would have to face this truth in herself. Eventually the music would stop playing and one cannot dance with effect when there is no music and no audience to give approving recognition.

As we were leaving I apologised to her for I needed to go home to Clare to spend the few remaining hours of that weekend with my family. I was imprisoned by the force of her presence and her wealth now flooding my business affairs as her unspoken conditional chains. These were creating insurmountable predicaments through the clouding of reason in my mind. Her psychology was amazingly sharp and it seemed that she never had failed in getting what she wanted. All my efforts of outwitting her were pulling me further in yet apart from all this a good friendship existed between us. Sometimes our relationship was played like a game of chess with each of us trying to outmanoeuvre the other, I for my freedom and she for her ongoing control. I went home wondering was this the cat and mouse game she played with her previous man, and why it ended the way it did? Was I to meet with a similar fate through myself? It all seemed so far removed from the piercing truth of Mary's guru in his words, "Be true to the situation".

In the confusion of my thoughts encaged in the conditional morality of right and wrong this game, this cunning game, was now appearing as blasphemy to the truth. My mind was placed in hell, as I was one of the players and yet behind it all it was me alone, me doing it to myself. This was the challenge that Mary's guru set, the challenge of recognising my role and letting go. The challenge of being true to the situation meant letting go of my continuous support of the false and this I had to do in whatever direction it took, even to the death. From here I was to set the course and allow it to unfold, however long it took, facing all the consequences that would inevitably present. This was to be a journey alone, this burning fire within.

Who could I expect to walk with me except those crazy enough to taste the passion of all of it, and face it in themselves. Now obviously Mary had also been at this crossroads of life and come to the same realisation. As one of the chosen few she had chosen the way, this path of truth, and she seemed to be light years ahead. I would need to find the energy, the strength and courage to catch up with her. In order to reach her state I set out on this ongoing quest, in my search for the 'Holy Grail', as the door had just been opened to all that was to come. This was reality directly facing me now. My friend James at the Source, in Dublin's Temple Bar, seemed to understand when I called one day and asked him to be a landmark in case others came searching for me to show them the way that I had gone.

Was I mad? It did not matter now. She was out there in front, her light of lights shining upon me lighting up the way and I had been touched by the grace of her master. Yet it was neither she nor the master that was now absorbing my inner focus, it was the illumination itself, this pulsing light of life coming through me in waves and lighting up all the falseness within me that raged as a blazing inferno that I could feel burning out through my solar plexus.

In the midst of the crazed world of wantonness my play of work continued and, even though I was there as before I was nowhere to be found, not even to the widow with all the schemes for business she placed before me. I listened and looked right into the depths of the minds of people being absorbed in relentless support of the false worlds of their own making. I too had been absorbing with each day of my life until I bit on the apple of knowledge that caused this awakening in me.

'She' who had now entered my heart by the gentle light of Mary and the forceful hand of the widow had helped bring about this awakening. Mary had encouraged me to look inward, to recognise the illusion of the world and the widow provided the illusion so great, so blatantly selfish, that I could hardly miss it.

Even the mythological tale of Oisin was opening its secrets in a way I had not previously understood. On the white steed of life that had carried the Goddess beyond the seas of consciousness 'She' had made room for me to discover the land of immortality, this truly ageless timeless land, Tir na nOg, across the seas of space and time. For this mystical place is within each and everyone of us but we do not have time to see. Our busy worlds that are mostly in service to the impostor that has taken up the psychic seat in our bodies, cloud our vision and are the cause of all our woes and misfortunes. But do not believe me, for believing can hinder the actual discovery in one's own experience. This is your journey unfolding, as you are impartially looking at mine, for we are all but mirrors of each other. One in all and all in one, there is much more to all of it than meets the restricted eye. This is for you to discover on this journey of participant observation, as it unfolds. To see this more clearly let us bring our minds to rest and without any analytical bearing enter the tale of Tir na nOg, open and free to receive, so we might have a clearer understanding of ourselves.

Once upon a time, a long, long time ago, and that time is now, there lived in the land of Eireann a brave young warrior called Oisin. One day when he was out in the clearing where the green land rolled down to the ocean Oisin saw, to his amazement, a magnificent white steed coming towards him as it appeared out of the mists of the sea. There was a lone rider on its back and horse and rider silently moved within a shimmering, golden glow. Oisin was frozen to the ground. The amazing apparition drew closer until eventually the white hoofs reached the golden sands and then the grass the steed moved without disturbing a blade, as swift as an eagle in flight yet without making a sound, until it drew along-side the spot where Oisin was standing. The rider was dressed in white with a band of gold on the fairest hair that Oisin had ever seen. Her beauty was beyond word and Oisin stood speechless as she leaned from the saddle and gently touched his brow. A surge of energy shot through his body as an arrow piercing the heart. Oisin's companions standing at the edge of the clearing were similarly stunned in the presence of such dazzling beauty. Then she spoke to him softly with the words, "You are my love, come with me to my land, Tir na nOg, the land of eternal youth, where we can be lovers forever".

Without a sound, without a reply, Oisin accepted her hand and she made space for him on her saddle. Then as swiftly as it had appeared the gallant white steed, now with its two riders, galloped into the mists of the ocean that edged the horizon of the human world. Tir na nOg is the timeless land where two lovers are as one together. This we cannot describe, for it is beyond all words for describing. It is as it is, never-ending, never-changing, in stark contrast to our world that is ever-ending and ever-changing, yet both are one and the same.

After some time a yearning to visit his homeland and kin arose in Oisin's heart for time was still in his body. His beautiful lover tried to persuade him not to return but the yearning grew stronger and stronger until eventually she said; "If you must go back then take the white steed but do not dismount or touch the earth or any part thereof, for if you do, you will never be able to return to me again in this land of Tir na nOg, this land of eternal youth".

Oisin promised her so and made haste on the steed through the mists on the seas until he reached the shores of Eireann. It had not been long since he departed, he felt, but strangely everything had changed. He arrived to his homestead but there was only ruins and all the familiar sights were no more. He was dazed and bewildered and inquired after his kinsfolk from a passing soul. He was told that they all had been dead for over three hundred years, those folk whose son had so mysteriously disappeared over the seas without a word of farewell. Oisin realised he had been gone for such time even though it appeared as just a few days in the land of Tir na nOg, it being a place of the timeless. His heart was heavy with grief. Everyone was gone, his kin, his friends, his hound, all that was life to him in the life that he played. All had returned to the dust of the earth, except he, alone, still in body of flesh passing over. He ached in pain now knowing that no more would he dance in the forests with the ones whom he personally loved, nor would he listen to their stories again, or they to his, the greatest of tales to be told.

Oisin wept and wept and in the midst of his weeping thought of his love most fair and beautiful in the land of eternal youth. She would heal his pain in one instant caress and he turned his steed for the sea. On his approach to the clearing, to that spot of his first encounter with 'She', when he, through the power of love, had passed through the boundaries of mind, Oisin now saw three old wise men struggling with a boulder they seemed unable to move for it appeared as part of themselves to themselves in their shadows. He galloped alongside and with one push of his hand moved their problem out of their way, for his heart was in sympathy with their feebleness and with the sorrowful state of their plight impeded by the lower wisdom to which they had become so endeared.

But for that moment he had forgotten his promise to his princess not to touch the earth, or part thereof. Yet the truth of it could not be denied. As Oisin leaned from his saddle, try as he could, he could not return, then the bellyband moved causing him to fall to the ground. Before the eyes of those three old men the young warrior instantly shrivelled and died. The winds blew the dust of his corpse all over the land calling it back to itself, as the white horse galloped out over the seas and into the mists of the horizon beyond the edge of this world and our minds. So it is, the passing through time into timeless.

This is how it was as the fable is told, how deep and how clear for those who can hear, this story of immortality. The dust of the earth is the matter in this consciousness that I falsely take to be 'me'. I cling to the matter as a rational matter of fact, then weep for its passing back unto itself, as it always has since time began, if there ever was a beginning. This simple understanding has taken me almost a lifetime to understand blind as I was from the dust of my mind.

Is it not all a mystical dance, the mad world of finance, the merry widow's mountain pageant, Mary and the surging energy of her words as an arrow piercing the heart,

Oisin's yearning to return to dust and 'I' being the one perceiving?

Oh how we try to lead the dance
As it plays its merry tune
Across the valleys of our lives
In woeful want of worldly highs
Regardless as to rule or ruin
We grasp to fill our belly-ache
Even truth we will forsake
That so we take to holy mountain skies
While deep intent we hold disguised.

Chapter 7

THE MASTER, SEX AND THE BEAST

It was a cold and sharp January morning when I arrived alone at the Olympia Conference Centre in London to attend a two day appearance being given by the Australian master. I trusted that I would find the next key through him on my journey through unmarked ground.

Mary was there to greet me. She was living in England now and nothing had changed within her. She moved in the same illumined glow of fiery gentleness as she attended to the flowers amongst this gathering of three hundred people or more. There was a man very much in her life as they had that aura of lovers about them in service to love, as lovers should be, when they were seated together. Now it was very clear to me that her concern was genuine and pure towards me as she opened her heart with her smile. And so was mine, I was now discovering, as I experienced the most unusual joy when meeting her in the warm embrace of this gentle man in her life.

His presence helped to clear out any notions of my relationship with Mary becoming a physical involvement that lay tentatively behind my immediate consciousness. Such thoughts usually occur between man and woman and can be a block to the finer message of transcendence. When we can only communicate through the shadowy imprint of past experience are we not forever denying the fresh and the new? Is this not the actual case between woman and man locked in the past with the claw in one recoiling from the claw in the other? Is it not so that we continually blind ourselves in this ongoing pain of our ignorance of past begetting more past? And we foolishly think that we know love, when it is this claw in ourselves that we are usually serving.

Mary had no ulterior motives, no hidden agendas towards me, just a genuine caring that I should find the light within myself, an angel in the flesh coming to my aid and a beacon of love in my life. In my own experience this is the rarest quality I have ever encountered.

The theme of the master's delivery centred on love, specifically love between man and woman. He was giving the sex in man a bashing and showing how this was the cause of all the problems we create in ourselves. With this I could well agree and understood from my own experience. I had come from an innocent childhood, before such thinking had entered my mind, to an adolescence of explosive worldly expression in which I was to discover that woman was viewed by men at large as an item of sexual pleasure. This too was becoming the arousal within me as I matured into the norms of the world, thus loosing this truth of love in innocence to the flooding of wants in myself. But fortunately for me perhaps at least my grounding was pure. In my home as a child there had been an equality between my parents that apparently was not the norm in the outside world, as I was to experience. In my later teens when I started dating I treated girls with the love and respect that my family shows to me by example. Although I was wild and exuberant and curiously interested in the mystery of woman, mine was the romantic heart in search for love, while the girls giving me wide berth were searching for pleasure. There were endless young men to fill them.

One night in Galway as a young student of life my girlfriend and I shared a whole night together in the local police sergeant's caravan. The mobile home was conveniently in storage in the garage where I worked as a part-time attendant. When we were both almost naked and embracing in rapturous delight, she took my penis firmly in both her hands, opening herself and guided it into her warm and moist vagina in that glorious pinnacle of love. This is how it first happened, when the world first stopped, totally stopped, in me. I was at one with 'She', as a circle complete in that moment of tasting the eternal. I was strangely home, in stillness, absolute stillness, as our bodies moved in their own natural rhythm. It all seemed so awesomely strange and yet so familiar, with a feeling arising within me of this being where I always am, as I always have been. The nectar of the Gods in that moment, that special moment of tasting, had entered my body. It is always within me for once it is seen it can never again be unseen. That moment of entering the love, and being love, at one with all the creation, and beyond, is this not our true essence of 'Being'?

Let us remember, dear reader, that this is a journey of participant observation. My journey is nothing more, or nothing less, than your journey for we are all but metaphors of each other in our passage through life. I speak to you from within you as I am speaking of this, in bringing both our attention to the primal fact that there is but one 'me'. This one 'me' within you now reading is exactly the 'me' at this moment writing. It is this one 'I', the only 'I', alone in itself, within you, as within me, that appears as the many in the outer side of existence. Nonetheless, it is but part of the inner. The glorious climactic of love, as experienced between woman and man in the making of love through the essence of 'Being', is this not the moment of two, melting together as one? Is this not the realisation through the light of the universal 'I' caressing the point of our consciousness that all is in one?

Love had spoken to me, through childhood, through

nature, through the beauty of being one with a woman of love. Then I took the evanescent lure of the world for reality as it carried me on its shoulders in a business whirlpool of greed and fear and eventually placed me on the rostrum of its charlatan glory. It wined me and dined me, and it embraced me with the bitter sweet curves of sexual expression rattling its bones about me. Believing it all I drank from its cup.

It was a lifetime later when the truth of Mary's words, "cleanse yourself as you come unto me", like a piercing arrow, struck me. I was exploded back into eternity. This was the second arrow from 'She' piercing through my being, the second coming, the first in the flesh, the second in spirit.

Mary's guru, the man of master consciousness, screamed at the sex in man. He exposed how all the world's striving and all the world's taking had turned this instance of truth into an instant of sex. He seemed to me that he was the precursor John the Baptist shouting in the wilderness, bringing out our awareness to the imminent coming of the message of Love. To me, this master immediate was coming from a place of experience, a place of sexual wantonness that appeared to me as his own hell that he had overcome. And this he was fiercely attacking. Yet are we not all but mirrors of each other? We may have different forms and differing ways of expression, but we are all participants of the one play and we are all playing the very same part, that is the part of life, in being life itself. When the mind comes to the stillness to hear what is really being said, then all that needs to be known becomes instantly known.

The sexual anger and sexual fear I was seeing in the face of this master was but the mirror of my own. This part of the hell I knew from within myself when facing myself in the presence of such light. For I too, had allowed myself to become a sexual man of the world, as also had the women who seem to be born into serving this sex, having forsaken their Goddess within. Is this not the image, the ugly distortion of myself, from which I cringe whenever I am confronted by sexual woman? In the purity of 'me' I can never serve that sex in woman, not once I am returned to the purity of 'me' within. From the very first moment of life in this body as man, from the very first moment of existence, is it not 'She' that I have been yearning to love and to serve, before I got lost through my mind?

This man I had travelled to London to hear spoke of the sexual wantonness in the male psyche and demands that it should be exactly seen as it is, for this is the necessary first step for man to stop feeding the monster in himself. If the feeding is stopped then the hungry beast in sexual woman will have nothing to feast upon. But does she have the courage to let it starve to its death thus allowing herself freedom from being the slave of its relentless demands and returning to her beauty within, to the sweetness of 'She', the Goddess of Love? This is where she rediscovers her true nature, as is yours, as is mine. Is this not the truth when the lusting of sex is cleansed from our being? Also greed that is but the same through extension?

In stillness I sat and listened for two days, my mind freed from thought, witnessing and sharing the grace of the light emanating from all in an emptiness to allow to come what may. I could see this man represented all that was good in the way he was speaking. Yet, even though he was calling himself 'Master of the West', it still appeared to me that he was still dealing with his own beastly nature and his battle was not quite over. This I could discern behind the mirror of my own beastly nature reflecting from him. He was fighting the battle majestically, as an example to all in attendance, this battle against the sexual beast not only in himself but in every man and in every woman who has forsaken her love within for a feline sexual lust.

I was going deeper now. I could sense that I was on the outer edge and picking up the vibrations from the tidal wave of the purifying essence of 'She' that is now sweeping this world of male projection. Now all of my past relating to 'Her' was flooding my mind. I found myself giving thanks to the Goddess for being so immediate with me, even to the point of a great sacrifice made when I was just seventeen which brought me crashing to my senses when I was about to abandon my purity of youth for the sexual depravity of the world outside then rising through me from within. I was on the streets of London with my male college peers and being driven by the curiosity arising from the same sexual desires this master was attacking in his efforts to bring the truth into our expanding consciousness. It was a warm summer's night, as five of us roamed the streets in Soho seeking to indulge in the sexual fantasies on offer within our limited budgets. One of my friends requested from a seasoned prostitute if she was giving student rates. We were that naive yet eager to discover the sexual mystery in woman and dump the psychological weight of our virginity in some lonesome dark alley. Although we were hungry to experience sex our money was scarce and there was a more immediate hunger in our stomachs for food. As we stood perplexed and gazing upon a window of barbecued chickens we counted our shillings to see what we could afford. Something caused me to turn around and I saw a young woman in a tiny blue bikini on a window ledge three floors up across the narrow street, almost directly above me. There was someone behind her in the room reaching towards her. She dived or she was pushed, I do not know. Her feet hit an elderly woman before her body crashed onto the footpath. The old woman ran screaming up the street taking everyone's attention away from the scene of the younger woman. For a moment it was just she and I, she laying there, face down, half of her slim white body on the narrow street and half upon the footpath. Her bikini straps had bursted open and her intestines oozed out of her opened side. I was with her as the breath of life departed from her young and still beautiful body on that night, that warm summer night in Greek Street, Soho, as she lay naked, delivered to death, and I to a frozen reality.

As she died I touched her cheek and my heart exploded in an agony I cannot put to words. I left London that night and took a train into the country not knowing where I was going, but knowing I had to be alone in open fields under the stars, alone, with her pain that I now had inside me. I found a field outside a little village in Essex. The following day I walked and walked in this rural place but could not escape from the paved footpaths even in those English green pastures and my heart cried out for the open mountain tops of Ireland, still untouched by man's folly, where I could release her spirit back into the bosom of nature.

Now back in the same city of London, as I sat listening to the Australian master battling with the torments of sexual hunger, I gave thanks to 'She' for all of it, for all that has been made known. The sacrifice made by this beautiful young woman, those many years previous, I now take as the message from 'She' that shocked me to my senses during my youthful and curious outward excursion to join with the sexual brigades of men pushing each other to unload themselves into recipient women in the dark alleys of living confusion. Now I faced it again in the presence of this master who was facing it within himself, on all our behalf, like the man who had done it before when nailed to a cross. It was a weekend filled with inspiration and it was plain to see that all he was saying, openly and freely without any text, was coming straight from a heart that seemed to be divinely inspired. He had descended to hell to show us how to get out. Each time I felt that I had got to the end of him, that I had him 'sussed', he would appear to move just one step deeper. He was always in sight, just that one step ahead of me, and this kept me charging at him as like a matador's bull.

There is a mountain in north Tipperary overlooking the magnificence of Lough Derg, the largest lake on the River Shannon, as it weaves its way through the hilly borders of County Clare. When friends come to visit I usually take them to climb its face. We start at its base, its peak is quite visible as it appears and the first leg of the journey is a beautiful climb through gorse and heather. The unsuspecting guests, on reaching this peak, discover a second coming into view and realise that only half the journey has been completed. Nonetheless, the breathtaking views of the surrounding countryside and the vastness of the lake with its many islands unfolding more and more of itself each step of the way gives enthusiasm to most of my guests and they proceed on to the second peak. But when the second is reached it happens again, there is a third peak ahead, of similar height. This is where many of my guests seem to falter. They rest and enjoy what can be seen within the limitation of one hundred and eighty degrees and then make their descent.

The rare and adventurous few who venture on are not told how many other peaks may appear before the real summit is reached. The summit is the reward in itself with a magnificent view of seven counties of Ireland. I know the distance up, although each time I climb it is a different experience for me, and I also know of the service road that winds its way up on the other side of the mountain right to the top. Yet one has to find one's own journey and one must allow the joy and awesomeness of the discovery to happen in one's own experience. Life is in the taste, through 'me', the only truth in oneself, as the secret unfolds, and no one should be deprived of its tasting.

Here I was sitting with many others in this Olympia Conference Centre in London being taken deeper and deeper into the centre of my being by this man of master consciousness who obviously knew the way. This was my mountain within, with summit after apparent summit coming into my vision in rapid succession, as mystery to me. He was showing me clearly that he had travelled the road where the truth became known in him. He was ready to die right now, he was saying, with nothing to fix, nothing to sign, he was ready right now to die, if that's what life demanded, as he was ready to make love right now, if that was life's demand upon him. Silently he looked at me with the question; Are you ready to die right now? I knew I was not ready yet. I needed to balance my accounts in my business world. I needed to render unto Caesar all that was Caesar's before I could bow and take my leave. As for making love, with this web I had allowed the widow to entangle me in, no I was not ready to make love as love should be rightly made. I was still feeling that I could not afford the luxury of dying to this self before my accounts had been balanced, still foolishly trusting the willfulness of self to balance the score of its own perpetual unbalance. I had entered the light, but I was still awaiting enlightenment. This man of total freedom I looked at through the bars of my self-made worldly prison. My dear mother used to pray; "God, let all our troubles be money ones" and here I was up to my neck in such. Yet looking at the bright side, I had burned out practically every worldly want that had possessed my body as I danced the dance of the worldly. My one remaining desire was to get back to that state of nothingness where real freedom abides, or so I thought. At least I was clear that I was in the right place, having been led to this master through Mary, and he entering my life story exactly at the time I was about ready to receive all he had to deliver. Nothing was going to divert my attention from this, or so I felt, as I left London after that weekend. But I was unaware of the extent of the willfulness that had taken possession of the widow. Willfulness bound her in her reckless pursuit to either possess me or destroy me through all the extravagantly deceitful communications that were having their play between us. I had sold myself into slavery by handing myself over to the measure that she had placed in my hand to manipulate me according to her want. This I had done in my blinded refusal to face the truth of the situation, as we played with the pretence that it was other than this, as in the disguise of business.

Is it not truly amazing how man and woman render such blasphemy to the essence of love in the course of serving the wantonness of self? The battle ensuing is the measure of her pain against the measure of his and the Courts of Justice are filled with such nonsense in divorcing each one from the pain of the other. When we are truly honest, when we take courage to drop our sham pretence, is this not what we are really doing? Still we refuse to awaken from our personal nightmares as we linger in our personal hell protecting our transient comforts. Is it not so how we are trapped in the fear of facing the truth of ourselves?

Chapter 8

THE BOGMAN'S BALL

What is fear? Do we ever really look deeply into this question when we are actually in the state of fear? Indeed is there ever a time when we are not in that state? Let us be totally honest with ourselves. Are we not always afraid of something, of loosing what we cling to in our lives such as our possessions, our image, the ones whom we think that we love, our bodies, our pride? You know the fear of failing to get what we want or of missing out on what others seem to possess? Is this not our ongoing state?

This is not just a question being aimed at the philosophical mind. The mind as such is the wardrobe of garments that appropriately cloaks the changing facets of fear. Is this not how the entire structure of the system of things has evolved on the face of this earth through the mind of mankind that is the human condition? And the only place since the beginning of time, if there was a beginning, the only place that I, the individual, can discover the truth of fear is to immediately face into it in this moment of now. This does not mean facing the cause of my immediate fear. I am asking to silently look at the fear in itself, without putting anything whatsoever upon it, like notions of fixing or changing the circumstances relative to the cause of it that pushes me along in my continual reactionary state.

Is not this reactionary state the incessant conditioning we place on ourselves as we stumble from one facet of fear, after much mental anguish, to another? We can but rest for a moment before the next facet arrives to the door of our minds? Is this not the actual case as we stumble along through our pitiful lives in a world of 'cause and effect' trying to find joy in our fleeting encounters of happiness yet always in the shadow of fear? Let us be honest with ourselves when we ask, what is fear? Silently looking through awareness seems to be the only avenue that is open to us to come to a clearer understanding. This demands a state of mind that is totally empty and free. We must be free of all thought, of all mental conditioning, with no need arising to change or to fix. This is the most enormous task as we are calling to something that is superior to mind in order to allow this stillness to be. I, the observer, am now observing fear and not as an object of fear that is always the trap of the rational and conditional mind thus keeping us imprisoned in a world of circumstances playing into the personal fear in ourselves.

The circumstances relative to the multitudinous facets of fear may seem to vary yet fear in itself is the common denominator. Let us continue to explore the escalation of consequences from the example of my own situation when we deny the opportunity in each moment arising to face the truth of the situation as we submit again and again to the fear in our minds. Fear is the obstacle preventing us from seeing the truth when we are unable in ourselves to face the truth of the situation immediate to us. For truth can only be found in the actual facing of the immediate situation of our lives. Everything we take to be truth outside of this is nothing but conceptualisation, which may or may not be true according to our interpretations, but it is never the truth, and this is where our denial of the truth continuously abides.

It was the night of the Bogman's Ball, an annual event in Maam Cross, Connemara. The widow was on the phone insisting that I should come and again reminding me that I had previously promised I would be freely available. Perhaps I had for I was finding it hard to recall as to what I had said in that bind of relationship that was hell expressing itself through both of us as we danced about the truth of the situation in our failure to face the truth in ourselves. She clearly knew that I had no wish to be her partner yet she would not take no for an answer. I clearly knew that I did not wish to go the ball and yet I failed to say no. She worked around my reluctance by saying there would be a group of us and it was to be an open night. "See it as business", she said, reminding me that mostly all the business people of worth from Galway would be there and it would be an ideal opportunity for extending my contacts. Also two of my own associates were coming. These two were a man and a woman whom she had actually won over to help increase the pressure of her hidden agenda to personally possess me. They saw it all as hilariously funny. I succumbed to her pressure against my own better judgement as I failed to fight off the force of her reasoning that was manipulating the situation between us. It appeared that the actual truth of the situation was still lost to a world of postponement.

I reluctantly arrived at the Bogman's Ball almost two hours late, the delay no doubt caused by my mental confusion. Everyone was seated and the dinner was just about to be served as I entered the room. It was a large rectangular space filled with three hundred people or more all laughing, drinking and waiting. I paused for some time in search of my group, still harbouring thoughts of bolting, and they spotted me and caught my attention by waving. I set out to cross the floor to the vacant seat waiting for me facing the curtains and the widow, when a lady whom I had never met before caught my eye and we smiled at each other warmly. It was a pleasant and sudden surprise as I paused for a moment to acknowledge her and then I thought no more of it as I continued edging around others until I eventually arrived at the widow's table.

I seated myself, made my apologies for being late, and quietly listened to the conversation through the laughter and chatter that was filling my eardrums. The volume was high and I had just entered from the stillness of the night outside. Everyone seemed to be in exuberant humour, but for me. Although I was there in body I was unable to be in the spirit of things. The widow was radiantly beautiful before me yet the pressure of her hidden intent felt like a strangle-hold on my very breath. But it was all of my own making for if I had been true to the situation I would not have been there. I would have chosen not to participate and thus spare them all the painful look on my face, a damper to their night of enjoyment.

The meal was served on large plates in large quantities and the drink flowed voluminously. It was feasting at its best, a challenge for the agile in body with fit and healthy livers. Balls of tension were twisting their way through my shoulders and I was painfully out of tune with everything served on the table and the immediate play about me. I sat in stupefied silence finding nothing to say until eventually the meal was over. What could I say, facing this woman who had everything she had ever desired with the force of her wealth except total command of my person? In her relentless pursuit of this she was capable of ignoring everything else. Although the play was enjoyable for the other two sitting at the table, I could only feel the pain of it all in my neck and waiting for some outside miracle to save me.

Then the strangest thing imaginable happened. As I sat with my back to the crowd, facing the curtains behind the head of the widow, the lady who had previously smiled at me warmly walked directly to our table on her way to the ladies bathroom. She paused for a moment, curiously looking directly at me, then openly asked, "Are you alone or is one of these ladies your wife or your girlfriend?"

I immediately found myself responding, "No, we are just friends who happen to be together for the evening" before anyone else had time to say different or intervene in the channel of communication this extraordinary lady had unexpectantly opened.

"Well if it is okay, I would like you to dance with me when the music starts", she replied, "that is of course if it is alright with yourself".

I could feel my face quite suddenly grow lighter, like the sun re-appearing from behind a dark cloud, as I responded with a definite yes. She gracefully smiled to all seated at the table then quietly left. Everything changed as I immediately came back into life. The pain in my shoulders disappeared and movement returned to my neck. The widow, however, was not to be so easily dismissed. She let loose with her tongue saying the woman was a prostitute on the streets of Galway. The other lady at our table encouraged her in nodding agreement to spur her on and hell itself could not spit more fire than all that I experienced out of the mouth of the widow that was not in keeping with her natural beauty. I excused myself and left the table to go to the toilet as it appeared that it was through my presence this woman was spilling out such outrage and losing her graceful balance. On my way back the band had commenced playing. I had been given the opportunity to face my fear, the dangerously manipulative nature of the widow. Then, finding the courage to break through the psychological chains she had skillfully placed in my mind, I walked over to the lovely lady waiting to accept me. As I approached she came to meet me with a radiance of fiery beauty emanating from her eyes and an aura of gentle femininity gracing her movements. The band was playing The Blue Danube. She placed her hand on my shoulder, I placed mine on her slender waist, and together as one we glided and twirled into the misty magic of the dance. Her soothing aroma for those brief moments cleared the cobwebs from my eyes.

When the music eventually stopped, I suggested that she should come and join us at our table when it would be convenient for her. Even now I felt obliged to return to the others still sitting and waiting in the shadow of the widow still fuming. When I returned to my seat the widow was at boiling point and I felt that I had to challenge her fury. Why was she so upset if our friendship was platonic as she was supposed to have accepted according to the theatre of our relationship? She avoided this issue of fact and her slanderous words against the innocent woman became more and more strident and vicious. The situation was beginning to get out of hand. Still I listening to it all, literally outside of myself, and selling every little bit of integrity remaining in the shell of my body into what was exerting itself through the rage of this woman.

I silently sat as my neck started tightening under the acute psychic pressure being directly imposed. Then the band started playing a fast jive and my other friend at the table, who had originally introduced me to the widow, was eagerly waiting to dance. I took the opportunity and the tension in me spilled out when we took to the floor. When the dance finished I felt that hell itself could not be worse than returning to that table. Return, nonetheless, I did. Then fear came into my mind as I thought of the possibility that the lady who had asked me to dance may accept my offer to join us. I sat facing the wild fury of the widow whose anger had now turned to a cold sarcasm.

"I cannot believe the cheek of her", she was saying, "I

suppose this is how she approaches her clients in Galway, when she is pushing her way through the other prostitutes bringing their filth to our streets". And so she continued, refusing to let go, refusing to face the truth of herself, or to challenge me directly for accepting the lady's request to dance.

The others at the table were beginning to grow weary of the subject. They had their fill of entertainment out of her anguish and they were anxious to get on with enjoying the rest of the night. As the widow was getting less response she gradually began to cool down as she talked about the sad plight of those loose women's families and how they must be suffering from such sinful behaviour. She was now on her righteous crusade, most familiar territory, turning the situation into another of her sad stories and refusing to look for a moment at herself. As for me I was suffering the guilt of birth as there seemed to be no end to the hell I was creating for this woman, even when sitting silently without moving an eyebrow.

Then it occurred. The lady came over and joined us but instead of sitting on a chair she sat upon the now vacant table beside me and placed her feet on the upper rung of ours. She wore a black tight dress that complimented her long slender legs, now crossed at the level of the widow's face and hardly a yard away from her mouth. She spoke directly and calmly to all about the pleasantness of the night and the joy of the music. Everything about her was calm and serene. To my utter amazement the widow was struck dumb. She was totally silent, with not even one word to say, and this silence of hers was sweeter than wine. Nonetheless, I could not help noticing the colour of red coming out from her ears and consuming her face.

The music for the last waltz began and, struggling with my chains of fear, I rose from my chair and asked the lovely lady to dance. There was stunned silence at our table as we walked out onto the floor hand in hand. I wrenched with the pain of the invisible daggers going through my back. I had chosen this woman instead of the widow in all of her beauty for the final dance of the night.

It was now just the two of us, together as one, and danced in a harmony that seemed unknown to the others still sitting and staring. As for me at that moment, I was caught up in a current alternating between the gentle bliss coming through this extraordinary woman and the acute strangulation coming through the mad rage of the widow, depriving her of her own natural serenity.

I endeavoured to hold my attention to the moment and to share in the joy of the dance with this amazing woman who had showed such daring as to rescue me from myself. The closeness of her body to mine dissolved the tension within me but that gripping claw of fear still remained for I knew in my mind that the widow had been pushed beyond the point of control. When the music stopped playing we embraced and enraptured in the magic arising between us we decided to return to Galway together.

One of her friends came over to join us and asked if she could travel with us also as the others in their party had no notion of leaving. It was agreed that the three of us would travel together and they returned to their table to get their coats and handbags and to say goodnight to their friends. I returned to my table to say goodnight to the widow and the others who were with her.

It was then that the fury of the woman started going totally out of control. She was screaming in a rage that brought her dangerously close to being physically ill. I stood there wondering how I could possibly ease her torment within herself, trying to find some way within me to be of assistance to her. But try as I could the situation was going from bad to worse. After all, I was the trigger that sparked the torment within her. It was I, it appeared, who had mirrored her state.

The two ladies travelling to Galway with me arrived by my side and, like two angels from some other dimension, they took me by the arms and gently led me out of the bizarre nightmare I was still foolishly trying to calm. As we stepped out into the sharp coldness of the winter night in the heart of Connemara, outside those doors of that scene, my head was spinning in confusion. I could still hear the outrage of the widow reaching the pitch of physical sickness coming at me through the darkness.

"Breathe in the freshness of the lovely air" this calm and gently firm woman was saying to me as we made our way to the car. But I was still torn with the guilt of abandoning the widow to her demons of torment. The two ladies now with me were conscious of this and tactfully tried to assist me. In my state of psychic shock I felt like a half-devoured fly being freed from the web of the black widow spider. They invited me in for tea and, in the course of my time with them, even when alone with this lovely woman, neither spoke harshly against the widow. There was, however, one warning, "There is trouble coming through that poor wretched woman that is difficult to see or understand, beware of it, it could destroy your life, it is already destroying hers".

As I later drove along the winding mountain roads on my way home to Clare in my aloneness witnessing the winter dawn breaking, my heart was heavy from all that had occurred. I battled with my mind in trying to understand how I had become the trigger of this woman's anguish, having seen the effects of her obsession that night. I wondered if I was some way at fault for the plight of her insatiable fixation on me. I felt I had never given her reason for this, to the best of my knowledge and I had always made it plain to her that it could never be so. She would verbally deny her intentions.

There had been numerous occasions before the night of the Bogman's Ball when she had acknowledged that our relationship was purely platonic. Even the weekend she had lured me out to the Aran Islands with the same two associates who had attended the ball, had I not then made it clear to her? When the bed and breakfast was arranged two rooms were booked. I requested that the men and women should have separate rooms. Yet I knew they were scheming otherwise when the three of them were in the other room talking and laughing. I got into the single bed still clothed and deliberately started to snore when she entered the room in her nightdress. She was obliged to use the other bed as I was already asleep and taking the easy way out rather than facing the truth of the situation. In the early hours of that morning I left the room without looking her way or acknowledging her presence and walked by the sea until it was time for breakfast. Still she refused to accept the message.

The Bogman's Ball had publicly confirmed that her obsession on me was dangerously chronic. And how had it started I wondered? I knew it was important for the image she put out to her friends that she be seen to have the best, and she was looking at me as one of the best in the game of the insurance industry with my crazy title as the European champion in selling. Oddly enough this title was bestowed on me through her city of Galway. By now I had become financially locked into the madness that was coming through her and her world. Whatever I had to do, I knew I had to find a way out, which seemed all but impossible through the utter confusion of everything that was happening, and in particular, the confusion that had taken over my mind.

I had entered this world, allowed myself to be crowned its king, and now all of it was entering me in my own experience. This woman seemed attached like a leech to its glory, as money was her world, having inherited her father's license as a bookmaker and all of his fever as well. Still I was anxiously concerned for the state of her health, having to leave her in such a chronic condition that night of the Bogman's Ball as I was rescued from myself by two lovely ladies. I knew she was physically sick as I left her that night and now I was struggling with the inner guilt of abandoning her to her sorrowful plight. But intenser than that, I was struggling more with the fear, that impassable fear, of facing the truth of the situation and officially ending my association with her.

The following day she had rang me as cheerful as ever and apologised about her bad mood the night before. She blamed it on something she had eaten. "Business as usual", she was saying. My God is there no end to this, this world of my own creation?

Charlie was alone in the forest one day with a puppy dog that had suddenly appeared on the doorstep one morning, abandoned by someone from town. This was a new experience for him as he never had a pup of his own before. The old collie dog in the family was usually busy on the farm and attached to its own importance would seldom accompany Charlie and did not even bother to respond to his calling as it had not yet given the significance of command to him.

Charlie was filled with glee as he ran and played with his new puppy dog in his favourite part of the forest. As he came close to the edge of a fence he caught sight of the woman with the peculiar stare walking in haste towards him. She was coming from the ivy-covered ruins at the other side of the adjoining field, and moving with considerable purpose. Drawing nearer to him she called out his name in a sharp squeaky voice. Charlie suddenly froze in his tracks. "I have some sweets in this bag for you", she said, as he looked at her in his confusion. "Don't be afraid me lad, can't you see I have some sweets". Her face was twisted in what appeared to be a smile as Charlie cautiously approached. When he reached out to take what she was offering to him she quickly leaned over the fence, grabbed him by his sleeve and proceeded to beat him on his legs with a stick she had for beating her cattle!

"Stay out of our land", she screamed at him as each blow left a mark where it struck. He twisted and turned and eventually broke free from the iron grip of this crazy woman that he could hardly see through his tears. For the life of him he could not understand, as he ran through the trees, the wicked intent of this woman with such a peculiar stare. Nor did he tell his parents what had happened to him, for he was sure he had done something wrong.

Chapter 9

THE SHE-WOLF, DAZZLING, POISONED
FANG, AND LOVING HEART

Time passed. The swallows returned, built their nests, taught their young to fly, then left again. Seasons came and went, yet nothing really changed. Although I had been physically freed from the widow on that one night of the Bogman's Ball, I was still bound to her play by the psychological chains of myself, imposing its will on this self of my being. Added to this the binding effects through the management of money made me sink deeper into the maya of this world as I continued my struggle of conditional self righteousness in my search for the illusive conclusion. But nothing concludes, I was yet to discover.

"What is the business of the day" the widow would ask as I was drawn in myself more and more to the city on the west coast of Ireland. What is this business about? What am I doing? Who or what am I anyway? These questions were arising in an earnestness that was growing more profound. The effects of Mary's words in her reference to 'me' and my time with a spiritual master were now taking root in my mind.

In dark contrast I had been absorbed by the insurance industry and skillfully trained in selling myself into greed and selling it to others. It was here I meet up with the widow endowed with the material wealth from the fruits of similar expression. On the surface this statement may seem to be a cop out, a passing of the buck so to speak, but one has to go deeper than surface thinking for the truth of it all to be known. Perhaps this widow's instant obsession on me was part of this discovery. We believe in a world of 'cause and effect' and in such a world everything is part of the act through extension. I had to be born for this obsession of the widow to unfold in a world forever unfolding. When experiencing this my guilt was the fact of my birth as I naively endeavoured to free her from her obsession on me, so I might sleep again in relative peace. I felt that even through my physical death there could be no escaping her obsession for I would be imprinted forever in time as another one of her sad stories. Karmic recurrence was the 'effect' that I feared. It had to be dealt with in the personified moment of 'now'.

In the field of social research the tendency is towards the analysis of 'cause and effect' when seeking the solution to a problem. Such research is usually within the parameters of time. Now I was looking at the holistic more than the particular. What was manifesting itself through the interaction between the widow and myself seemed enormously greater than the personal. It felt as though this was now the purpose of my birth. It was not the journey I would have personally chosen but it had exploded itself upon me in unavoidable form through the circumstances of my life. In the presence of the spiritual master a sharper awareness was made accessible revealing my mental limitations. Now I could see myself as a product of a world of rational logic that tends to obscure the logical. There is logic and there is rational logic. Logically we can ascertain there is but one 'I'. This one 'I' is the universality of all. But rational logic is part of the rational mind that weaves out the world of duality into an endless stream of 'cause and effect'. Such is the illusion we serve.

When I first entered insurance, directly after graduating

as a mature student, I had no real knowledge of the business nor had I any intentions of pursuing such a direction. Even the advertisement in the newspaper was cunningly disguised and once I was in the programming commenced. This programming was literally pumped at us by people who had been totally brainwashed and believed against their better nature that all the scheming was true. Indeed it was true to the scheming although it had little in common with truth. These people are at the raw, market face of the life-assurance industry where new entrants are used as fodder to feed it. According to the statistics of the industry itself these new recruits have a maximum working life of three years before they 'burn out'. Thus recruitment is the survival line of the life-assurance business. The new entrants are wound tight and programmed to sell to all their friends and when eventually they have no friends left the system tells them, in a way of its own, that they are the failures. The rest of their lives is usually spent trying to come to terms with this within themselves while the industry continues sucking in more recruits in its relentless play of greed and human destruction. So it seems to continue, the wheel keeps on turning with no one in particular accountable as the system itself convulses along through the mayhem of its own misconceptions.

And what were we selling? The vast majority of the products were of little or no real benefit to the consumer but it was all part of that particular dance. Whether needed or not needed the job of the seller was to show the customer the defined benefits and sell as many products as possible. I had seen all of it, the marketing of the products of practically every life-assurance company in Ireland and the international companies as well. I had now spent close to five years studying the industry in depth and applying my knowledge to the markets. I was able to see at a glance how every unit of money a customer invested was used up and could easily calculate the time-span that was needed for that unit of money to be even partly returned. The glossy brochures and the high marketing profiles at hand served the illusion being placed in front of the expectant consumer. People actually believed that they were getting value for money but this was rarely so as every system of application that was used, from mutual houses that share profits to those playing on the stock markets all had the same underlying common denominator. To clarify this now is not right for the flow of the text and indeed there is much more to all of it than the life-assurance industry's merry dance, itself just a part of the wobbly world of finance.

But there I was, in that moment in time, in the middle of it with a ready-made sales team well conditioned into the play. There was no one to blame, not even myself nor even the widow when she first met me at the pinnacle of my success and persuasively edged herself onto the scene, we were all part of that crazy expression. We were all fodder and each of us was suffering, or about to suffer, according to our level and measure within it.

The official thirteenth member of the team arrived by her own appointment. She was in her mid twenties, tall and beautifully elegant, a part-time actress of sorts who had been working in an administrative role with a financial services company. Obviously she was under the impression that I was the highly successful entrepreneur and the launching pad required for her own lift-off. It all started suddenly. She met me for a midday lunch date and before I knew what hit me we were in the middle of a passionate affair that was to last for several months. This beautiful young lady, highly intelligent and versatile, became the most colourful chameleon in my life. With her daring and vivacious personality she dictated her own letter of appointment to the business and proceeded to enjoy and organise herself within the group according to her own rules and liking. But on such licentious terms it could not last, particularly when her aura visibly turned from a colourful light to a dark and troubled black when she brought her ex-liaison on to the scene and finally a gigolo who seemed to have a hold on her from the past.

In the middle of this affair the Australian master returned to Dublin to give two day seminars at the Blackhall Place Law College and she demonstrated her capacities in being able to compete with this. I failed to attend on the first day and was late on the second after she and I had spent an intimate morning together. Even during that seminar the morning with her was full in my mind and the sweet and hypnotic aroma of her presence was still in my nostrils. I was out of tune with the master, with Mary and all the others, having submerged in my own temporary heaven in the foolish belief that I was serving love wisely. In truth one needs to be astutely aware to know when love is being served.

It soon became obvious that love and the business we were in were poles apart, indeed, we had mistaken another mask of the demon of greed for love. One cold November day the affair exploded to an end as swiftly as it had begun. I realised that I had allowed myself to be lured a million miles from my search for the truth. I had been chasing shadows from within myself and the darkness about me had become denser than ever. I could not find an answer to deal with the growing confusion, not even through experiencing the death of a dear friend at that time who departed the world in her prime, just days before my affair came to its end. Now I was alone, my body and mind chilled back into a stunned silence as the sheep caught up in the briars awaiting the fangs of the hungry wolf.

The widow had been biding her time and within days came pounding on my beat. She placed some money with me to transfer to the tax-free zone of the Isle of Man and it still had not reached its destination. She now turned this into her new line of pressure. There should not have been any immediate problem as she knew we were waiting for new regulations that would allow free movement of money offshore. Her transfer was to be balanced against an overseas sterling arrangement that I was working on at the time overseas. No actual transfer of funds was to take place. This was to facilitate her request for privacy. It had started out as an apparently straightforward arrangement. Her money would go into my business account and part of the overseas sterling transaction on completion would be directly put into an account for her in The Isle of Man. Interest was paid on her money at an agreed rate until such time as the transaction was completed. No actual transfer of money was to be made rather an account balancing arrangement put in place. Although she fully understood this, yet it all became distorted at will in the dishonesty of the communication between us.

She arrived in Dublin, booked into an hotel and arranged that I should meet her there for dinner. Her demands were immediate and heavy. When she eventually acknowledged that the money matter needed some time to conclude and having commanded all of my attention for the evening she relaxed into her usual sweetness. She suggested that money was not important in our relationship and that I should spend the night with her in the hotel. I had entered her scheming, without her training, or being born to such, as I allowed the energy of her money to immerse in my business, and her mission that night was to bind my mind with her psychological chains. She was strenuously telling me that black was black and white was white and with the account still not opened for her in The Isle of Man, I was guilty of making use of her money without her permission. This disregarded the fact that her interest was being paid in the interim and indeed disregarded everything else in the arrangement that was unacceptable to her particular way of perception to suit her deeper intention. And this is how I sinned. I sinned against life, against myself, even against this beautiful woman by allowing her to turn the situation to her advantage. After all, the initial objective of the entire money arrangement was to facilitate her request to avoid any detection of her overseas funds.

After a heavy supper and wine she succeeded in breaking through my resistance and I found myself succumbing to her demand that I go to her bedroom with her. Now I truly entered hell for being lacking in discernment. The week I later spent in prison was paradise itself compared to the inner torment of that one night's dreadful situation. I had allowed it to come to this with this woman, for she was unwittingly demanding that I prostitute love as I lay in her bed. She pulled my body on hers, but I could not respond. Then an unexplainable incident occurred. I heard the piercing howl of what seemed like a she-wolf among the trees outside. My body froze. I had sunk to the depths, had no further to go, and with this realisation was catapulted back into my senses. I got out of the bed and left her, having been torn open within by a torment that cannot be described. Hopelessly lost to all that was sacred I walked from the hotel. The agonising howl still rang in my head and I felt broken and finished. Suicide was not on my mind but I was willing myself to die for allowing the integrity of life in this body to be mortally abused. It was not the fact that this woman was going to set out to destroy me as far as our business was concerned that caused me such grief, but the fact that I had so sinned against love by allowing her to do this to my integrity. This is the greatest crime of all, for it is a crime against all that is good. I had betrayed love by entering the world of this woman in pursuit of her wealth and allowed the most vile to occur, where all of the creation died.

Now I was ready to die, but this was not the readiness the Australian master had spoken of, my readiness was a despair. I thought I had stood firm against the forcefulness of this woman yet I had chosen to ignore the reality of her desire for me in order to pursue the commissions to be had from her wealth and to satisfy my own self-interests. Even the facade of ours being a platonic relationship was part my own creation in acknowledging it as such so I could maintain the relationship without taking responsibility for her hidden desires or mine. She was about to use the money she had placed with me, which was about ten per cent of her wealth, to seek revenge by setting out to destroy me. Nonetheless, it was too late for her as her revenge could not exceed my destruction of myself on that cold and terrible night. Indeed, that night was truly the death of this wretched self in its final climacteric expression.

I had become aware of the force of whatever it was possessing her person and the subtle cunning of her mind. Yet I strangely knew this woman in her heart to be pure, as if she was calling to a purity in me to rescue her from herself. It all seemed so strange to comprehend yet the fact of the matter remained that the fusion between us was flushing both our impurities to the surface. She had come with me to listen to the spiritual master for the first two days he attended in Dublin and challenged him on the truth he spoke relating to death. She dismissed him through his own particular weakness in dealing with sex, that she, unlike the many, had seen in him through seeing from herself. Yes, there seemed to be a particular fury in this woman that had not been met before. Who is teaching who? Can there be resurrection from this? These questions churned through my mind as I walked on the streets of Dublin that night. The resonance from the piercing howl of the she-wolf touched my spirit as a piercing cry from the heart of the Goddess of Love and it was still vibrating my being.

I spent two weeks in a shocked state of numbness after that night until I took time out and sought good company in an effort to get my mind and body together. I started meditating again, as I had been doing sporadically for some time and then one night, when totally unexpected, the healing occurred. I was sitting alone in a restaurant in Leeson Street waiting for the chef, who was a good friend, to join me after he had finished his work in the kitchen. There was a lady seated facing me two tables across and we simultaneously became aware of each other. That magical feeling I had not experienced since I had been a teenager was suddenly re-kindled within me through the tingling of blood in my veins. I could not help but notice it also in her. I tried to stay calm as my friend, the chef, came up from the kitchen to join me. We talked for some time about the usual things relating to work but my attention was still with this woman, and hers was with mine. He noticed how I was not focused on what he was saying, which was quite annoying to him, and he followed my eyes to hers.

Taking his glass of wine in his hand, he straightened himself back on his chair, with the words, "She is nice", then tasting the wine he followed by saying, "But the wine is nice too". My attention remained in her presence for the remaining time I shared with him, to his discomfort. Later as she was getting ready to leave, with another lady in her company, she called to the waiter to phone for a taxi. On his way over to her I asked him to request her to join my table for a glass of wine before she should go and he delivered the invitation quite eloquently. She looked over at us in surprise then spoke for a while with her friend. I assume she explained to her that it would be reasonable to join us for she smiled my way then gracefully accepted. We spent an awesome hour of mutual exchange together while her friend and mine also found joy in sharing their stories. We could sense all that was about to take place between us. It was that spontaneous first meeting of pre-destined love that had suddenly and unexpectantly exploded its brilliance upon us. We could hardly contain our eagerness to be fully together. She seemed immediately sensitive to my silent dilemma, as if she already knew, without any words being exchanged relating to anything past. We were both in that shivering magic and fully open to each other. The creation in its wonder had again re-opened its heart. Love was still there for me it appeared, but I had not yet forgiven myself. Through my own personal sackful of guilt from all of my past, I was still out of tune with the harmony of being with the moment.

Indeed, is this not the usual problem we create for ourselves? We become our own judge and jury according to the measure of the impostor within and we set about whipping ourselves accordingly. This wonderful woman had suddenly entered my life and there was less than half of me present to receive her. Most of my space was swallowed with my pain of being born with the torment of the widow stamped on the front of my mind. Yet it was myself who had allowed it to happen.

Then through it all came the explosive presence of a spiritual master that allowed the dawning of truth to enter and the break-up of this 'psychological me' to commence. Now I was being suddenly presented with the strangest occurrence in meeting a woman of love.

Life is filled with coincidences and we should pay

particular attention to such for through these the subtle aspects in this play of living our lives can be more clearly understood. Everything has relationship and each aspect of one's life has a direct relation with all the others. As we move from the courser to the subtler realms of existence it is vital that we are awake through this awareness. Without this awareness we are moving in an ignorance that is the ongoing barrier to the message of truth. All the assumed knowledge and intellectuality, no matter how well it may seem to have correlation to what is taken for reality, is seldom anything more than the polished expression of this ignorance in another guise of itself.

I was still entangled in the courser expression of communion, while those people entering my life were more in the subtle. Then things seemed to begin to move at a swifter yet finer pace demanding more alertness in order to stay with the moment. I was becoming amazed at the amount of coincidences now happening to me. The most amazing of all happened that night as the taxi she had ordered arrived. I asked where we could meet again and she paused for a moment in thought then mentioned the foyer of a particular hotel, at a particular time, for the following evening. There are countless hotels in Dublin, yet the one that she mentioned was the one of my previous anguish and the time for our meeting was exactly the same as the time previously set by the widow.

Yes, life is beautifully strange, when I am awakened to its fullness and the 'psychological me' with its world full of woes is transcended. What are these woes but the fears that we harbour within as we fail to face the truth in the immediate situation at hand, the only place where truth abides. In the universality of 'Me' the creation is endlessly spectacular.

All of this world I seem feverishly bound
In serving since first uttered sound
Is not even the shadow of truth to begin,
As darkness I am dissolves from within
From the inner 'I' thus cleared to see
The omnipresence of all that is 'Me'.
When this pearl of wisdom be realised
The false no more in its dazzling disguise
Can lead me on its merry-go-round
With nothing of truth out there to be found.
And even the beauty of nature I see
Is but a reflection of 'Me',
This 'Me' in this heart as in all others too
The 'Me' that is the Heart-Centre of You.

Chapter 10
MONEY, A COMEDY OF ERRORS

I was living on the edge of a volcano, as the costs of maintaining the business were mounting and a gap had developed in the accounts between the money coming in from clients for eventual re-investment and the actual amounts being invested at times appropriate to the fluctuating market conditions. This situation arose when the anticipated flow of business from my clients and the associates clients came to an unexpected halt as the industry itself went into a decline. The costs were further increased by the excessive interest rates needed to be paid out to clients whose funds were temporarily caught in the gap.

Indeed the situation of my business had become the general condition of the time as the entire financial services industry was undergoing radical change. Throughout most of the decade of the eighties the industry was driven on the hype of excessive returns that had been the cause of one serious stock market crash. Uncertainty of direction had by now become prevalent and the general push in the life-assurance sector was turning away from investments and focusing more on life-assurance protection policies. It was becoming more and more difficult for the large financial houses to sustain the illusive air of financial mystique and superiority that they had enjoyed as new legislation was geared more towards transparency in regulatory efforts to clean up the declining image of the market. Speculation on currencies was rife and nobody seemed to be clear where the markets were heading.

In my own effort to overcome the imminent crisis developing in my business situation I sought to purchase money to bridge the expanding gap in the business accounts. The flow of the larger investments that were to realise the much needed commissions to balance my books had suddenly disappeared into currency speculation. We could not compete with this. Marketing support from the industry itself had seriously declined and an acute negativity was developing among the life-assurance companies as the returns were sharply falling and drastic cost-cutting measures were impending.

The widow had placed some of her money in my business with the intention of binding me to her and, this having failed, she now set out to destroy me. Rightly so perhaps, according to her way of thinking and if I had been clear in myself I would never have accepted her presence in the manner I did. The business arrangement we had earlier negotiated was quite clear. Her money was to be balanced by funds held abroad and interest was being paid in the interim. However, my business became vulnerable due to the changing market conditions, although I doubt if she was aware of this. She demanded a detailed account of the inner mechanics of my business and foolishly I succumbed to this in my naive assumption that she was only concerned about the security of her money. To alleviate any undue anxiety she may have been feeling I offered her further security on my property but this, at the time, was not her direction of intent. My financial vulnerability offered her a way to avenge the scorn her image had suffered through my final rejection of her as woman. This was her weapon to destroy me and she wilfully set out to do so by using the force of her wealth to engage a private detective, among others, to create serious disturbance around me. If her concern had been for her money she would have accepted the security of my property there and then or have honestly assisted instead of wilfully agitating the crisis.

One could say I had scorned this woman by walking out of her bedroom that fateful night in the Dublin hotel and she was merely seeking revenge. Yet what I was now experiencing seemed to be much deeper than that. There was no equilibrium in her feelings towards me. She needed either to possess me totally or destroy me totally, regardless of financial cost to herself or to anyone else. Money was not the real issue nor was it merely revenge. It seemed to be much deeper than that but I could not figure it out. I wondered was it something from her past she had placed upon me or was it something from mine re-asserting its presence. Whatever it was the psychic pressure I was feeling was becoming unendurable.

I found it acutely difficult to hold on to my sanity in the thick of this state of affairs. The sales team were not generating business and the industry itself was at an all time low. Morale was weak. The decade of the eighties was truly over, that decade fuelled by greed right across the face of this evanescent world. Now the storm blew from another source. The nineties commenced being fuelled by fear. The new insurance products coming on the market were largely aimed towards protection. Transparency had become the buzz word in the corridors of legislation. In those early years of the nineties I began to see that everything happening to me was but a microcosm of the larger reality. The insurance industry itself must have been in serious problems as it measured itself. Then one insurance brokerage firm collapsed sending shockwaves across the field. Was mine going to be the next? Could I sustain myself much longer under the relentless pressure coming from the widow's brigades?

The Australian master had stated that the solution to a

problem is always within the problem itself. So the answer to the dilemma arising around me must be somewhere within it yet through all the confusion it was nowhere to be found. I felt that the only avenue open to me was to buy myself out. I needed to borrow money for this. The banks, however, were now moving into this end of the market themselves and it was in their interests to wash us out of their way rather than negotiating favourable terms of assistance. There was nowhere in Ireland to logically turn, neither did my sales team have the capacity to support themselves. Reality had to be faced. It was time to wind up the business. I told them individually that the play had to end and that I was definitely not playing anymore. The amount of activity, outside of the immediate sales team, that this generated amazed me. It became clear that some about me had been creating their own credibility on the tail-end of my own illusive wave. There was a lot of shouting and even some court cases were sent my way in the wild expression of it all. We were like school children too long at play in a field that had turned into mud. Our costumes had become too dirty and torn for the usual washing and mending that had been sufficient before. The star persuaders of the large life-assurance houses who had for some years enjoyed the colourful road-show of their marketing seminars could no longer sustain credibility in themselves when they were looked straight in the eye.

Eventually everyone went home and I stood alone to face the reality of the situation. If I had done this two years earlier there would have been less of a problem. Yet if I had postponed it for a further two years the problem may have been much worse. But such thinking was not helping. Working and living in the past and future is how one keeps missing the truth. The world of life-assurance and investments seems to sustain itself from the fruits of marketing a conceptual future basing its merits on past performance. We were the sellers of time-related concepts perpetually racing ahead and away from the truth of the moment. If one was to stop and earnestly look at the situation this reality was there to be seen. However, having swallowed the illusive dream the industry permanently weaves the dream of fulfilment seems to be always around the next corner. Practically everyone in the financial sector still wished to believe this and at the same time were scared to hell of their own shadows. It was indeed a comedy of errors and I had danced their dance. Now the music had stopped and the industry itself only had one way to go deprived of the spinning momentum that sustained its illusory trance.

I felt that the best way to bring my part of the play to an amicable end was to buy money from the money markets and move it into investments myself. This would need to be large enough to allow me to bridge the deficit gap and secure the concluding clients at risk with the money guaranteed on commission payments, plus any gearing that may be required on the new parent fund. No other solution was visible to me from within the problem itself, except to allow it to continue as it was and that could no longer be justified, even though some of the large life-assurance firms may have been doing just that in hope.

The truth, however, was not yet being faced by the life-assurance companies themselves. Some of the larger mutual houses were facing uncertainty as their annual bonus declarations could not be maintained and some of them seemed to be indirectly borrowing from their terminal bonus funds to disguise the grim reality of the situation. Such action was taken in the hope that the following year might be better. They could do this because of the freedom they afforded themselves in their internal system of accounting, and it enabled them to protect their face on the market.

These were the difficulties I faced as the external conditions seriously changed and the widow's force continued to intensify about me. I was, nonetheless, still concerned for the welfare of this woman in my foolish assumption that I could rescue her from herself in bringing her to acknowledge reason and still balance my books for the protection of my clients. She was playing the card of I being her mentor as her contact with me continued while, in fact, I was little more than her puppet on the end of a precarious string.

Shakespeare's words, "One man in his time plays many parts" echoed in my ears. The widow's part was very definite on the cold stage of this particular play. My part was to suffer her presence in my life as, in some unseen way, she had significance towards my own awakening. Some of the great masters of the East have clearly said, "I am the world. The world is, as I am". This, I must accept. It is as it is. This is the philosophy of life wherein lies the truth, for I am this world immediately about me. Its confusion is my confusion, its pain is my pain, and its solution, whatever it is, must also be my solution. This was also what the Australian master had been saying, the answer to every problem being in the problem itself. Yet I was still searching for the solution in the world outside, a world that was but the reflection of myself. This is exactly how we partake in the chasing of shadows. If I am in confusion, then everything I call up from outside will be but an extension of that confusion through my interpretation. This is the world we create, this world of ongoing conflict where all of our vested interests endlessly clash, as we chase our personal shadows through shadows. For such is the human condition it seems, to be perpetually trapped in its own perceptible limitations. I was locked within its confines through the hell of my own creation as I had as yet failed to live the wisdom of truth that was coming my way.

Raising money from the money markets was not as straightforward as I had thought. Here I was to discover a far greater web of deception and intrigue than I could have imagined. It started with a character from Galway who actually knew the widow and her involvement with me. He introduced me to a British establishment in the north of England that promised, through him, to accommodate my needs wholeheartedly. But after I had spent some time and effort flying to and fro over the Irish Sea, it turned out to be other than it first seemed. It appeared that they were actually using my problems to help advance their own vested interests. I was fortunate to discover their play before I had made any commitments, but it did cost at least three months of valuable time.

Another character from Galway came on the scene with a proposal for an elaborate range of money instruments that he had knitted together through the currency of the Deutsch Mark, which, if it worked, would be the answer to all our problems. Unfortunately his scheme needed heavy priming and I came close to loosing a quarter of a million pounds that was being made available through me as a short-term primer from a commercial bank. This Deutsch Mark loan scheme was so elaborately complicated that it baffled the brains on the Dublin banking circuit and it took me considerable time to get to grips with it. Apparently forty million pounds would be necessary to create the momentum for it to successfully work and then the legality of all its parts would need to be certified under European Law. I had confidence in the formula and it could have succeeded if there had been a unified commitment between all the participants involved but, unfortunately, conflicting interests came into play and the human condition caused a malfunction again. After giving considerable time and effort to the proposal it had to be abandoned. Other loan schemes came to my attention but after thorough research all proved the same, takers of money and givers of none. The world of the money-men is a mercenary one where everyone is out to take immediate advantage without consideration for the advancement of good.

However, on the positive side of my dilemma, I acquired an indepth understanding of money, this abstraction of reality, and the energy field that it amasses from all who serve it. This is an insight into what is real and what is not that few people have had the privilege of receiving in the way it was presented to me, and for this I give thanks. I know now that all that was presenting itself to me as hell, was in fact just that. This is the blindness of humanity, this human condition, locked in its self-perpetuating ignorance. I had served all of it and believed in all I had served, but every system, every scheme, every individual idea I encountered, when tried and tested, proved false. There was nothing more I could believe in to serve. I had claimed to not know, when listening to all who claimed that they did, yet I was looking again at the force of greed blinding the vision of those in the money-lenders world refusing to face the truth of themselves.

I had now entered limbo. All avenues of recovery I pursued to solve this problem of money, which I had felt I had personally created, took more of my energy and ended in the same way. Eventually I woke up to the knowledge that these problems were not my creation at all. I was merely a part in the play of the elaborate complexities created through that what falsely appears as service to man in the world of finance, but is, in fact, service to the greed that is the reincarnating condition of the human psyche of ignorance begetting more ignorance.

I continued to accept what the master had said, that the solution to every problem is within the problem itself then another of his statements, "If there is nothing you can do, do nothing", entered my mind. I had tested every other option without positive results and indeed the one option left was to sit things out and accept whatever was to come. As I came to a halt, after those years of exasperating madness and relentless speed, I was awesomely amazed at the energetic movement of money. The only movements I made were in response to requests and, strangely, the deficit gap started decreasing. The amounts were insignificant, but there was a decrease. In addition, the value of the property still in my possession was now beginning to increase. This was my only real asset and it had become part of my business account. But even with that, and if the stillness I was now trying to uphold should remain, it could take years to conclude. I was still out there convulsing in the depths of this human condition with people about me in fear. I had now totally immersed this self of myself in experiencing the depths of its world.

Yet I was to truly discover, as the master from Australia had said, that stillness is the way, the only way. In this stillness of mind I began to realise that money was not the real problem at all, it was really a mask hiding the deeper truth of almost everyone immediately concerned. Now I looked from a different place and I saw with a clearer light. I could see the widow's anguish, her real torment within, and her particular cry for help in the only way she knew how. I started looking directly at others, even the meditative friends who gathered together as seekers of truth. We were all suffering from that fear to let go, I mean totally let go, of everything. All the beliefs, all the attachments, are the clinging illusions we mistake for reality.

We endeavour to mend our worlds in our own particular way and in the course of our mending become prone to replacing our discarded beliefs with others more suitable to our shifting rational logic. We are still philosophically groping in the darkness from within the field of thought, for all of this field is conditioning. All the arguments, the rigid assumptions, the imaginings from where all the formulas and beliefs emerge are nothing more than self-deception. In my efforts to correct my own specific part in the play of the life-assurance world I was but one hole in the sieve confusing myself in my particular search for my own particular truth in accord with my own particular conditioning. This was the problem I created for myself.

Some argue that reason is the way. With this I agree when reason is pure. But is not the reason perceived a faculty of thought? Descartes stated "I think therefore I am". Yet all thoughts are conditioned and the reason being used, however subtle, may be nothing more than pre suggested conditioning. Nonetheless, 'reason' can bring us to the threshold then the reason perceived we must also let go of in order to transcend our conditioning. In this way I realise the heart of truth, where reason and truth are one and the same in the light of clear intellect. But I must have freed myself from all opinions, all beliefs and all assumptions before the heart of truth can be realised.

I hasten to add, however, that you should not believe me, for believing is not knowing. This, I must say, can only be discovered from within. If it is not in your own experience, it remains as secondary knowledge and merely a speculative theory, and theory is never the truth. How does one attain it? In my own experience I discovered that stillness is the way, the only way, where there is no thinker separate from thought, no duality as such. This is the true essence of 'Being'. This stillness cannot be forced, it can only arise from within when the mind is fully at rest. The minds that we have become in this world of becoming are never at rest in the continuous churning through the peripheral sensory perception where the false impressions occur. It is through our sensory perception that we create our illusionary worlds where the ignorance of this 'psychological me' conjecturally abides endlessly changing its tune in avoiding the end of its own conjectural self.

The state of absolute stillness is attained through negation, that is, once the 'psychological me' is totally dissolved. When this happens what becomes known is known, and everything is as it is, not imaginary, but exactly as it is. I had been trapped in the illusion of everyone else in my belief that the false was true, even to the point of trying to bring this 'psychological me' to the stillness within, until my earnestness in seeking brought me to the master and I was set free. All that I had previously heard through the words of the wise I now discovered in practice, in the actual experience, where it becomes known. My journey to truth, the real purpose to life, seemed to be holding its course.

Chapter 11

THE REVENGE OF THE WILFUL WIDOW

I could feel the wind of the widow's scheming when a man, using an assumed name, was on the phone with the message "I have money to invest, can I make an appointment to come into your office to meet you". In my years in the business this was the first time such a call arrived from a stranger in this manner. I instinctively knew this was somehow connected with the widow and I wondered what she could be up to now. Since that night I rejected her at the Dublin hotel her sporadic behaviour at times would reach that uncontrollable explosiveness she demonstrated at the Bogman's Ball. The so-called business meetings she was having with me were keeping me spinning in circles. On one hand she wished to destroy me and on the other she showed a willingness to financially assist me so I should acknowledge my dependence on her. The relentless psychological pressure seriously affected my work. I was loosing lucrative business projects due to my over-anxiety for expedient completion so I could conclude my financial bind to her money. She was aware of this and knew it would be the absolute end of the relationship should I succeed in regaining my financial freedom from her. Whenever we met I could never get her to be direct as she nurtured the pretence that the forceful demonstration of her hidden intent had never happened. What could be next? I wondered.

The appointed morning arrived for the prearranged meeting in my office with this stranger and in she walked with this man. At first he looked like a priest in a civilian suit or perhaps a polished second hand car-dealer. In any event this was not a social call. They had it figured out, she the deprived pennyless misfortunate widow and I the thief who had stolen everything form her. It was so sudden and convincing I believed it myself. They already had made a statement to the police they said and they demanded an afternoon meeting between me and their appointed solicitors. This meeting took place in my own offices with her solicitors and mine attending. They demanded that I give her security on my property and I advised them that I had already on several occasions offered her this. But my own solicitor, a woman of insight, requested time alone with me and she advised me against doing this as she saw much more going on than what appeared on the surface. Nonetheless, after the widow showed me the pills she was taking to balance her nerves I decided to go against my lawyer's wisdom and provided the required security by signing the papers they put in front of me to sign. I still lived under the assumption that this was but a question of money.

Neither did it rest there. She went after the property to force it to be dumped on the market while her messenger man bombarded me with threatening phone calls, day and night. It was a mental assault of a most twisted and sinister nature that I could never have even imagined. Indeed this was the most bizarre introduction to depravity that I had ever experienced and it was capable of breaking the most positive mind. He set out to get at my family by phoning my father in the early hours one morning and dumping the story on this innocent man by informing him that his son had robbed a misfortunate poor widow of all her money and was about to be put into prison. It was fortunate I arrived home that morning to help my father deal with the anguish and shock of such a wilfully sinister attack.

The wisdom of my own solicitor was becoming clear to me now. There was obviously much more to this than met the eye. Behind the holy facade of the widow dwelt her association with this man of vicious intent. Then she phoned me again in assuming concern asking me to call to her house as she had something she needed to discuss with me urgently. What could be more urgent than what was occurring, I was trying to imagine, as I knocked on her door that last time. After inviting me in she proceeded to tell me from her feminine side that it had all gone out of control. She claimed to have had no idea that the man was so sinister and said that she had never met him before. According to her story he was introduced to her by a friend and she did not know where he lived, or how to make further contact with him. The friend had apparently left the country. Once again she had me believing her. She said she had handed over thirty thousand pounds to him to get back the money she had given me and now was unable to reach him or stop him. "Not only that", she then said, "but he has now paid five thousand pounds to professional gunmen to have you shot".

She was very convincing and I believed her, as I had always foolishly done. I had been by her side as she told her sad story so convincingly to all those participating in the mountain pageant now some time in the past and particularly in relating to her spouse who had tragically drowned while she was on a religious pilgrimage. As part of her audience I was shown first-hand how skillful she was in painting the picture to her own particular suiting. Still I assumed she was now being truthful with me when she told that she had no way of contacting this man. I blindly overlooked the fuller extent of what appeared to be happening, but engaging assassins to kill me I found too bizarre to accept.

Subsequent to this meeting with her I saw the man in question leaving her house one day as I was driving past. It was obvious from what I saw with my own eyes that they were both good acquaintances. Then I wondered if she could possibly have been lying to me. Yet even when the lie as such was exposed I convinced myself that she may have come to know him following her last meeting with me. I still could not think clearly or act appropriately as I was too confused to distinguish the wood from the trees believing myself to be the cause of this widow's torment.

What had prompted all this, I asked myself. The extraordinary clarity that I had previously caught sight of in the presence of the spiritual master vanished beneath the dark and sinister cloud pushed over me by the widow and her male accomplice. The two could be taken as twins, for the rhythm of their continuous assault seemed to be so much in tune. I felt that I was at the brink of calling on immediate death for release.

A woman had entered my life, a wonderful loving woman I had met in the restaurant that night when I went to visit my friend, the chef. Then the notion began to arise that this widow's appointee, using an assumed name, had been shadowing me and reporting back to her, Now I began to see what may have really been happening. If she could not have me in her life the way she wished it to be, she would not tolerate any other woman having me in hers. This seemed obvious now and her capacity for doing it had already been well illustrated.

It was not just a question of money. It was much more intense than that and the weight of it had driven me financially offside beyond apparent financial redemption. She had for years been bombarding my very existence and manoeuvring me with her business propositions. Why was I the one to be experiencing all this, I asked myself. I never invited her into my life, or into my personal affairs. I was first introduced to her by the life-assurance woman who was trying to sell her a pension. But she instantly took over, skillfully manoeuvring the other woman from the scene. Ever since that first meeting she would rarely look me straight in the eye, no more than she faced the look of the spiritual master when he challenged her personal interpretation of death.

I had not spoken against the force of her presence to anyone before that day she told me that a contract had been taken out on my life. But now I was obliged to respond. She had publicly declared herself the martyr, and indeed it was true, for she had become the martyr of the demon possessing herself that had driven her into doing all she had done in the guise of her holy crusading. No one, until now, had opposed her and she had her eunuchs at hand, selling their souls to be her muscle at will.

Now it seemed it was me she had chosen to face and expose our monsters within. I was just only coping with the slaying of my own. As I set out to take up this challenge she has placed before me I knew I must first be freed from everything false that may still be hiding within me. We had danced the myriad interpretations of wilful minds. The only way the affray could be rightly resolved was through seeking the absolute truth. My precarious business dilemma in the world of finance is part of that world and can only be true to itself. The complexity of the dilemma arising through my involvement with the widow had found its continuity as being part of that world. So where, I asked, could this battle be fought? Where can truth be served?

The only apparent avenue for the discovery of truth, I had come to realise, is in the discernment of all that is the false. Truth cannot be bought. It is the source of all that is 'Me' and, through this body and mind, I can never even hope to know all that I am. As I silently look at myself I can only know what I am not. Truth is in the discovery, it appears, not in the discovered. Whatever appears as true can only be true for now but is not the perennial truth. I had been living my life through the measure of pain and pleasure up to the time I met up with the widow. The very nature of my personal self was in the continual search of pleasure and avoidance of pain. I discovered that the psychological suffering which had become unavoidable in my life had arisen from my non-acceptance of pain. I had been brought to this. There was no other avenue open to me now other than the acceptance of the situation of my life exactly as it had become. Suffering is due to non-acceptance. Acceptance takes one deeper. It opens the door to that place of stillness within. The seeking of pleasure and avoidance of pain keeps us outside of ourselves in our sensory world where our false impressions occur. This is usually due to lack of discrimination. The personal self is constantly seeking pleasure and avoiding pain in its world of self-made duality. The ending of this division is the ending of self. Now I was obliged to accept the pain. There was no other way. This personal self of all that I had become in my world of becoming was brought to the ultimate point of facing the pain of itself. This is entering the personal death where beyond lies the perennial truth. It can only be discovered by discerning the false as I, the observer, am the experience where everything is as it is.

But let us be light in ourselves as we return to the boy in the forest and his adventures unfolding the truth therein to be found. Some time had passed since the incident between little Charlie and the strange woman with the peculiar stare. Nonetheless, Charlie could not forget the beating she imposed on him that day and her deception in offering him sweets to lure him into her deceitful web.

Now this day, Sunday, he was the new altar-boy, dressed up in vestments trimmed with lace, about to assist the priest with communion. The woman with the peculiar stare was kneeling in the front row directly behind him. This was the closest he had come to her since that terrible day. He had not returned to the forest, nor even to his secret sanctuary, for he was consumed by fear. Indeed as he lay in his bed to sleep the fear was there eating up all the openness of life that he had previously enjoyed without question. The sound of her praying from where she was kneeling directly behind him was so loud that he wondered if she could be heard throughout the chapel. He felt that the entire congregation could see the terrible dread that had him consumed. The sharp breeze he was feeling on the back of his neck he was sure was coming from her as she gulped in mouthfuls of air through her flurry of prayers.

The time for communion arrived and the task of attending the priest had been pre-assigned to Charlie. When it came to the strange woman's turn to receive the host he was shivering in dread. He was trapped in this place with the source of the fear in his life now motionlessly standing in front of his face. He looked on her tongue as the tongue of a serpent when it reached out, curling upwards, to jerk in the host. Then, he was utterly amazed as his courage returned for he had passed through the terrible dread of meeting her again. The fearful images and sensations stopped, apparently disappearing as if they had never been there. He realised how silly he had been in succumbing to the fear and how no one had told him, for there was no one but he who knew of this fear that had stood like an invisible monster blocking his natural path of spontaneous life. Where is the difference between this fear that had taken over his space and the fear possessing the adults of what the neighbours might say, or indeed the fear of Hell as spoken by the priest in his over-winded sermon? His thoughts turned back to Church, to God, to the infinite. If all this is the world's answer to ten divided by three, he surmised, then definitely the world does not know.

Chapter 12

THE DARK SHADOW OF DEATH.

WHERE IS MY LOVE?

I knew that the woman in my life should not be exposed to the serious danger. When I told her of the situation she was shocked but insisted on standing by me to give me support. She was the only one I told as I had felt it unnecessary to involve the police. After all, I had only received a threat from a widow who had trusted her heart to my care. This is how it would have appeared. Also I believed that the widow would not be party to such or be in any way associated with hired killers.

Then an extraordinary coincidence occurred. It happened one morning in Baggot Street, just around from where I lived in Dublin. I parked the car and got out to buy the newspaper at my local newsagents. A stranger was waiting by the bus-stop shelter and on seeing me approach came towards me with a gun in his hand. Then the most amazing thing happened. A car suddenly screeched to a halt outside the parked cars. Two men jumped out and seized another man who was standing a little away from the one approaching me. These two men were casually dressed but carried guns and handcuffs and I immediately knew they were policemen. Within seconds another police car arrived with two uniformed officers and the man arrested was handcuffed and bundled into this second car. As suddenly as events began they stopped and everyone had gone, including the first man I saw.

Now it was confirmed to me. I knew it was real. There was someone engaged to kill me. Whoever it was, whoever had engaged them, there was imminent danger to my life. But I could not accept that this was the work of the widow. I had been dealing with many clients and this threat could be coming from a source unknown to me. I knew I had to take immediate action to preserve the life in this body. I did not go near my office that day nor go back to the place I was staying. I phoned my girlfriend at work and arranged to meet her in the city centre instead. When I told her how serious the situation had become she found it hard to accept and suggested we go back to my flat, as we usually did. When we pulled up outside my place on Waterloo Road, three men got out of a parked car two spaces up from where I had just parked. She noticed them as we climbed out of my car and I locked the doors. One of them had opened the boot of their car as the other two approached me. I would not have seen them if she had not been so alert. At that very moment she definitely saved my life. The car keys were still in the door and I immediately unlocked it. We jumped in and drove off leaving the three men looking after our exit in amazement.

We found a bed and breakfast that night in another part of the city. The following day I stayed away from everything associated with my work. It was now obvious that these hired killers had been given details of my normal day to day movements. There was literally no safe place, and now I was experiencing what 'going to ground' actually means. I was being hunted like a fox or any misfortunate wild creature in fear of losing its life. Do animals know fear, I asked myself. No, obviously not. Fear is the product of the thinking mind. The animals respond from their natural instincts. This is how they survive from moment to moment. That day was my test in dealing with fear, the chilling and awful terror and the human condition of this personal self.

I went into a church I had not been in before, found a quiet place and sat in stillness for hours. I waited for the panic to subside and the wild raging thoughts to pass. Gradually, I could feel myself descend, back down into my body, re-entering my hands, re-entering my feet, re-entering my veins and felt the flowing of blood. I went further, further down and there it was, as it always is, that absolute calm flooding up and out to meet me, beyond me, to where I had been, outside of myself. The beauty, the love, the awesome ease arising through the stillness, was now gushing through my body.

Evening arrived casting her colourful shadows through the Gothic arches about me as I sat there returned to the awareness of life. The mind realigned itself to the bliss of the moment. The storm within was stilled. Then gentle thoughts of my childhood years began to arise, like little white clouds in a clear blue sky, with the feeling of life I had seemingly abandoned when I entered the world that swept me out into its turbulence and away from the natural spontaneity of my early childhood when every experience was immediate and whole. But the stillness of the moment at hand was absolute bliss for it had been enriched with an awareness unknown as a child, as I now realised in the preciousness of every breath. I had come to be at one with life, not alone in my body, but in the shapes and forms about me, where there seemed to be no distance between, nothing outside, being fully at one with all else observed.

Nightfall arrived. This night I was spending alone, totally alone. I needed someone to help me, someone strong enough and logical enough, without emotional attachment to me. I phoned a friend and we arranged to meet in Glendalough, a place of ancient monasticism in the mountains of Wicklow. He loaned me some money for food as it was not safe for me to access my bank. There was someone he knew, he said, someone he had worked with on a building contract who actually knew some of these professional killers. He told me he would make enquiries to see if there was any possible way of making contact with the ones after me in the hope that someone could reason with them. "In the meantime try and hold yourself together", he said as he departed, leaving me alone to myself.

That night I spent alone in Glendalough where, for a thousand years or more, monks had slept, lived, prayed and died in another time, another world, somewhere beyond these monastic ruins now silently speaking to my troubled mind. This was a night of reflection. In the stillness I wished to connect with the spirits of the wise and the holy who had once lived and prayed in this sacred place. I ached to connect with their presence I thought I could feel still shimmering through the ancient stones of the place holding the secrets of time. Were they going to hear my pleading for a clearer understanding of all I was now experiencing? But there were no voices from the past to comfort me. Only silence prevailed. I was alone, the only 'I' in the creation, in the silence of this place, stunned to attention by the madness of my living nightmare and the crippling fear arising within.

What is fear? Where does it come from? Why had it put my body and mind in such a terrible state? From the darkness of life, in that darkest night of no other, these questions started arising, all clamouring at once for attention. Yet somewhere behind the deafening noise of my mind, my heart pounded the message, "I am not this, not this".

Then I started to look at the situation. My fear abided in relationship to my physical life. This ultimate fear I was now experiencing was the fear relating to total extinction. This was not the fear of death in itself, for that I could accept, it was the fear of not being. From this root, I discovered, all the other branches of fear were frantically and simultaneously arising and expressing themselves. The fear of never seeing my family again, of never being able to love again, of never being able to conclude my accounts, and all the others now clamouring for immediate attention within this body facing an imminent end.

Being totally alone in the sharp coldness of that night I was seeing that life itself can only exist through relationship, as was the final relationship then expressing itself through this fear of final extinction. All of my problems to date were coming through fear. There was the fear of losing my image. Now I realised it had to be lost. It had to be totally abandoned before the answer to the original question, 'Who am I' could enter my understanding.

It seemed I had come to that place where I was ready and willing to die to all my personal fears. My personal world and personal image could no longer be sustained through the immediate insurmountable pressure that I had seemingly brought upon myself. Was this to be the ending of fear? No, alas, there was the fear of the widow and what she might do to herself should she be forced into facing her own reality. Now my fear of not being able to conclude my life in a manner acceptable to myself was the most immediate. So it continued throughout the night, as each time I felt I had conquered a particular fear, after an exacerbating battle with it, again it returned in a different guise and caused me further anguish.

Dawn eventually arrived, cold and damp on my shivering bones now rattling with the fear still coming through me in waves. I was to discover that fear cannot be overcome by conquest, in fact all my resistance seemed merely to give it more power and created ground for further conflict between myself and my fear. Then, without trying in any way to oppose or to change it, I was obliged to enter it. As I did, the vibration of its presence enormously increased. It was as if my flesh was being torn away from the frame of my body. There was no other way, apart from losing my mind. I entered into its root, as walking into the mouth of a lion, and amazingly I discovered that I was still holding my resonance. I moved within its enormous bubble and passed through its centre point. All of it now entered my understanding.

I discovered that fear cannot be overcome through resistance, as this can only give rise to further expression with another circle of happenings through which it continues its smothering hold. Most of our lives are lived in bondage to such, time spent in the wastefulness of being its victim and its instrument as well, when imposing it on others. The willfulness of all of it feeds on itself and all that I had taken myself to be had been nothing more than its instrument as such. How was I to gain freedom from it? In my direct experience I came to realise that it can only be transcended by true understanding, which is not conditioned reasoning, but the understanding that only comes through the self-knowledge that is self-realisation. Any understanding less than that is still in the realm of fear.

I returned to the city later that day and met my love at a cafe in Grafton Street. After spending the evening together we went back to my place in Waterloo Road. I was to go to England to attend an appointment that had previously been arranged with a commercial bank for the following day. This was to be our last night together. No words were spoken to this effect but yet somehow it was known. There was no way I could give her assurance that these terrible circumstances would pass. This was our last embrace, this one beautiful night of tender and special love, this night I experienced the warmth of 'She' to the innermost depths of my being, a place that was too sacred for any gunmen to violate or for anything worldly to reach. Morning arrived. We embraced and we kissed our last goodbye. I left for the airport under the shadow of death and she went her way in her journey of life after giving to me the greatest gift of all that night in giving herself up to the Goddess.

When I returned from England after that weekend, she had gone. Nothing of hers was left just a note on the table that read, ' Please do not try to find me, it must end this way.' I stood in silence, stunned at the emptiness of the presence of nothing and accepted this terrible fate. So much had gone into our love in such a short time, even with so many pressures from outside crashing upon it. This final pressure from the fear of unknown assassins engaged to kill me, the worst of all, was the breaking point of this wonderful passion we shared. Now she was gone, driven away by the state of my life. I was numbed into empty silence as I walked into the tiny kitchenette. Where our toothbrushes had been together, now there was only one. Even from here her presence was gone. My heart exploded in pain. 'What, Oh God, what has this toothbrush done that it too should be deserted so?' I broke down and wept.

That night I slept alone in Waterloo Road. My instincts, even in a troubled sleep, were alert to every sound. My God, this was a terrible situation that had overtaken my life. I was facing immediate death. Any moment it could occur. If they were to break into my room with guns there was no way I could prevent it. This is how it was, as I lay in silence on my bed awaiting whatever was to come. I listened to every sound on the street outside and every sound in the house. Then suddenly, in the depths of what seemed like despair, that awesome calm, that absolute stillness of mind returned. It swept over me like an enormous wave, coming up from the depths of my being. Immediately the words of the master were a living experience within me. Yes, truly then, I was ready to die. Nothing to sign, nothing to fix, if it must happen, then so be it. I was truly ready to die as I was truly ready to make love if she should return.

The following morning I was up at six, showered, packed my belongings and went into the office before the city awoke to its noise. I collected my post and the list of persons who had called on the phone then quietly left to find a safe place to deal with the facts of the day. I had now entered that place of acceptance where each moment happening is the only moment there is.

This is how it was for me under the shadow of death reflecting the state of myself. But must I not be thankful for all that occurred, for it had brought me through the depths of hell to my own awakening and one glimmer of the Light is worth more than all the sufferings experienced, and all those imaginable as well. This I can say from the depths of my heart.

Charlie was still less than ten when two policemen called to his home. It had been reported by the woman with the peculiar stare that he was the one who had stolen her apples. "But how could they be hers for they were growing wild and free along the dykes of the field and all the children at school were eating them", Charlie pleaded.

"But the field is hers," his father said, "and the apples growing in that field are hers as well. Those you have taken you must give back or these policemen will take you away to a reformatory place. Stealing is a crime and she has told these policemen it was you she saw entering her field".

"But I cannot give them back for I have eaten the lot with my friends on the way home from school", Charlie argued. He felt quite confused as to what was happening. These policemen appeared to be her servants and he suddenly felt that all of the world was in service to the madness that seemed to be taking hold of this woman.

"How could she own these apples? They appear on the trees by their own each year. There is another tree on the other side of the forest. Does she own the apples on that one as well? Does she own all the apples there is, this woman with a peculiar stare?"

It all seemed so strange, he was thinking, this fuss being caused over a handful of apples for eating, especially when last year's crop were left to rot on the ground. Yes, this world that seemed to belong to this woman with a peculiar stare was becoming more than confusing to Charlie.

Ripple stream with soul of wrath,
Cherish deeply sweetest thought
On vain upheaval surging free
From darkened tombs celestially
Shining brightly shaking sights
So 'tis, it seems, in grimmest nights
A howling wind on growling sea.
Let loose thyself upon the wind,
On fruitless pleasures hearts shall bind,
Yet bind themselves momentarily;
Subconscious thoughts wish to be free
Thus it is as time rolls on
Leaving distant thoughts bygone.

Summer, 1966.

Chapter 13

RIDING THE STORM

I knew I had to become illusive, to be, yet not to be. Every call I received and every appointment I made I looked into deeply, even calls from my friends who could be unsuspectingly used to flush me into the hands of these professional killers. Yet, strange as it seemed, the circumstances of my life had brought me to the awareness of being in the moment, fully alert to each moment happening, the quality to life that the spiritual master was zealously expounding.

Usually when we say we are present we are still loading ourselves with thoughts of the future derived from the past, are we not? We are planning for tomorrow, or next week, or next year, or our next dinner, to be as good, or better, or not as bad, as it had been before. And this is what we usually accept as being present. Our minds are endlessly filled with this idle chatter, until eventually we die and the vacuum of our space is instantly refilled with silence! Now, through the immediate circumstances of my life, I was in that void where no such chattering thoughts could be entertained. All my attention was absorbed in an awareness to everything immediate about me. There was no space in my mind for transporting my past in the shaping of future, as each moment of now could well be my last. This situation was making me acutely aware of the blessings of life in everyone and everything I was meeting. I had entered the ice-cold stillness of reality, and it had entered my understanding. This is the rarest thing on the face of this earth. Up to that point in my living experience even coming to stillness and being in the present was but part of my mind. Indeed, those moments in silent meditation, that had become a twice daily occurrence in the stilling of mental activity, were more like a stunning in comparison to the light of the awesome awareness of eternity in each moment of life where life actually is, regardless of space, or place, or time. The 'psychological me' had entered its own dissolution. I was being swallowed by the Logos, the first uttered sound of the point in the void, the perpetual beginning and ending. This is the state of 'Being', both inside and outside my body, this body, that is merely a spacesuit of time. 'It' was being personified within me, as all that I was in the world I created was finally dissolving, and dying. Strange as it seemed, I had been flushed out of the cover of my personal self through the word of a living master and the hand of 'She', in the wrath of the furious widow. Was it not the 'I' from within who called both of them up, when this personality of myself was ready to die?

This realisation is the most astute moment in one's existence, hence my warning to the reader as we set out on this inward journey through the terrors of the inner self. If you are still with me, dear reader, not just this me now writing, but the 'me' within you, the only 'me' known to you in all this creation and beyond, you may now see that the one who earnestly seeks the wisdom of life must inevitably be dissolved in the seeking. This happens through the gnosis, as is already known from within you, and is re-cognised as the cognition of truth once it is illumined through the grace of a guru, as appearing outside you, that is in essence the reflection of the guru within. This is the crossing over, the transcending, the stepping through that invisible door, where this self of myself is never, ever to be seen again. Even in our folklore the key is presented in the tales that are parables illustrating the reflection of the true reality, this key to the door of wisdom, the way of transcendence. As we travel through the facets of time this key is always at hand for those who are ready to enter this door, a passage always invisible to those who are not. Should it be otherwise? Did not the wisest of all once tell us that it is easier for a camel to pass through the eye of an needle than the wealthily possessed to enter? Or do we still equate the lesson as merely referring to the hoarders of money?

During the next meeting I had with my friend he told me that the going rate for a life on the streets of Dublin was just five hundred pounds. He also learned that these hit-men were loyal and dedicated to their task. Once they receive payment to do a job they usually do it. It is a matter of principle with them. The feedback he got from the streets was to advise me to disappear completely for at least three months to allow the heat of it all to cool down. It would give them more time to 'suss out' who was actually paid for the job and perhaps reason with them. He did discover that the hit would be more than likely in Dublin. He told me that I should stay clear of the city as there could be more than one assassin involved depending on who had engaged them. I should change my car and also change my appearance, if I could.

I took my friend's advise and I lived for some time without routine. I would arrive at my home in County Clare unexpected to visit my father and family and then suddenly be gone again. I found some work in England for a while and travelled over and back, but found it difficult to earn enough to cover my costs. Although my body was still in the flight of action occurring each moment about me yet I had entered that state of stillness within. My outward appearance was all physical movement related to my efforts to keep some balance in my accounts. This was becoming impossible as I could not rest, or stay at any one place for too long. Inwardly there was relative peace, as I accepted all as it was.

Then the widow pounced again, this time to seize my assets. A date was set for a hearing at the Four Courts in Dublin. Now I was pinned down to a time and place. I considered the imminent danger if it was someone who was aware of my problem with her who had engaged the assassins without her knowledge. This could have been possible for many were aware of our friendship. I had been working on a close personal basis with most of my clients. There could well be someone among them with something deadly serious to hide of which I was totally unaware. The precarious nature of the situation between the widow and myself could be causing them panic.

But when I attended the court that day I was surprised to discover that her appointed legal representatives, a top firm of solicitors in Dublin, were not handling the case. In any case matters were resolved out of court. The bartering and re-securing of her money took place between her representatives and mine outside the Law Library. It was a comedy of errors, securing what was already secured as she dodged around the truth of her main issue. She agreed to withdraw the charges she had made with the police and also agreed to allow me six months to dispose of her financial claim. If it was to go beyond that time then interest would accrue at an agreed percentage. I agreed to put my property on the market and dispose of her connection with me as swiftly as possible.

I knew that she had no immediate need for the money as I had been working with this woman for years. I was aware of her income from her properties and of other assets she had secured for herself. Nonetheless, I had an urgent need to be rid of her presence in my life once and for all for it was now very clear to me that I could not hope to correct my state of affairs while she continued her schemes to disrupt them. This seemed to be her ongoing intent, for she was still very much in the expression of her mental obsession on me as been her torment.

When I left the Four Courts after the meeting I walked down Ormond Quay, the river Liffey to my right, and crossed over Capel Street Bridge. In defiance of would-be killers I had momentarily walked into the sun. I found my way to The Source in Temple Bar, I was offered a steaming black coffee by James, and listened to people talking about normal things, about love, about life, about truth. The wonderful freshness of this entered my being as nectar from the most high. The sun was shining again. I was aware of the contract out on my life and these people needed to be acknowledged with respect. This one moment's freshness was not total freedom from my burdens.

Some time passed, and details of this additional court agreement brought about a temporary ease. Nonetheless I was still obliged to stay out of sight, out of Dublin, and to avoid any type of detectable routine for I did not know who were these killers nor was I sure who had engaged them.

The procedure of dealing with my business, by bringing my accounts to a balancing stage I tried to do by phone and by proxy. My life was still on a razor edge. Any moment it could be suddenly finished. My main concern arising was for the clients who were innocently exposed to this turmoil in my affairs. This was the one purpose remaining in staying with the flow of my business and for this I needed to stay alive, apart from the natural instinct of preserving the life in this body. I still needed to be there to conclude, however long it would take, and in the meantime to serve their immediate needs in whatever way I could.

Now the rules had clearly changed, for this was a matter of life and death. It had evolved into a balancing situation, my inheritance from the brokerage business I created once I accepted the sales-team that had knocked on my door. Yet through accepting them everything else ensued. Many had come, and joined and played as the bubble had grown and grown and then, as the markets turned, so did everything else and I stood alone with the deficit. Everyone else had gone. The few loyal ones who had remained, I now personally sent away due to the critical state of my life. This was no place for innocent folk. It started with me and with me it must end, but surely not by the hand of professional gunmen on the side of a Dublin street.

Now I had entered aloneness as a solitary soul on the face of the earth. The emphasis of my work seemed to be moving more towards listening to people's personal stories and showing them ways of dealing with their problems rather than talking finance. Basically I was sitting it out, riding the storm so to speak, and waiting for an issue large enough to facilitate a way out of my own financial dilemma. I observed that my vision was growing deeper and deeper. Being with persons for just a few minutes I was seeing right into their lives. Problems they may have been carrying for years, the remedy would now almost immediately present itself. I had no time for loose talk. They either accepted the solution I was presenting, or allowed me to fold my brief and be gone. Each moment now had become this precious, for the knowledge of life, I had now discovered, can only be in the moment. I was dealing directly with truth that so few of us are ready to face. This is the root cause of our problems, as it had been in my own experience, until the widow entered my space and blew everything that was false in me right out of existence through the weight of the problems she harboured in the depths of herself being with a reflection of my own.

For this she has been my archangel in disguise and, who can tell, perhaps she has also been my salvation, in whatever needs to be salved. Yet the truth of my own situation to me was still bizarrely complex. There were so many issues at play that seemed conflicting, yet each was true from a particular point. I was beginning to realise that the real truth in this gigantic jigsaw of living confusion is more holistic than particular. I had stopped responding to people's unnecessary narrow desires and unwarranted fears. All my energy was now being absorbed in facing every situation as it presented itself and finding what was available to remedy each moment. The past was past and what was done was done. This was not a time for tribunals. The answer to the problem lay in what could be done now, right now, yesterday is done, tomorrow is not here, the answer is always in the moment. If nothing can be done right now, then that is the immediate answer at hand and is to be acknowledged as such instead of forcing what is not, in trying to appease the want or the fear of another.

This awakening was like waking from a dream where I had been lost in illusions and bound in service to yesterdays. I was back to square one, nothing could be done, except to ride out the storm. This can be most painful, can it not? I was trapped in the relationship with the widow and desperately wanted to end it, for I knew it must end, as everything does in our dreaming. Yet nothing ends before its time. Is this not so in every experience? In moments of clarity the witness seated within me silently asked who is this person wanting to end it, and I would instantly see the ghost of the past and drop it. This ghost of myself is the human condition of infinite past still foolishly trying to conclude. But do not believe me, just listen to the people about you, to the politicians, the social scientists, the economists, and everyone else, listen, from that place of silent listening. Is theirs not the ongoing story of past fixing past, while perpetually creating more of the same?

Is this not how it had been in my life? I had to get this job at hand completed before I could enter love, before I could be the joy of life in itself. Does it sound familiar? This is my story, my contribution to this tale of madness, in which the essence of life is wastefully absorbed in endlessly dealing with yesterday's problems. Each day adds another yesterday to my overweight sack, as my own personal contribution to the mental derangement expressed as the human condition. Is this what we accept as being normal? Are we thus deluding ourselves? It may be normal as in being the norm, but can we really assume it is natural, as our true nature? Can I hear it from the place of silent hearing? Can I see it from the place of seeing through stillness, with no thought arising?

This was my life of looking, silently looking, as I drove through the night from one situation to the next, rarely resting, rarely laying down in the same place twice, with the likelihood of death on my heel and my business dilemma before me. My sack was let go, no more to be filled, yet this ghost of my past, the ghost of myself, was now the ghost of the world around me.

Where now dark night?
Where is the sun?
Where is the seed
From whence begun
The sprouting of this tree
That I assume is me?
The fruit that's bitter sweet in taste
Through pleasure-seeking haste,
Is this how it must be,
Resprouting seed, resprouting tree?
Must all I am now lie to waste
Forever dark through sensual taste?
Where now is sight of 'Me'?

Chapter 14

THE MASTER RETURNS

Summer arrived again and the Australian master commenced a round of seminars in Europe. Although my funds were low I managed to get to his first call at Leicester University where I attended four and a half days of a residential retreat with approximately three hundred others.

Since my first encounter with this man he had seated himself in the middle of my road of inner discovery, my journey within to meet with the terrors of the inner self. The illumination from his wisdom had already spun me deeper than the philosophical field where I had been focusing my search for a clearer understanding. The light that flowed through the grace of his presence caused all my world to become transparent and I faced the incredible subtlety to the finer masks of the demon abiding in the human psyche behind the consciousness of our immediate selves.

By the time of the seminars in Leicester I was over two years into the burning hell and things were somewhat different now. Night after night as I lay my body to rest I could physically feel that scorching fire and the blood pumping through my veins to the sound of a garrison drum. This I experienced directly beneath the conscious state when the body is on the threshold of sleep. Even when I entered deep sleep there was still an awareness of it. There was no escape. This was the truth of my situation for I had called it up when previously in this master's presence. I accepted his challenge in calling to life to deal me whatever it should to make me pure. I had ignited the fire that was by now a raging inferno devouring the psychic demon of my psychological self, as I had placed my trust in his words.

The human condition, that is 'the psychological me' in all of us, is what I had been serving through my reactionary state within the confines of this reactionary world before the burning commenced. Once the gates of hell are opened, they are opened to swallow. Even if all of my financial dilemma immediately dissolved and the widow withdrew her threatening behaviour, there could be no turning back. When this fire is commenced within there is no stopping it. It will burn and burn until everything is burned out. The deeper it burned in my own situation the clearer I was coming to life. Now I was sitting in front of this man of extraordinary wisdom and absorbing his every word. Yet not just the word, but what was coming from behind the word, and deeper still, his pain. I was connecting with this as it started clearing itself to me. Most of the people present, it appeared, had also entered this burning while some of them, saints in the flesh, seemed to be physically glowing in the light. There was a beautiful gentleness, a grace, permeating through the entire assembly that visibly expanded each day. This grace was a cleansing, a letting go of the fears, as this master, in fecund and lion-hearted style, pounded the truth of the situation into each problem declared. To me this was my reservoir of light, this outer confirmation of all that was happening within.

The outer mask of the personality that I appeared to be, and what I served, had now melted down, and what a melting it was! This personal mask, this impostor to life, had even been declared a European champion in selling life-assurance and all the energy of my true essence was sucked out in support of it and its consequences, the brokerage firm, its illustrious team, and its insubstantial impetus face. As this mask screamed for more food to support its falsehood the deficit of itself grew larger and larger. Then it screamed for my life as the only way out, as it had succeeded in doing to others. Some people I knew still living, supporting their own, were soon to be dead by their own hand under the impetus weight of its psychological pressure. This is man's own self-made monster of living and yet it is not personal at all, for all of us born, whether saint or villain, are part of its continuing story. Whether we care to accept it or not, we are, as one, this human condition.

Nonetheless, the natural rhythm of life, as is nature itself, brings all to an end before the next beginning. Without exception this psychic demon, this creator of the human condition, breathes in and breathes out across the frontiers of time. As its monstrous outer shell grows larger and larger its mask grows thinner and thinner until eventually it becomes transparent to all. Then, when exposed through illumination, it dissolves, but alas, is reborn again in another one of its cyclical masks, another hell in the making, for the un-vigilant reborn to serve it. Is this not the repetitive story in our history of time?

With the light I received I was now seeing into the presence of this psychic demon in others, as myself and not just in individuals but in corporations as well, particularly the insurance and money business, for this is the heart of this world where the illusion we serve is mistaken for truth. As we become lost to our own individual struggles to satisfy our individual desires, whatever they are, we are the fodder for this demon re-asserting itself within us. However noble my personal goal might be, even in desiring to become a saint, it is but another facet of this 'becoming' that immediately generates another division of 'me' and causes the arousal of what is not saintly. All the trying, all the 'becoming', is the demon re-asserting itself.

This spiritual master had become my silent mirror and I

brought myself before him. Just by pausing and looking without question or judgement at this false image of myself through the light of his seeing it was clear how this image had taken my life's blood to support. This silent looking carried me into my third year of burning through the terror of my inner self, through my own personal layers and personal masks in the impersonal world of my immediate making. In discarding the outer I simultaneously discarded the inner and I found myself stripped naked within, standing on the edge looking straight into the abyss. I discovered the actual hell, that is the negative to life and the essence of being. This hell is directly behind the psyche, the root of the human condition and feeds itself through the outer masks of expression, relentlessly sucking the vitality of all humankind.

Some of us may fervently believe in a hell hereafter and this may or may not be true in accordance with one's conditioning in one's particular world of beliefs. There is, nonetheless, a distinction between believing and knowing. Believing in anything is conditional on the fact of not knowing? One does not have to believe in the known. The hell I discovered is right here in this eternal moment of 'now', just one layer beneath the personal psyche, this raging abyss, the bowels of the human condition. This is merely the beginning of what is made known to one, with no bags or baggage, still venturing on. So let us continue, and earnestly question, as we step into the depths of this hell.

The 'psychological me' is the personal expression of this hell in ourselves. It is here that we have become lost in the wilderness, having lost contact with reality. This is the world of duality where a hell must be for a heaven to notionally exist. The rule of measure is the chasing of pleasure and the avoidance of pain. It is so how we continually strive in our relationships in our efforts to ease the psychological pain of ourselves where we can never discover that heaven and hell are one and the same as part of the human condition.

The widow remained imprisoned in her personal hell through her obsession. The continuity of this had become dependant on me for we are but mirrors of each other. The false that she unknowingly served had found its dependence in the false in me. But the light that flowed through the grace of the master has caused everything about me to become transparent where the hell of oneself can be seen. This was her greatest challenge in bringing her face to face with the hell of herself, as had happened to me, thus aroused the fury of her own personal jailer. This jailer, her outer mask that validated itself on my masks before the burning of mine commenced, is the hell she was suddenly obliged to face.

This is how we set about living, using our energy and time supporting this image, this outer shell of ourselves, for the approval of a world we deem to be other. When we earnestly look from the place of silent looking let us ask ourselves: Is this where relationship is sought, even between lovers still seeking mutual satisfaction, as the demon of hunger looking out through the eyes into the eyes of itself in another?

This is the world, the outer shell of the abyss and the only avenue to freedom is through the invisible door. I discovered the personality abides on this shell where all the pains, the fears, and the narrow perceptions clamour for individual attention. I believed in a god created by man in the image of man. This god of fear I had received as a child and then later I was given the modern day god of false love, that is the false love with its claw of personal need, consumer wantonness and self gratification. We race from one love to the next screaming for satisfaction. Is this our fulfilment? Can such be the purpose of life?

The ultimate consumer desire is the want to secure a personal place in heaven for this outer wretched shell, this false image we serve. Is this not the greatest blasphemy of all against the truth of immortality? How great it is to die, totally die, to all of this, and still be alive to know it. How great it is to hear the word, as it was in the beginning, is now, and ever shall be, and greater still to enter the word, and be as one with the Logos.

Mary had not changed any. She met me with her smile still walking in the same light, that warm glow and ease of posture. Each time I met her at these seminars, the last one six months before in London, she was always in that same calm, that awesome calm that momentarily cleansed me of fear that day I sat in a Dublin chapel in terror of losing my life. To me this was my coming home, this was the cleansing of me. I must thank the widow, as the part she played in it provided fuel for the fire of my cleansing. Here also gratitude is deserving.

Is this not the true reality? When relating to this play of life in my own situation, if any of the acts were excluded, then all that happened would not have happened as it did. I had been struggling so much against all the parts that were seemingly unpleasant in the blind ignorance of picking and choosing. Then I appointing this wretched self as judge and jury of my own apparent failures. Is this not our usual problem, as we are endlessly trying to eliminate those parts of our lives that are not to our immediate liking, while those could very well be the most relevant if seen in the context of the fuller story?

Nowhere is this more obvious than in the world of the saintly, where denial is stacked high upon denial, and bound tight with the bonds of fear. Then some teacher arrives with a glimmer of light and everyone runs for cover while all the stacks of denials turn into a raging bonfire. How glorious it is to be able to accept it all as it is, the good and the bad, the pleasant and ugly, as being but one and the same.

Four and a half days in this place of retreat among three hundred people or more, all emanating like Mary, allowed an extraordinary awakening to happen within. Now all of the madness of my personal story made sense, the egoistical glory, the indifferent insurance industry, the wilful widow, the hired killers dedicated to their task, the Courts of Justice, and all that was necessary for my awakening to occur.

Is this not the silver lining in the cloud? Is it all necessary? Yes, and more, or whatever it takes to dissolve the ignorance of self. This I can freely say from my own experience even though I was still walking in nights darkness with a torch for a light. Recharging the battery through the presence of the master may have brightened the field, yet my vision was still restricted to the length of the beam. To see all, I knew I had to patiently wait for the dawn and for the glorious light as the light of the sun. Trusting the word of the master I had entered the abyss with this torch. I was now in the inner realm. The albedo was beginning to show its measure over this volcanic apparition, this 'Master of the West', still sitting firmly on my particular road, as its glow was now flooding out from behind him and reducing his presence to a shadow. Or was it but another reflection of hell I was seeing, another reflection of another part of myself?

My energy and enthusiasm was raised sufficiently at Leicester to create the opportunity for me to attend an extended group at the following seminars in Eindhoven, Holland. Here the master was even more elegant, and his magnetism was all-consuming. In this large gathering I noticed how centred he was, as the axle of a wheel with all spokes leading from the outer rim to this inner place. I could almost visibly see the lines of energy flowing in his direction, as if his lights were being charged by these people quietly sitting before him. There was no cross correlation to be seen as everyone's attention was directed towards him. I noticed how personal relationships were coming under strain from the magnetism of his presence. There was no space for pretence before him, no space for lovers serving themselves instead of serving love. No outer mask could endure the burning power of his penetration.

Truly this man, who claimed to be 'Master of the West', was accepted by all as the captain of their cosmic ship. And truly he had helped me to grow through the years of mounting crisis that lead to my personal death. Listening to his tapes and reading his books had been my only sanity. All that he said had given me the key to the inner door, seeing the human dilemma exactly as it is and greatly contributed to my inner awakening. He had indeed been the mirror reflecting the false within me. It was through the illumination of his presence that my psychological masks were dissolved. Now I looked at him silently and my vision passed right through him. No, I did not wish to come to the end of this man, yet I could not deny what was happening. I had no question to ask. Indeed, during those moments, there was no questioner left who needed to know. All action now seemed to be coming from that place of stillness within.

Then a man from Denmark came to my notice as he had been quietly observing me. We sat through lunch together and he confirmed to me all that he could see through the light of his teacher, a Maharishi from the East. He had been with his teachings for some years, he told me and that the Australian master bore testimony to all that he had received through the light of the Maharishi. Then he continued to tell me that there was light even brighter than the Australian master's in our assembly that many had not yet the vision to see. It is the greatest privilege being at one with all of it. This is the well of our being. This man from Denmark introduced me to the works of the Maharishi which later became my daily companion and opened me even further to all I received from the 'Master of the West'. Now it had truly escalated, the bridges I had crossed had all burned behind me, there was no turning back as there was nothing to return to. The bubble of living the confusion of the human condition had exploded back into the nothingness from whence it had come. If the aching was to arise to return to that state, then I would be as the mythological Oisin succumbing to the earthly desire and returning to dust.

I was dying to each facet of this 'psychological me' through all that was occurring in my own experience. My inner consciousness was transcending the human condition of mass ignorance that had been my personal condition before the illumination from the master's presence flooded through the falsehood of this world of myself. There were no other courses at hand, or no university to my knowledge that had attained to his state of enlightenment. This wisdom flooded from this man and I was freely receiving it in the stillness of listening, among the many others now seated in silence.

I knew I had to continue in the earnestness of seeking as the seminars in Holland were coming to a close. I had discovered the purpose of life, having been cleansed of my illusory world, which is the rarest of occurrences on the face of this earth. Colorado was his next call on his journey back to Australia and, if it was to be part of my own journey of awakening, then I knew that I would somehow be there, as I somehow had come to be in Eindhoven.

I?
Who am I?
Am I none?—Or am I all?
The archangel or the fall?
To existence am I the intrusion?
As I trudge wearily onward,
Searching, searching—For a way out to find
Of the dark forest,
Feeding its endless confusion—From the bottomless pit of my
mind.
The signs of approaching night—Again almost upon me,
Another corpse.
Another beginning?—In this endless spinning
Of night followed by days.
Then lo!—A torchbearer—With a flickering light.
I will travel by him to the end of his journey
Should this be what life doth say,
Until the evening dawn
Lights this forest within
This one dawn
This last dawn
This tree
This 'Me'
This,
This,
This
'I'

Chapter 15

AMERICA CALLS TO ME

It was my first visit to the United States. I had never had any desire to visit this land. In my naivety I had assumed that it was already lost unto itself, as it had evolved into a place of consumer vulgarity most chronic, and gave little sign of redeeming itself. Of course this was just another of my personal, lingering opinions about to be challenged. Every opinion one holds is a barrier against the truth and in my own particular case, having been a student of Political Science as part of my past, I was dominated by the analytical opinions of the Euro school of thought. We, as individuals, are seldom more than the mass opinionative expression that is most immediate about us. We foolishly play hardball with our personal opinions, even those scientifically proven through professional analysis, yet we are locked between the permitted parameters in our structures of thinking, as in accordance to the limitations of mind.

I set about examining my own personal opinions of what the United States seemed to have become. I was now consciously looking so I might see these opinions for the unnecessary baggage they were, and leave them behind me. I felt that I should travel to this land with the freedom of open mind, otherwise I would be nothing more than another pawn in the ongoing conflict that is the human condition of war declaring itself on war. Is it not the usual story, even through the courses of Political Science in the field of Conflict Resolution, as delegates circumvent the world of cause and effect, forever dissecting the problem in the other, where there are endless others, while failing to grasp the fundamental truth that conflict commences at the very first opinion that I, the individual, hold? Is this not the root of all conflict among humankind, this opinion of mine imposing itself on another? And if I am the analytical scientist now feeling the hairs of my neck rising to this challenge to my opinionated, intellectual self, then should I not look at what am I immediately defending? Is it another opinion?

The flight from London to St. Louis and then on to Denver was pleasant, relaxing and presented itself with the ease of destiny unfolding. Having spent about ten action packed days after Eindhoven in attending to my work, getting my visa and my first transatlantic ticket, it amazed me how efficiently everything worked out. It was as if the clarity of that man of master consciousness also flowed through my immediate affairs.

My first overnight taste of America was a low budget motel on the edge of Denver City. I slept soundly with the windows wide open, there were no hired killers after me here and no business dilemma to crowd me. This wide open place, with clear air and Rocky Mountains was nirvana to my heart and my temporary release from that insanity and madness behind me.

The following morning, after taking a cab downtown for a breakfast that was American and massive, I returned to the airport to join with a limo that had been arranged for the group. We were taken high up in the Rockies to a resort in Winter Park where the seminars were to take place. As the mini-bus wound its way up through the mountain ledges and precariously positioned pines, we eventually came to the peak that is of special significance known as 'The Continental Divide'. Apparently from this point of this great turtle continent, all the waters flow either East to the Atlantic, or West to the Pacific. What a magnificent view to behold. It filled me with awe, as I am sure it fills everyone standing on the crest of such an enormous geographical expression.

Two weeks previous I had been on the flat lands of Holland with no idea that this day I would be in this magnificent place on top of these Rocky Mountains, and tasting its wonder. Such is how things happen when one is swallowed in the earnestness of the search for the truth. An avenue suddenly opens and the obstacles of the world are obliged to make way. But nothing happens before its time, and my time had now come to be in this land.

Here on this peak I took my first silent pause as the engine of the limo was released from its laborious climb. I had been brought to the stillness of this special place of purity, the perch of Aquila. The waters beneath me flowed out to the East and the West impregnating the great mother earth, my lungs were filled with the clear mountain air of the Great Spirit of this sacred land. My first landing again so it seemed, and I was made welcome. With the blue sky caressing the lower peaks of the summits around me, the midday sun shimmered through the clear valleys and danced on the green hue from the tree tops below while the birds of the air soared beneath them disappeared out of sight. Such was the beauty to behold in the boundlessness and natural freedom this land of mystery presented to me in that moment.

The limo continued on its journey, now mostly downhill, until we eventually arrived at the Conference Centre. We booked in, had lunch and made our way to the seminar room. It was bright and airy with a magnificent view of the trees and the peaks from all the windows that were opened to the freshness of the light, mountain air. This was an intimate scene as there were only about fifty attending. The rostrum up front was neatly prepared with the master's seat just high enough for all of us to see him, and with a beautiful display of native flowers to his right. Needless to say he was pleasantly surprised to see those who had travelled from Europe. As it was such a small gathering everyone had space to ask their questions. As for me, I still had nothing to ask. I had connected with the awesome grace of the moment in the stillness of being. This was a pause, a rest for my spirit, nothing less, nothing more, a time of absolute bliss, my release out of hell, being fully in this moment. Each day on these mountains was a journey into deeper and deeper stillness, a step in the ongoing dissolving of the personality of myself. I was there to bring an end to this 'psychological me' through the process of cleansing that had commenced on that evening following the funeral procession in Ireland.

One majestic night of clear skies and soft winds, as I walked up the side of the slopes with the sounds of the wild in my ears and the trees to my left and my right, the full moon seemed to be resting on top, as her beams were reaching down to caress me. I stood there in this timeless expression of stillness and beauty and the glistening aura of the trees, of the mountain, and even the moon, was clearly visible to me. That moment, as is every moment, was a privilege to behold just in being, spilling out into it, with all of it spilling into me, where there are no boundaries, no barriers, no personal me, in that oneness, beyond words, beyond description, beyond, yet within. This is not speaking about past, for what I am describing is exactly what is always present in you and I, when we are purely in the 'now' to receive. Being in the presence of a living master, which is the rarest occurrence on the face of this earth, allowed such stillness to be clearly perceived. Alone on the mountain that night was the most wonderful welcome of that place of magical innocence and all my opinions through my conditioning of past were discarded, and hopefully dissolved, thus allowing me the freedom to receive.

Another night we went to a rodeo, and one of the wild bulls broke loose. He came right over to us, pounding and snorting, and we could see the fire in his eyes, as fierce as the fire in the spiritual master's. This is the closest I can come to describing what looking into the eyes of a spiritual master actually is to behold. It is so, like being eyeball to eyeball with a wild raging bull. The master's intent is just like the bull's, death, immediate death to whoever or whatever it is starring in the eye. To the master this is the outer shell, the personality of all that we blindly support, where we carry all our pains and woes, even to the pinnacle of unloading this baggage at his feet. He will keep charging and pounding until it is smashed and dissolved and so this personal death occurs. Then, only then, is one truly born to be one's own master. Is this not the wisdom of life given to anyone truly a seeker?

My own outer shell had expanded beyond true recognition. As part of the insurance industry I had become top salesman and forceful persuader, persuasion and the application of pressure being the survival line for that business. All its refresher courses and its particular concepts of positive thinking were all geared towards improving the techniques of this forceful creed. They crowded the minds of the innocent prey for wilful and selfish advantage. Then, as new legislation appeared, the techniques became more sophisticated, but with similar intent. My own outer shell became a microcosm of the marketing face of insurance and investments but we have more layers than one to our particular shells, it appears. When one sits in the presence of a spiritual master, which I am told less than point two percent of the world's population is ever likely to have the privilege of doing, then layer after layer is set on the course of self-destruction by the grace of his presence. This is the challenge to all that is perceived to be hell, for as one layer dissolves another is exposed to be faced, and each layer being faced is but another hell of myself.

To me, it was like the swinging of a pendulum. The higher it swings to the right, the higher it also swings on the left. There is a law of physics that states, to every action there is an equal and opposite reaction, or, the higher the climb the greater the fall. These statements illustrate that the equilibrium is always served, and this too had been my dance. I had taken the life-assurance industry to the limits of its own application. All it had fed into me I had become. Although it has laws and suitable formulas to disguise itself, I was now obliged to operate with none as I set out to compete with it in my efforts to conclude in the interests of everyone immediately concerned. This was the equilibrium I sought in my business. But my childhood, my family and my upbringing were the anchors of love and my true equilibrium in life. As my pendulum of existence swung so high in the outward direction, it was logically necessary for it to reach such a contrasting height as to be seated in the presence of a spiritual master in the flesh. I must not deny any part in the play for all is but part of the dance of the life being examined.

Now my own outer layers of personal image were exploding, one after another under this constant and persistent pounding of the spiritual master. In stillness I observed. The following morning when he entered the conference room and took his seat, he sat in silence for a while, then looked at us one at a time with a similar look in his eyes as that of the raging bull expressing its anger on the previous night. This was fire, this was death, with "no bullshit here please", as his spoken words coming to greet us. This is the greatest giving, for we can take it or leave it, it does not matter to him. How privileged we are to receive this greatest gift, when we are opened to see, all in one, one in all, the rodeo, the rider, the bull.

This great turtle continent had opened its heart to me although it had taken the presence of a spiritual master to lure me here. The people were warm and friendly, and openly sincere wherever I went. I discarded my sackful of opinions On route back to Ireland I was detoured from St. Louis for a week on invitation from a friend I had just met through meeting with John who was now lecturing at Missouri University. I found myself attending an annual convention at an open camp in Connecticut with economists, political analysts and sociologists, among others. Here in this place of varying convictions, among social scientists from the highest calibre of intelligentsia, I was amazed at the openness and sincerity and their eagerness to seek out the truth. There seemed to be a willingness to acknowledge the cause of all conflict to be rooted within, among those to whom I had spoken, even though all the research issues being displayed were on findings that were always relating to the 'other', in ongoing evasiveness of that fact. Individually they spoke from their hearts, while collectively they spoke from their minds. It takes extraordinary courage for the one sleeping under the shelter, in the collective mind of the intelligentsia, to discard the familiar in favour of allowing the unknown dawn through clear intellect.

Yet there was a willingness to pause between the stressful necessities of impressions being made to protect the insecurities of image, there was a willingness to briefly acknowledge the human condition. Our minds, still locked between the permitted parameters of thought of each particular field of research, deny the openness required for the shift in consciousness to occur so that we can transcend our particular wheels of cyclical repetition. Must we not challenge this state of being locked in the past through consensual opinion? Or are we not yet ripened to the maturity of moving away from the endless analysis of the 'other', not yet having come to the realisation that all others are but the reflection of self? Can there be understanding in shadows? Or must I forever conform to intellectual opinion, as this 'psychological me' crouches in fear of the unknown? Perhaps it is easier for the camel to pass through the eye of a needle than for this 'psychological me', we each relentlessly support, to pass through our accumulated wealth of information. Somewhere deep in my heart I am probably aware of the flimsy lining in this cloak of knowledge, cushioned by consentience, that I have wrapped around the insecurity of my transient self.

Even as the plane departed for London I knew that I would soon be returning to this great land again, for it had unfolded itself and it had shown me its love and its pain through the heart of its people. Their sense of adventure, now coming to the end of the exploration of matter, is still very prevalent in its eagerness towards exploring beyond the frontiers of mind. There seems to be a willingness to pause and to question, a willingness that has flowered beyond the apparent complacencies of the philosophies of the East and the re-shuffling of European Christianity. Here in the West stands this moment's harvest of the Athenian seed, the raw purity of what is to come. And this coming is already here, is it not, as it always has been? For this is the awakening, beyond the permitted parameters of the opinionated mind, this awakening to the recognisance of our true nature. You do not have to believe me, as it glows from your centre, this cognisance beyond all opinions, that you, in your heart, are the center of all.

Whatever being there is glorious,
prosperous or powerful,
know that to have sprung from a spark of My splendour.

Bhagavad Gita X 41

Chapter 16

MONEY MADNESS

It was a cloudy and misty morning as the plane flew from London to Dublin on the last leg of my journey from the USA. I could sense the unease in myself.

I had no idea what reception would be waiting for me. Fear returned to the thoughts flooding my mind. It appeared as if I was being re-programmed back into that state of fear, now that the two weeks release from its clutches were spent. I did not oppose it or deny it. It was there. It was real. I remained as the participant observer witnessing it re-entering my body. I could see that it was clearly coming through what was entering my mind. It was not outside of me. This fear was the shadow of the past re-asserting itself through my thoughts. In this moment, the one now happening, there was nothing immediate to fear, even so, rising thoughts came to mind suggesting what might happen as the past re-asserted itself and the fear was now being expressed as part of my lingering attachment to this.

This I could see as the 'psychological me', the ghost that it is, entangled in the analytical web of a world that has been. But I was openly looking at it now, and it was clear to see that there are no segments to fear, as we are usually led to believe from our own self-delusions. Fear is and all the objects it creates are always of the mind coming from the memory of past. All the different forms it takes are but forms, there is only one fear, fear is. I was now looking directly at the fear re-asserting itself within me and in the light of this awareness it did not have space to objectify itself in an outside form. Herein, I discovered, lies the door of transcendence. And it can only be understood in the actuality of experiencing it.

I found the question arising in challenge to psychological thought as to why we only seem to think of past and future in relation to pleasure and pain, which is the womb of fear in itself. Is it possible to be in the present and to be free of such linear thinking? In my experience I had already discovered it in the presence of a living master, beyond the self-imposed permitted parameters of thought. Having been opened, can I be closed again to have my actions governed by fear, as had occurred through every action I had taken before this opening, even the washing of my face?

My play of life is as your play, my experience is as your experience, in another form, another sequence, but yet exactly the same. I am the participant observer and I had been wasting my energy in trying to distance myself from fear. What is this observer but the accumulation of past, with its dogmas, its theories, its cushions of beliefs. Through these we have built false security and placed ourselves in the protection of a society of our own re-creation, as it perpetually battles with its fears. Let us honestly look at it. Am I not endlessly trying to distance myself from my objects of fear? From my first moment of waking each morning, am I really anything more than a reaction of fear? I am afraid of being late, afraid that my lover might stop loving me, afraid of not getting what I want, afraid of losing my job, my status, my child, my image to others, as I am scrubbing my teeth, without even noticing the scrubbing. Does it not sound familiar? Then why can I not face the truth that I, the observer, am the fear? For the facing of this truth is the ending of it. But do not believe me, this can only be known from within oneself, as all that I am relating from the outside is but another idea, another theory, that can only be true from within you, in your own experience when there is no distance between you the observer and the object of fear being observed.

As I went through customs, collected my luggage and exited to the car park, I was acutely aware of anything suspicious. I had just been two weeks out of Ireland and nothing had changed as far as the hired killers were concerned. Points of entry, such as airports, would be particularly dangerous if these people were aware of my movements but the trip to America had been arranged on the spur of the moment, and it was unlikely that anyone should be waiting for me. Nonetheless my mind hugged the possibilities and it fed me its quota of fear as the plane approached the airport and later as I cautiously made my way through customs, then on to the car-park to eventually exit this human bottle-neck and arrive once again in the open.

Is it not usually so when the mind is being used by the imaginary self? This imaginary self is all that I usually take myself to be. Is this not the psychic invader that inhabits each and every one of ourselves in our daily lives? Is this not the play of the demon within, that is the human condition, cascading itself through the realms of time, as we endlessly seem to be reborn to be bear it? Now this day, as I swiftly passed the airport, I observed it attempting to rebirth once again within me.

The usual calls were on my answering machine and the pressure was the same as it had been two weeks previously when I called to the office. There was no positive advance on the loan application I was working on through a commercial bank. If this loan was to be granted it would clear the deficit in the working account and I could visualise three years business in front of me that would stimulate sufficient income to meet the interest repayments. After that time the remaining principle with modest growth together with my property assets should be sufficient to balance the final accounting. But in spite of my marketing record and all I had achieved before, my overall criteria was not fitting neatly enough into the narrow band of the bank's requirements. There were more forms to be filled and more securities demanded. It was beginning to become so expensive that I was obliged to seriously question the feasibility of it all, and I was on a dangerous tightrope. Although there may have been less than seven per cent of the overall client funds loose in the system when the market nose-dived yet this was seven per cent too much. Dealing with this was taking up all of my time. This left me with very little space for applying myself to productive projects. I considered that the situation was in urgent need of a successful loan approval to bridge the gap and, trying as I would, the loan would not appear. I seemed quite skilled and efficient in dealing with other people's problems, yet I was still proving unable to get a handle on my own. I felt obliged and committed to all of my clients but particularly the ones whose investments were now exposed. Yet when I stood back from the problem there was nobody in real immediate need for money, but still people were not giving me space and I could fully understand their fears.

The widow's case was different. Her money was now totally secured on property assignment and was only a modest percentage of her overall wealth. I could see clearly now how her persistent personal demands had initially contributed to this deficit situation, her unending persistence had used up my time. I am not passing any blame on her, for it was my own doing that allowed her to get such a hold on me when I accepted the lure of her wealth. My own dilemma had arisen by going with the tide

176

of it all in trying to deal my way out of the problem instead of being absolutely direct with her. There appeared to be no other way I could see at that time, apart from folding up the business completely and allowing innocent parties to suffer. This was not an option, so I had to stay with it as it was and seek out every new alternative.

I could now clearly see the precarious nature of the money markets and investment funds. For most of the gains they showed, it seemed that a similar amount of losses were present. Nonetheless, the large institutions made profits but individual investors had much less of a chance. Except, of course, when they were prepared to remain in a particular fund for sufficient years until they had covered the costs that were levied on them for being there. But this is common knowledge and it is logical that a price must be paid when one engages others to perform a task on one's own behalf. In the world of money management all is accepted as fair, even to the point of reckless speculation on countries currencies when their economies are exposed through signs of weakness. This is the macro expression of the human condition, as the acknowledged role of the fund manager, in being the head of the macro beast, is to take instant advantage of the weak using the force of money, regardless of suffering incurred by the ones being exploited at the far away end of the equation. This might seem like a loose, sweeping statement to the economist but the fact of the matter remains this is exactly how it occurs as the system itself dictates. We are the cause of the distant millions dying each day of starvation and it can never be otherwise as long as our underlaying motives are solely for individual, corporate and fiscal profit. But we have mechanisms for distancing ourselves from this truth. It is all very sophisticated now. We have grooved ourselves deep into convenient norms, with convenient religion and convenient god to save us from accountability, like burying our heads in the sand.

This generation, like every generation, is less than one speck of dust in time, while time is not even a speck in the timeless. Yet we continue to polish our children's shoes as we march them forward, through our blindness of convenience, into this world of pitiful exploitation. How long must we wallow in this darkness of mind?

I was discovering the truth in the most extraordinary way and yet I was to remain in that financial prison denying the truth of itself. Could anything be more bizarre, I asked, as I lived each moment as my last. I had come to the end of it in myself, having had this revelation of hell but the roles of my play had not yet come to their end with me. Now my only real and apparent desire was to serve others and the only place I could do this was in the midst of this money madness. I was still tied and bound within its confines.

Nothing was happening to break the dilemma and worse still, a banking institution through its own incompetence was now taking from me. I had another unnecessary court battle on my hands and the civil courts of the land are the instruments of the money managers. This is not intentional, one might argue, but it is as it is through the force of business. The legal council representing the bank squirmed through its own interpretation on facts of convenience. This had become their acquired nature. It is so that the pitiful human condition finds temporary solace through fooling itself. Yet we must not loose our direction by placing fault on another, as all others are but the reflection of self, where all of us in our hearts have become lost to illusion in taking the false to be real.

Why am I here at the centre of such apparent confusion, and what am I now supposed to be learning from this, I asked. Am I here to balance the final accounts in satisfying a 'want' of myself? Or am I here to balance the final accounts as a 'need' of my clients? When seeing this web of complexity being spun by the money world I had absolutely no 'want' left in me to be any more as a part of it. Nonetheless, the situation demanded that I remain as part of it to fulfil the 'need' of my clients. Truth demands that I must be true to the situation. I knew I must stay for the solution to eventually arrive and stay open to whatever form it should take.

This financial problem before me was my grounding and all of it was necessary, as one must enter hell and be hell to know hell. I can only serve others according to my own experience. As the good man said, "I am the way, the light and the truth" and as there is but one 'I' in all of the creation, the 'I' that is writing this, as the 'I' that is now reading this, in serving others, in serving you, am I not truly serving 'me'? Mary's words still ring in my ears when she spoke at her brother's funeral; "Cleanse yourself as you come onto me". As there is but one 'I' there is but one 'Me'. Yes, I say, in all of the pain of it, in all of the agonising hell of it, let this cleansing be done.

Charlie is hardly twelve years old and yet his parents are planning to send him to secondary school. They want him to choose a profession in accountancy or business, something congruent with the ways that are the ways of the world. But Charlie is hesitant, even though he feels the excitement of the strange world of the city about to become a part of his life. He feels that the short time still left to him as a country child is more than precious, for it will be lost forever when the world of the city takes over his body and mind, as he sees it has done to the others who have gone before him.

Charlie escapes to his forest one evening in May and walks through a carpet of bluebells. He is amazed at the vividness in the new leaves on the trees. There seems to be so many shades of green that he had not noticed before. Beneath the new wild growth on the forest floor he rediscovers the little shelters of flat slab stone that he made for his tiny invisible friends, when he was less than seven years old. So few others had entered those parts of the forest, his own secret world which he has shared with his invisible friends, that nothing had been disturbed. Nothing has really changed, while all the world has been changing about it. Now he is back again in this sanctuary. He enters his private domain between three trees drooping with ivy. Here he sits in silent listening to the birds singing and chirping profusely, they all but perch on his nose when he is long enough sitting without movement or sound.

His young mind comes to rest as he slips back into the harmony of nature expressing her beauty about him. This is his heaven. This is the place of peace that has always been loyal to him, even though he knows that his visits have grown less frequent as he is becoming more and more involved in the demands of the adult world. Yet he has not forgotten. He sits for a while and ponders as again he feels in his heart that this is the true reality. This is his home, away from the maddening crowds, away from the demands of the approaching time of decision.

Then, as the evening shadows descend, he walks through to the other side of this forest of life and on making his exit out onto the road adjoining, he reads to his horror a sign that states, 'Forest Trees For Sale'.

The music has reached its crescendo
With fury of speed I lorded the dance
Now the magical lure her veil is unfolding
To the money mad world she has webbed in a trance.
For this I have given all of my schooling
Like all the souls lost out under her ruling
Is it but justice I get what's deserved
From this god of illusion I've served?

Chapter 17

THE PSYCHIC REALM

What we normally understand as the psyche is immediately behind that what we class as normal day to day consciousness. I have seen through my experience that the psyche, this ethereal part of one's being, is the seat of all the false imagery, the illusions, the rigid beliefs, the divisiveness, that continuously rise to surface expression in our day to day living.

Unfortunately we take these surreal impressions that we blindly impose on ourselves to be true. We enact laws pertaining to the societal expression of them. We try to define justice from them. Our universities have set their courses of psychology and philosophy from within their confines. This is the blind leading the blind across the surface of time as our delusions skip from one generation to the next? But do not believe me, for believing may not necessarily be understanding. It is only through understanding that the mind becomes spontaneously quiet. This becomes known through experience, as the problems in one's life cease to be problems when they are fully understood. In other words it is only through the lack of understanding that problems arise. Whatever one's problem is that is the level of one's consciousness. Understanding is the food of consciousness. The affectionate awareness permeating consciousness is the supreme reality. When I am silently aware in the place of silent looking I am the supreme reality and it is absolutely clear that there are no problems in 'Me'. All the problems before me are of the psychological world, this outer shell of myself. This outer shell is the psyche, the cosmic vapour between 'I', the supreme reality and my sensory body of perpetual life. The psychological self is consciousness within a cloud. Awareness pervades the cloud, to be only experienced through the absolute stillness of mind, when mind and body are fully aligned and fully aware of being aware, in the stillness of 'Being'. Only then can I be that I am, the supreme reality that is 'Me'.

Merely talking about the supreme reality is nothing more than a theory. This is how we trap ourselves by creating differentiation between a higher self and a lower self. If I, the observer, become absorbed with the notion that my supreme reality is the higher self then I will look on the lower with distaste and enter a world of trying to fix it, change it or transcend it. I am back in my world of conflict. Love must be present so I, the observer, can understand that the lower self projects itself out of the higher and the higher out of the lower, they both being one and the same manifestation. In truth there is neither higher nor lower self. There is only self. When the self is fully aware of its own superficiality, its hidden layers of discontent, delusive desires, judgemental dissatisfactions, its wounds that are still unhealed, when it is fully aware of such, only then is it ready to understand, through its own dissolution. Is this a matter of fact? Or am I still being deluded by myself?

After my return to Ireland from the USA I began to notice people who had become tangled in the web of the psyche. Indeed we are all entangled but I saw clearly those consciously tapped into it in particular the magicians, the healers, the spiritual mediums who make themselves known with their formulas and remedies. All seemed most sincere in what they were doing but it is just a form of patching and temporarily mending this space of our egos and imaginary souls for the ongoing appeasement of the demon within us ourselves. Is this not more of this self-projecting self indulging in superstitions through the confusion and misery of mind? Can a monkey understand the principle of a camera, I ask? Or can the mind of the scientist, when splitting the atom, really grasp the wisdom of the mystics when relating to love? Only when one experiences that state beyond mind can the understanding I speak of be known.

When I first sat in the presence of the Australian master in Dublin to flush me out of myself, there was a lady sitting directly behind me. She spoke of her psychic experiences and how she had played with the occult in performing exorcism to another whom she had deemed to be evilly possessed. One clear question arose, Who or what is doing the perceiving? Who or what is doing the judging as to the nature of good and evil? Could we again be burning the innocent at the stake, through our newly acquired ignorance? I have found the answers to such questions in silence.

Buried beneath all the healers and all the spiritual mediums I have met, seemed to be their own particular denials. I found that when I pressed any of their buttons relating to this there would be an immediate explosion, as there had been with me when I failed to face the truth of myself and came into the presence of someone who had. Did someone not say some thousands of years past, 'Healer heal thyself'. This is particularly true when dealing with the psychic realm, for it is filled with traps, filled with shadows of shadows where one can become totally engrossed. This can be the greater hinderence to self-realisation for here is the play of plays, the real comedy of errors, being re-enacted often by bewildered bodies self-seeking their own particular enlightenment. Is this not again the psychic demon with shining halo now saying, "Hi there, I am your psychic monkey sitting on your shoulders. Do you like my new disguise?"

The psyche is the root of all ignorance and what it extends to the outer shell, the personality of the body, is its own karmic recurrence. Children are born to parents to serve it. The educational systems of societies are tailored within it, thus determining the ongoing condition of all sentient beings. We are all so fully occupied in keeping up with this repetitive past that there can be no life in the present. What a shame it is for one to discover this eternal truth only when drawing the last breath that life is only in the 'now', always in the 'now'. It can never be in the future, that is but the repetitive past. But do not believe me. You can only know by discovering it in yourself. Indeed are not all the psychic cures but mere projections towards the shadows of a better future? This dance of the psychic realm can be mischievous and grossly misleading, for if one cannot deal with the facts of one's life by facing the situation, whatever it may be, then how can one deal with the shadows?

The psychic mystique being eagerly illustrated by those devoutly pertaining to it is like the children in a kindergarten eagerly showing their paintings. But the children are pure and their hearts spontaneous and free while most of us adults are calculating and laden with past. In our curious indulgence in the psyche we are merely the conditioned conditioners reconditioning ourselves. This is the reincarnation that has implanted itself as immortal belief in theosophical thought, this reincarnation of ignorance begetting itself, with bodies being born to serve it, like fodder to be pulped for pigmeal and recycled through the intestinal gut. Is there an end to this, or are we forever bound within these confines?

There were no magical formulas to solve my business

dilemma. Even if there were, then solving it so would deny the rest of the play. I had discovered that being true to the situation is in fact accepting all exactly as it is and allowing the story to unfold in its own natural way. Even if I am to be branded a villain in the financial world, then so be it. I do not have anyone's crock of gold under my bed. I have nothing to hide. I am that I am, having danced this dance as part of their show. Are they ready to face the truth of the situation, not partially, but wholly, exactly as it is? But let us be aware, for in truth we may all be one and the same. What holds any of us back is personal fear. We are so close to heaven on earth yet it is still denied to us by ourselves bound by our own misconceptions. We need to be awakened from this preposterous dream. For this awakening I thank the spiritual master and I thank the part of the wild and furious widow, who, through her obsession had left me with no place to rest. My time had come to be flushed out of myself and I accepted my personal death. It is worth all of it and a thousand inflictions more, to walk in the Light.

Now there is no turning back for self knowledge, once attained cannot be denied and all impressions dissolve the instant they appear. It is like watching a movie fully aware that it is all but impressions on a screen that is itself always unchangeably white. In this movie of life, 'I' am the participant observer, apparently acting but truly observing. I am aware that all of it has already been done, the observer, the observing, the observed. If you, dear reader, are following me through, you may notice by now it is happening in you.

Once the mind has attained to stillness, absolute stillness, with no thought arising, then what needs to be known becomes known, and this is the way, the only way in my experience of transcending the human condition. Is this not the fundamental revolution that is facing us all as the social order is visibly decaying? Is this social decay not the outer manifestation of the psyche of all humankind in its cascading, karmic recurrence? The transcendence that I speak of is not another concept on which to structure a theory, nor is it another idea. All of such exist in the realm of thought and are the base for further conflict. This understanding is the most radical revolution of all. It demands a shift in human consciousness out of the confines of rational logic in which the human mind is locked. Our thoughts come and go within the permitted parameters of societal acceptance and are simply the macro image of the microcephalic and 'psychological me' dancing with the mirrors of its pitiful self. This is the futile battle of you and I in our personal clinging to our personal selves and each of us feels that 'mine' will be different. Facing the reality of this is the greatest revolution of all.

How is this revolution to occur? The seers of wisdom agree that stillness is the way. This stillness is not an endeavour of stilling the noise of a world outside, for that is but the chasing of my own shadow that moves as I move and stops as I stop. That is but a stunning of mind. This stillness I speak of must be re-cognised from within, where the cognisance of all is stored. It is beyond thought, beyond mantras, beyond the psyche, beyond the spoken word, beyond, yet within.

Charlie was shocked into silence. The world of his childhood was to be sold. His one place of magic was facing immediate destruction and, not only that, but the trees, including the ones that formed his tepee, were each marked with a number to enable them to be individually auctioned for firewood. The date for the auction had been set and now the unbelievable was imminent.

"Who can be doing this?" he inquires from his father.

Title to the land has passed to the man on the mountain and his sister, the woman with a peculiar stare, he discovers to his astonishment. Apparently they have inherited it through the changing laws regularising ownership.

"And now they are selling the trees, some one hundred years old or more to dead people for firewood", Charlie protests to his father. "But these people are not dead", his father replies. "Everyone is dead for there is no one who sees. None can hear the voice of the trees? Is there anyone who cares? Is there anyone who understands?"

"For God's sake they are only trees", he is told. Every family around, including his own, attends the auction to buy up their share of wood. Charlie stands alone to one side as the multitudes gather about the man with the auctioneer's hammer moving from tree to tree. There is not even one person present who sees the wonderful world of magic being trodden back into the ground.

Chapter 18
RAJAS, THE DEMON JAILOR

It was a cool September evening, the days were getting noticeably shorter and nights cooler. I was travelling to Galway and on this particular evening after crossing the river Shannon at Athlone I noticed the clear air and freshness, in stark contrast to the congested city of Dublin I had left over one hundred miles behind me. I was now in the western province of Connaught and a feeling of relative calm entered me, having been temporarily released from the stuffy capital and not yet close enough to Galway to be re-absorbed by the urgency of its wild intensity.

Indeed, this miniature city of raw energy seemed to be in a permanent mould of tempestuous expression. In the sixties when I was there as a young student it was such an exposure to my being, after an innocent childhood on the rolling hills of Clare, that it blew me wide open. It was in the city of Galway that I first made love to woman on a beautiful winter's night. It was here I wrote my searching poems as a teenager facing the mystery of life.

Those were my unbridled days I spent on Lough Corrib boating with so many exuberant friends shortly after my first arrival as a total stranger to that historic place of perpetual activity. Everything was a dare-devil challenge, even the times when the winter flooding would rise to the tops of the arches that form the bridges. We would still get our canoes down the swollen river by laying on our backs in the boats and walking our way through upside-down against the tops of the arches. Nothing was impossible then and everything had to be tested. Such is the nature of youth, and such is the nature of the raw energy that never seems to change in this city.

This raw energy abounds as each year the 'freshers' of life are enrolled in its colleges. As a student I was whipped up in the wave of it, day and night at extraordinary speed, as if my entire being had been taken over by its perpetual spinning until eventually my body collapsed with exhaustion. The siren of the ambulance brought me back to life as it sped past Saint Mary's College. I was obliged to take three days compulsory rest in its hospital in the good care of my student nursing friends, who were also in service to its wildness in their moments of freedom.

At one stage I had a very odd experience in the old house that I was lodging in. One night, deep in the darkness, I awoke frozen in terror by a strange presence on my bed. As I lay on my back with my hands by my side, I could feel its hot and damp breath on my face and its hard and forceful hands clasping over mine. Its fingers locked through my fingers and the weight of its presence pushed me into the mattress. It seemed an eternity before my throat could utter the words to order it to begone. Was it real? Or was it a dream? Yet as I sat on the old wooden chair by the window recollecting my reason the strange odourless smell it left behind was a conscious experience of that smothering encounter with whatever it was. How strange it all seemed then in that vortex of living. Such rawness of hot blood pumping through the veins of existence, as the disembodied and the incarnate seemed to be one and the same.

After two college years I had to leave that city and take up work in London as a labourer on the railways in order to grind off that wild, wild energy that I seemed to have absorbed to the point of exploding my mind. There seemed to be no other way. I remember holding to the dream of returning some day to stay there forever as I left. Yes, it seemed Galway had taken my heart in its action and indeed today I can still see, after travelling the world, that this city has got that something special only to itself.

Oddly enough, my current business dilemma including the widow had arisen there in the space of the Galway client-bank. How strange it all seems. Was it something I did or something I missed in my first encounter with this place? Or was I as yet caught up in its whirlpool of action as though being permanently bound in rajas? These questions faced me that night as I drove west through Connaught and its albedo edged over the horizon to greet me. Was I other than the moth flying into the flame of the candle, as I seemed to be endlessly pulled back to this place? This was obviously a story of recurrence.

The Managing Director of the insurance brokerage firm, the man I had overthrown as European champion in life-assurance selling, had adopted this city over his native Donegal. He was hailed from this western seat as the King in his field and he firmly believed it himself, until I arrived on his team after replying to an advertisement that read, 'Are you sports-minded?' Yes, I took it in sport and in my blindness I took his record as well, and his team and his glory, and danced it all over the cliff. Such is the madness of living and such is the pulse of the life-assurance business when it sucks in the salesmen and saleswomen to dry out their veins. It sucked me into its web through this city of Galway, now greeting me with its particularly noticeable fresh Atlantic air recharging through my veins and blasting me up to its speed.

This night I was to meet a man still in his prime who had spent eleven years in the life-assurance industry and eventually found the courage, with assistance, to break from it and repair his damage within. This night was to be his regrounding, his re-affirmation of his sanity after serving eleven years as its pawn. Now he was on the road to rediscovering his true self. To me it was a joy to behold, for here was the living proof that this tidal wave can be confronted and turned. This man had been with me from the first moment I entered this field of life-assurance and he showed willing himself to test its extremes, although cautiously at times, but test it he did.

Initially he had persuasively introduced me to it as his final grand expression still clinging to its glory. He had been trained as a recruitment and sales manager by this industry. In his relentless drive for personal success he had unknowingly tapped into the energy lines of the new recruits and dragged them down to the point of destruction as they came to him, joined with him, spent their energy, and left in the confusion of not knowing themselves, or how they had been used at the hand of one so skillfully trained to use them and waste them.

What is this nonsense about energy lines, one may ask. Let us use an example. Once upon a time on the seas surrounding this island a fisherman lost his trawler after his fishing nets became entangled in an unidentified submarine. The stricken boat, having lost its control, was dragged backwards at a speed way beyond its normal capacity until it was eventually submerged and lost to the depths. Such is how it is when one's energy lines become entangled in an unidentified blight from the depths of the psyche. The life-assurance business finds its survival in the sale of concepts, it is a psychological play of mind upon minds. Many come to partake in its lure, some survive for a time through the ignorance of not knowing but the ones who dig into its depths are inevitably faced with the urge to go deeper, or burn out in the searching. This the man had discovered, and now he saw how he himself had been damaged by the life-assurance business. He had believed in it, was blinded by it and had given away his authority to it. Now his personal battle lay in regaining his integrity and, for some unknown reason, he was looking towards me for direction to lead him out of its web.

Each time I ventured to put my head in the lions mouth he courageously proceeded to follow. It seemed that he had come to realise that he too needed to have it burned out of his system for now we tested the industry together as he left behind his destructive traits of recruitment, having become the recruit in himself. We had worked through new formulas and complex financial packages to increase our share of the market but deep down he had known we were still its pawns working within its confines, and denying this truth to ourselves. Yet the mathematical equations we devised to increase the speed of the marketing dance were amazing as it seemed necessary to increase its speed, if only to bring it to its end.

This man had bravely undergone the testing within and exposed the fears of himself to himself in his quest to face the truth of the situation. His greatest test where he would be stopped at the wall of fire that I had apparently burned through had yet to come. He had chosen, now life was setting the altar for this sacrificial lamb, this final letting go and exposing of the monster within. He had the courage, he had the daring and he had taken up the sword, another stage, another play, as part of the grand play of life. Such is the nature of the creation for once its forces are invoked for good action then one must be prepared to accept whatever it takes for that good action to come into play, even if it means losing everything one clings to as precious, as indeed is often the case.

But this was going to be a night of discussion. We met on the outskirts of the city, went to eat in the centre, and then went on for a drink in a crowded bar of locals, tourists and musicians. We spent the final hours in a crowded nightclub where we remained until dawn as we continued our dialogue. While we had edged through the crowds of bright colours and cultures there was none other to be seen or heard outside of ourselves in the fervour of conversing. Such it is in this barrage of talking from thinking through a mind that is shrouded in fear. Yet it needed to be done. It had to be talked out and it had to be dissolved in the futility of its own expression. The following morning we met after breakfast and the discussion continued at a deeper level. Then we walked by the ocean, taking in the freshness of the wide open Atlantic blowing onto our faces and we were brought out of the tumultuous mind into the consciousness of life in the body and the bliss of the present Harmony was temporally restored. Reason prevailed as the anxious, dense clouds were dispersed. The intensity was over for now, being swallowed by calmness, once again the equilibrium was served.

In the late morning we parted and he went forward courageously to follow his quest. After having attended to my affairs in Galway that day and before I departed for Dublin, I drove out to the lake to replenish my peace. I sat on a stone in silence for some time to allow the stillness to raise from within. The waters were softly lapping the edge of the pier as the reflection of the sun danced on the miniature ripples being gently stirred by a faint breeze. Its beauty consumed me as I re-entered through silence to be in the oneness of it all. Two lovers walked by, hand in hand, laughing and loving with their five year old son. It was good to see there can be more to love's story than the honeymoon, and more to life's story than the anxieties of greed.

The silence was disturbed by an old lady's two dogs barking and jumping on the water's edge. Having placed her will on their minds they accordingly responded. She sat and momentarily settled in herself to the beauty of her surrounds and the two dogs, released from the force of her command, returned to their own natural state of silence. Her stillness, however, was short as her body contorted to her personal barrage of thinking. She jerked to her feet and the dogs immediately responded with their barking and jumping, as the outer expressing the inner. She sat again, and silence returned to the beauty of Lough Corrib. And so it went on through the waves of her mind, until eventually it forced her to leave. This poor wretched woman, my calamity to life, such is the human condition, as it is in me when I am lost to the willfulness of thought. The peace, the stillness, it always is, when the mind is allowed freedom from thinking. Even one minute a day is better than none when it enters one's awareness, that is when the awareness is allowed to arise from within.

What is awareness? Is it enough just to be aware? Coming to stillness it can be seen that even awareness itself is but a mirror, a reflection as such. There is always a distance in the awareness we know, we are aware of things outside of our immediate self. I was aware of the woman and the ongoing anxiety of her mental state. I was also aware of nature's beauty giving her but an instant's relief, as she submerged in her anxiety again. Then a deeper awareness allowed me to see her problem as my problem. Is it not yours? Yes, I must see my condition through the deeper awareness before I can understand the consciousness of life that is always immediate with no distance involved. This is the awareness of 'Me', that is the essence of 'Being'.

Who is this 'Me'? Is it the formless within, as within you, the one now reading these words, from the formless before it enters the brain to become the form in body? Is this not what you are when you are looking into 'Me', the 'Me' that is you? Are you formless life? Is this body of yours your first form from whence all other forms of life appear, before it becomes lost to mind, as the woman with her dogs, deranged by her thinking? Indeed all confusion in my immediate world is all a reflection of myself through my thinking. The name of myself is fear for in order to enter 'Me', I must pass through the fear of myself.

But I spend my life considering myself, considering what is likely to bring me personal happiness. Is this not the usual story? Nonetheless, the personal self is forever unhappy, happy for some moments perhaps but this is followed by the opposite as it is bound up in the web of activities in serving its wants. This is how I imprison myself through the maya of the transient world where the desire for life that just is, is turned into wanting by thinking? But should I, through awareness, keep the focus of my intelligence on the stillness of 'Me' rather than the screaming of myself, then, perhaps, myself may become the willing disciple of 'Me', as it ceases in its becoming through the wantonness of itself.

Stillness is the way, as we are reminded by all the seers and all the masters who have made themselves known. "Be still and know that 'I' am God". What a blissful place this is, when I am connected with 'Me' and there is but one 'I', dear friend, the 'I' within you in your experience, in the body of all that you are. We discover from ancient Sanskrit there are three constituents that form the creation. These are known as Sattva, Rajas and Tamas. Sattva denotes being, existence, true essence. Rajas denotes energy, motivity, activity. Tamas denoted darkness inertia, passivity. All three must exist in the cosmic substance, each through the manifestation of the others. Acknowledging this, should we not let rajas be servant to stillness rather than an instrument to the demon of the psyche that is endlessly screaming through the wants of ourselves? Is this the message of Galway for me as I am being aptly cascaded to the end of myself? What is life's message to you, dear seeker in action? It is only in absolute stillness that 'It' can actually be heard.

Charlie is crossing the fields when he spots a yellow machine in what remains of the forest. Some trees are still standing awaiting the ones who claim ownership on them to come and chop them. But this machine is doing something else, he sees as he draws closer. It is digging up the stream in the centre and putting large concrete pipes in deep under the ground. The man from the mountain is there and also his sister with the peculiar stare. My God they are burying the stream, this beautiful stream of life, as it always has been, glowing, and winding its way through the stones. Now this woman and man have used the money they got from the trees to hire this machine and bury alive this stream. Charlie is moved in himself to take action. The son of the man driving the machine, sheepishly standing nearby, starts beating the ivy still hanging from the one remaining of Charlie's three trees. Charlie leaps over the fence to challenge this one, who is bigger than him yet the nearest to his size, but is met by the woman with the peculiar stare. With shovel in hand, she screams at him, "Get off our land".

The life-assurance industry creates its marketing kings of extravagant action and wild exuberance. New business piles upon old as the concurrent result. Each bubble grows larger and larger as the moment grows fat at the seams. But all bubbles inevitably explode, as did the bubble of Charlie that day by the stream, and indeed his magical world of trusted permanence in a forest returning through ashes to dust.

Chapter 19

THE TRUTH SHALL SET YOU FREE

Things had cooled down somewhat. I could sense calm returning yet my friend on the Dublin scene advised me that affairs involving hired killers are never concluded until everything relating to the issue is actually cleared up, one way or another. Although the widow had warned me that her consort had paid five thousand pounds to someone to have me shot yet it was probable that this was not actually true. It could well be some other issue with someone else that I was totally unaware of that had triggered these attempts on my life. My personal issue with the widow was far from over although I was now beginning to understand it in more detail. I had not been harassed since she accepted the legal agreement in the Four Courts in Dublin. Yet, when taking into account the depth of obsession she had well demonstrated in so many ways, it was logical to assume that she would be preparing her next course of action. The shadow of death was upon me causing my movements to continue in an illusive pattern.

I had come to love life dearly, each moment as it occurred, the freshness of the air in the breathing, the aroma of the flowers, the touch of soft rain on the skin, the vividness in every sight to behold, the sounds of the birdsong, and the taste of the porridge, all of life in each moment, as each moment is alone where life is. When travelling back from England with a friend on one occasion, we stopped in North Wales for supper in a country pub. It was late on a Saturday evening and I noticed three young men enter the bar. They were in their best weekend attire and their faces were shining as they met with their three pints of ale. Young men had been there before, a hundred years or more gone, and so had the ale. And then it struck me. Man is born, he lives and he dies. The ale is brewed and it's drank. But the tasting, the actual tasting is constant, as here sat these three young men taking their first sip in their service to the taste. Is this not where life really is, in the taste, each moment in the taste? Bodies come and bodies go while life just is. Is it not amazing how we seem to keep missing this point of fact? We are so preoccupied with our personal worlds of our mental creation that each dawn and each sunset, and all that is between, passes unnoticed. Yes, this shadow of immediate death, my blessing in disguise, had brought me to life, and to the self-realisation of life in each moment.

In the futility of worry I had been depriving myself of this fundamental truth. All worry is caused by uncontrolled thinking. In the still mind, not the stunned or the drugged, but the still mind, there is no worry. This I discovered in my own experience, and through the stillness came the dawning of immortality, where there is no longer a need to believe in a particular god, for God becomes known in the truth of all as it is. Then everything comes to life, as practically all the religions of the world have been trying to express. But we are so busy, so pre-occupied with living that the actuality of being life is missed. Even the masters of religions themselves, when propounding their dogmas of conflict, are too busy.

My own particular busy and pre-occupied living had been danced to the extreme. I had believed all I had been told, tested it to its limits, and caused all of it about me to explode. Then the mad world in all it's fury came chasing me with guns for exposing its nature. Yes, I came alive to the realisation that I had to be awakened from the preposterous dream even though it had taken something as crazy as this to jolt me back into my being. After spending a life of becoming, in accord with the ways of the psychic demon that is the human condition, it now seemed my time had come.

The phone calls kept coming in from people in fear and demand. I had become a juggler in trying to keep the balance of accounts together until this deficit gap should close or something unseen should occur to bring it to its end. I could do nothing else but stay with it until it would conclude, accepting whatever was to come. In the journey it was now taking me this was to continue being a journey alone. I could not expect anyone to fully understand. The truth of life was at one side of me, the world at the other and I was somewhere in the middle. I found some helpful words from the scriptures sounding like trumpets in my ears; 'The truth shall set you free'. It was then I decided that whatever it takes I must face the situation exactly as it is. I must accept the ways of the financial services industry as according to my current position, just as I had accepted its ways in the past when it had crowned me its marketing king. Obviously there would be many others on the face of the industry in a similar dilemma and each one must be thinking, dying and judging it as a personal failure, while the industry itself, through appropriate legislation, was conveniently avoiding any accountability. It was not long before the heat was really turned up for my roasting. Things became so crazy, even the clients that had been relatively quiet for some time, as we waited for the markets to improve, began to call demanding why the funds were still losing.

These calls added to the basket of my crisis but the shift within had occurred. Instead of responding to panic with panic, I was now responding in calmness, regardless of the urgency of the immediate problem being presented. I discovered I was dealing with fear and the varying levels of its expression coming from different people. Sometimes it was so well disguised that it was almost undetectable, even to the ones affected. But once exposed through the illumination of stillness it lost all its masks and then was it possible to deal the facts of the situation. I have found that when attachments, emotions or panics control the mind and cause the clouded turbulent thinking, then the truth is inevitably avoided. Even after such fear is exposed and expelled, returns again newly disguised, riding on the crest of another emotional wave. It seemed to have an entity of its own and the only place I can truly understand it is in its presence in my own body.

As a child I had spent seven years in its terror beginning with my first day at school. I was placed under the hand of an authoritarian woman whose clinched fists had no mercy. Her uncontrolable temper regularly exploded on my innocent and unprotected head. When I walked through the wide open fields each morning on my way to that first prison of hell the birds sang freely and danced in the trees and I wished that I had been born one of them. Yes, I had been introduced to fear and since then I had been challenging it, or running from it, in all the facets of my life. I discovered that by staying in the stillness and being fully aware of it my fear, without fighting it, trying to expel it, or ignoring it, then it would eventually dissolve and never return in that particular mask again. Yes, fear is our greatest barrier, for fear is the name of myself.

In order to answer that great universal question, 'Who am I', one has to fearlessly face the terrors of this inner self, this manifestation from the volcanic depths of the human psyche that is the human condition at large. One has to pass through the face of this before self-realisation can be re-cognized. But I hasten to add, please do not believe me, for it can only be true in your own experience and not in what I say, or in what anyone says. It can only be found within, within you, within 'I' as in you, the only 'I' there is. And in this formless universal 'I', you and I are synonymous, believe it or not. When you examine it closely is it in your own experience that the 'I' is not just the form? The form, the spacesuit, the body of time, it changes, but 'I' is always here. Has there ever been a time in your knowing that 'I' was not here? The re-cognizing is the returning to the cognition of what is already known and what is always there immediately behind the turbulent thinking mind. It is universal knowledge free to all and one.

And how do I discover it? Stillness is the way, and it can only be in the 'now'. One can immediately drop into it by totally letting go, or be exploded into it as in my particular case, by becoming so hyperactive that it erupts into a scorching inferno dissolving all things relating to it back into the nothingness from where all things have come. This has been my scene in the play, my particular dance, as the merry dance of life. What has been yours, dear seeker of truth? What is your dance of discovery? Silently pause, and 'to thine own self be true'.

When man escaped from nothingness
Its clutches no more bound him
He was condemned a world to face
Forever all around him.
Let not temptation cast an eye
On frail humanity
Reflect on what shall never die
(With mind not asking reason why)
Man lives immortally.

Summer, 1966

Chapter 20

DESIRE, THE WHITE STEED OF LIFE

What is desire? When I entered the life-assurance industry my manager told me it was the greatest business in the world. I only had to apply myself to the system and I could have practically anything I desired. All the possibilities were placed before me. What are you uppermost desires? I was asked.

Of course my most immediate aspiration was to have enough money to pay off all my bills. Next to that I sought a decent car and creative employment. At the time there was a wonderful woman in my life and, oddly enough, she had no such money desires. Her one desire in our relationship, only now apparent, was for me to mature to a state in which I could love her properly. She was a highly educated, highly sensitive young woman of life in all matters.

The manager pumped his seemingly limitless desires at me. Everything was made attainable. The immediate sale of thirty life-assurance policies would be sufficient to have enough money from commissions to buy a brand new, executive car. One hundred and twenty policies would earn the price of a world cruising yacht. So it went on each week, backed up by the video tapes of the super dynamic and turbo-charged Australian sales expert who had all the desert nomads buying up his sand! I admit I was not particularly moved until the manager brought my attention to the European life-assurance sales record, then held by his boss whom he did not seem particularly happy to serve. That I bought, and to break the record became my immediate desire. By the end of the month I was the new champion. Then came the trophies and glory. No, I did not desire that but it was part of the package of success and there was no escaping from it. Little did I know this was but the introduction to the fuller story. My lover, the beautiful woman in my life, stayed on for a little while longer then, seeing the pitiful state of it all, packed up her belongings, threw out her memories and left. Now I had unwanted glory and fame for the price of my love. She had arrived to me in her fullness of womanhood from Paris and departed as my tango of personal desire commenced. Why should it take less than the widow of misplaced love to sting me to the actual truth of what I had allowed to happen? Perhaps the widow's obsession on me was the reflection of my own obsession with the insurance industry. Perhaps I had appeared to my lover as the widow had come to appear to me. The sting of pain and personal death which had to occur was a necessary part of the play as I had placed the world, the transitory world of illusion, before the woman of love in my life.

At that time I was being carried along by the tidal wave of my illusive desires. It was a road that introduced me to many people, some lost, some slowing down, some running out of fuel, some stopped and dead on the way, some coming back on the opposite track, some travelling with me at great speed. As the momentum gathered and gathered, fuelled by the unheeded desires of greed, piled high on more greed, the leaping flames grew higher and higher only to scorch me to hell when the momentum ceased to save me from the hell of myself.

What is desire? Is it an illusion that must be entered if it is to be tested and known? Desire always seems related to something outside of ourselves and desires fulfiled breed more desires to be fulfiled. It is as if we are beguiled. It seems that we must fulfil our desires in order to be free of them. Is it not usually so? We spend so much of our time planning our course of action in order to satisfy a particular desire. The wedding day arrives, the desire is fulfiled but soon the honeymoon is over. The fulfiled desire is swiftly replaced by another desire arising. The financial adviser knocks on the door and spreads out a magical display of possibilities. There seems to be no end to it. We seem to be endlessly bound by our desires and fulfiling them does not satisfy. It only serves the illusion.

Neither is it possible to satisfy or understand desire by suppressing it. In fact, suppression may have more serious consequences. Did I not suppress my desire to be with the truth when dealing with the situation between myself and the widow? I could see her obsession on me yet I lived with the pretence that it was not there so I could fulfil my desires to increase my score with the insurance industry by selling her life-assurance and pension policies. This is how the dilemma commenced. So desires are not only complex but they can also generate conflict and mis-understanding. Yet, desire is nothing in itself without the intention to fulfil it. Ultimately, there is no desire. When the intention is to satisfy the personal self then the desires are endless. But when I intend nothing for myself then all my desires disappear and when my intentions are for the good of all then I am on the road to truth and the universe works with me. Once in the light, in truth, there is no desire. Desirelessness is the highest bliss.

If my desire is to be free then I must not neglect what is immediately before me. This is my first step to freedom. Before the white steed appeared before Oisin in the mythological tale of Tir na nOg he was not even aware of the greatest love to behold. But when it came to his attention his decision was immediate. The white steed is the intention of the desire to be in the desireless state. On my own particular steed of desire galloping at great speed on the highway to hell, Mary suddenly appeared. She glowed and pointed me to the arrow that read; 'Cleanse yourself as you come unto me'. I was stopped and dislodged from my saddle of paper glitter that filled the shelves of myself. As my feet hit the ground I was dazed by her smile for my body had not yet felt the fine piercing arrow of the Logos cutting through the centre of myself. My mind was filled beyond capacity with the countless desires conveniently stored on the shelves of the life-assurance world. "Beware of obstacles" I had been told. "Keep your sights set on your desires and let nothing get in your way. Obstacles are what you see when you take your eyes off your goal". These were just some of the sayings the life-assurance industry used to wind up our minds, direct our energies and blind us to everything other than the sale of life-assurance policies. I swallowed the pill and was crowned with its transient glory.

In Mary I had suddenly discovered a pearl of the greatest light. She spoke to me from that other dimension of knowing as I lost sight of the transient world. Like a wound-up clock I asked her to lend me her light so my companions and I could increase our speed on our particular highway to nowhere. She smiled and said, "No, but I will lead you to one who will show you the way". Instantly, this became my all-consuming desire.

Mary, in her ease and stillness appeared as a mirror in which I could see my disguise. I was as the others gripped in tumultuous noise, galloping through the smothering dust of our minds. On this highway of worldly desires I was stopped by her presence in a place so strange, yet so familiar. She took me by the hand as I stood dazed and bewildered. Suddenly the madness of clattering sound was gone and silence, beautiful silence prevailed. A bird sang.

Stillness spilled over me, then through me, until I was stillness itself.

This is how it is, exactly as it is, in my own experience. But again I wish to remind you not to believe me, but see if your experience is different. Truth is in the experiencing and experiencing in itself is boundless, as I have discovered through this greatest experience of all.

> *Let no man leave a hand*
> *Unkind on her. She alone,*
> *Alone, alone with love for 'Me'*
> *Pure, majestic, free,*
> *An angel bathing on the strand,*
> *As blossoms on an apple tree*
> *But ne'er to face the death*
> *Which they will have to face.*

> *Summer 1996*

Chapter 21

AUSTRALIA OR BURST

October had arrived too soon, and one of the most important events of my life was suddenly upon me. I had planned to spend a seventeen day retreat in Australia with the master and his group to stay with the pulse of earnest inquiry that had been ignited within me. This was a momentous undertaking.

I had already bought an army tent in Wicklow for the occasion and my registration fees had been paid but the flight ticket had yet to be purchased. It was only a matter of weeks to departure and there was no money coming in and no commissions arriving as I had expected. Not only that, but everything of business on the horizon was postponed. My only option was to sell my car, an old classic mercedes that should be worth something in the region of ten thousand pounds. Or so I imagined until I advertised it and got no replies. Indeed everything in the world about me seemed to be in resistance to this Australian trip but the decision had been made in the light of clear intellect and this I set out to respect. Over the following days I re-advertised the car and steadily reduced its price until I had reduced it by half. At that point all sorts of people started phoning, but few of them intended to purchase. One man was sincere but became unsure of himself because he was getting the car too cheap. He had to check out its history and everything relating to it before he would make up his mind.

Time was running out fast. The appointed day for departure to Australia arrived and nothing had happened. It now appeared that it was not to be. I felt I had done all that could be done and yet it was not falling into place. I had to acknowledge the situation exactly as it was, not as I desired it to be. Even though I knew my desire to go to Australia to be in the presence of the spiritual master was taken with the intention of good and not just good for myself but for everyone about me. This is how the decision had been made yet it was not happening as I had expected it would. There was nothing more I could do so I accepted the fact that I was not to go, for this was the truth of that moment before me. I sent a fax to the organisers stating I was unable to attend and offered my place as a gift to any late comer who might be anticipating a cancellation. When I phoned to check if they had received my message a softly spoken lady on the Australian end of the line encouraged me to come anyway saying that I would only miss the first weekend. I phoned the travel agents with this new encouragement on the following morning, which was Friday. They offered me an alternative seat on the Sunday flight with Singapore Airlines to Brisbane but I would have to have cash to pay for the ticket before five that evening.

I phoned the would-be car purchaser. If he were to take the car that day I would give him a special deal. I offered him the bargain of a lifetime and I eventually got his cheque at three thirty that afternoon. But the manager of his bank would not convert the cheque to the cash I required. I had to track down the managing director of the banking corporation to exercise pressure on this intently awkward manager. With just fifteen minutes to spare I eventually got the transaction completed and at one minute to five o'clock I was in the travel agents office literally seconds before my reservation was to automatically disappear off the computer network to be taken up by the next standby client. This was the effort I was obliged to make in order to get to Australia and my old classic mercedes, a pride and joy to behold, sold at less than half its market value, had found itself a new home.

These were the difficulties to be overcome to clear the passage for my journey of a lifetime and my life-assurance training in the manipulative overcoming of obstacles had paid me its greatest dividend that day. The intention of my desire was good and it was fulfiled when I applied the assertiveness of my marketing training. The universe was working with my intention, myself being aligned with 'Me'.

Sunday arrived. It was a beautiful fresh morning of late Autumn colours as I drove across Ireland from County Clare to Dublin Airport to catch the London flight. It was happening, against all the odds I seemed to be on my way. I was Australia bound and eventually seated in what can only be described as a luxurious oriental restaurant in the sky flying out over the Middle East to the first stop in Singapore. The calm and awesome vitality of the retreat I was about to experience was now flooding into my being, even before I arrived. Singapore was a two hour stop and then onward to Brisbane. On arriving for the first time in my life to this open land, I entered with the early morning sunrise on that particularly special day. When my feet touched the ground I could feel the energy of this continent surging upwards through my legs and filling all of my body with its welcoming warmth. From Brisbane I was flown down the Gold Coast in a little aircraft to Coolangatta, where the territories of Queensland and New South Wales meet on the Pacific Ocean. To me, that moment was truly a coming home and when I stepped outside the airport buildings in the early morning coolness I knelt and placed my hands on the first patch of green grass that greeted me.

It was as far back as 1968 that I made my first abortive attempt to be part of this land. I had been offered a permanent position with an Australian bank, and three times they had called to me. But on each occasion I was knotted in my own personal worldly affairs. It had taken twenty five years of living before I came to understand the scourge we place upon ourselves through our attachments to the familiar. Nonetheless, this day I had finally arrived. I was here, fully present to everyone and everything I was meeting, and knowing there was nothing but hell in the psychological world that dwells in the first thought outside of the moment.

This is Australia. It strangely felt on that day as though I was returning and not arriving for the first time. The house of my birth in Ireland was built by a man who had returned from this land with his wife and two sons well over one hundred years ago. My own grandfather had spent twenty years of his early life in this place. It was as if they were within my veins, now in this land twelve thousand miles from my own place of birth. The taxi driver who drove me the last leg of the journey gave me his address and invited me to his coming barbecue. Indeed, everyone I met were just as open and friendly. Then I arrived at the end of my trek and it was like entering paradise. I was greeted by a wonderful couple in charge of the camp-site nestling in a natural rainforest close to the ocean. If the Garden of Eden had been truly lost to mankind, this seemed like heaven itself being regained. I was shown a spot to pitch my tent between three native trees and then I was alone in the stillness of that place, so strange yet so familiar, listening to the birds singing and chirping to my presence.

I undid the plastic wrapping from my tent and I searched for the instructions. There seemed to be a lot of parts and this was the first time I had opened it since purchasing it in Wicklow. After spreading the tent on the ground I proceeded cautiously, one step at a time, until eventually there it was, fully erected as it was designed to be. A lady standing a little over from where I was working it watched the procedure with some amusement. She was the only person around, as almost everyone else was down by the beach or by a majestic lake surrounded by tea trees at the other side of the forest. We smiled at each other and spoke. I noticed her skin, her arms, and her ears and found myself silently saying no to that warm sensation rising within me. I was there on my spiritual awakening. This was my quest with no room for personal engaging. Yet my interest was much deeper than that. As she smiled and went back to what she was doing I found myself saying almost aloud, "so be it, as it is to happen then let it be so". What a happening it was with this beautiful woman who had journeyed from America to be in that spot in the Australian rain-forest to greet me!

I had been travelling for thirty hours before I arrived at the camp-site and, strange as it seemed, any tiredness upon me was instantly vanished by her attentive smile. The seminar commenced at two thirty in the afternoon and the harmony prevailing with the three hundred or so people attending was immediate within me, even though I was a late arrival. In the presence of all, in the light of a spiritual master, was the most momentous occasion of my life story to date. Having connected with this woman was like connecting with a fellow cosmic traveller on this journey through time. Everything was unfolding as it should, now that initial resistance of the financial barriers had been overcome.

There were people here from many parts of the world and from a variety of professions. To name but a few there were doctors, scientists, teachers, university students, carpenters, journalists, healers, physiotherapists and even a squadron commander from the American Airforce with his beautiful wife, a moon goddess to behold. It was a privilege to be in the awesome presence of all of it, the gentleness, the stillness, the knowing, the extraordinary knowing that was shining from the eyes of all.

Words were not necessary, strange it may be, as communion was happening in the silence of being. Indeed, words are too heavy and turgid in this remarkable speed of cosmic consciousness and beyond. What it is cannot be described, yet describe it I must attempt. It is like a being in another dimension, out of space, out of time, at the other side of the outer sensory perception and yet without there being another side. There is a moving beyond the limitations of the discursive mind in its thinking and worrying about yesterday gone and tomorrow another day's yesterday. Yet there is no movement but a stilling instead that opens the door of this space-time machine travelling at a speed that is light years beyond the speed of light where there is no time, or even timelessness. It cannot be described in its immensity that is infinitely beyond the limitations of the mind. The assuming, worldly educated mentality tries to analyse it, discern it and measure it in a calamitous ignorance that can never be seen in itself by itself. To know it one must enter it and be it. It is 'Being'. Yet, this is but the first step.

Here we were gathered, camping in the openness of this Australian rainforest, in nature most spectacular and attending this 'Course in Being' with the Australian master in his native land. What could be more real? What could be more true to this moment, the eternity in this moment of sensory time.

The radiance of your smile
Wildly blows me open
To receive all of you
Into this heart
It is wild wild life
Wild wild love
Let all the creation dance
To its wondrous tune.

Chapter 22

THE REALISATION OF IMMORTALITY

Each day in Australia was a journeying deeper within. All of the master's talks were a movement towards this stillness, or rather a movement away from moving. This is negation, entering the absolute silence behind the spoken word, the state of nothingness, and immensely consuming. The understanding of this is not possible to the discursive mind by the nature of the discursive mind in itself. The opening can only occur in unblemished stillness when there are no thoughts, where there is no searching, only total trust in letting everything go. Even one thought of divine expectation being present is one thought too many.

Human willfulness always resists and the closer to the opening the more astute this resistance becomes. Ninety nine point nine per cent of the time we get stuck at the finest point that the mind can hold firm. Even some holding to the knowledge of master consciousness apparently transfix here. At this point it is seen but not entered. One has to go through the point and in order to allow it to happen there must be an absolute willingness and a letting go in an absolute totality, of everything. In existence it is not possible, it seems, for to be in existence there must be something. This is a passing into nothingness, into a void, an emptiness, yet an emptiness so vast it is pregnated with everything that is, including this speck that is all of the world and even the world of one's own creation. It cannot be reached with the five senses, not even the sixth. It is absurd to even try to imagine. Being, as such is being on the point, motionless in mind and body. This, what I endeavour to speak of, is beyond being. Being is the point. This point is the last point in existence. One can go no further. Until it occurs. One must be spontaneous and free.

In my own experience I had absolute trust in the divinity coming through the master and my earnestness sought out the truth. I had no prior knowledge of what was about to become known nor could I have had any desire or expectation. As it occurs the passing through is so immediate, so swift that forty seven years of living becomes less than a millionth of a second. This is how it happened with me on a particular afternoon in that rainforest in Australia and it became stamped on my countenance for all time. The awesomeness of 'It', the enormity of the wave of 'It', washed all that I had become in this world of becoming out of this presence.

I found myself walking deep into the forest through brambles and bushes and eventually sitting beneath a tall tree. This body convulsed and convulsed in a flooding that washed through all that I had become. It is undescribable, unimaginable, this passing through. It never needs to be repeated. It never can be repeated, for once it is done it is done. Who am I? Now it is known, in this body, in this experiencing, having been imploded beyond experiencing itself. As spoken through Mary from my altar of worldly disturbance, "Cleanse yourself as you come unto Me", now I have seen this last point in existence where this cleansing occurs, and the truth is forever made known.

Eventually the wild life of the forest began showing their presence, some strangest of creatures just inches from me, as though I had dissolved into being as one with the brambles and trees. The birds hopped on branches within hand's reach. The sun, the evening sun, cast its rays like pillars of gold down through the tall trees onto the forest floor. The returning of man to the Garden of Eden, it is so. How many thousands of lifetimes must I have wandered bewildered and lost in the parched deserts of my own creation, and hopelessly searching, even through reason collecting imaginary sand with a sieve. Now Genesis regained, it is done. In an instant, it is done. I walk back through the forest, now for the first time, I am met by 'She' in the camp-site.

She instinctively gives me my first embrace. The end is in the beginning and the beginning is in the end. Oh woman most fair of the northern star, I acknowledge your love. I acknowledge you, man, for the second embrace and you, lovely woman of the flowing hair, for the third.

It is light, the wonder of light, it is everywhere and in everything, even in that what appears most foul to the senses and the mind, the light is there too. There are no divisions, there is no other, in the oneness of being, where all is in one. To anyone coming into the presence of 'It', with clear eye and mind, 'It' becomes immediately known, once the death has occurred. That is the communion that takes place in the silence, where no words are spoken, for 'It' is beyond word. All the doctoring and healing is the farcical dance of the lie supporting its own refusal to exit the gates of hell. Even the teachers and gurus are part of this farce, before this implosion within, when the truth of it all is made known. Existence begins as it ends. It is already done. We, you and I, in this sensory world, we are doing it now. It is forever now, as it is forever being done, and forever is eternity, but eternity is not immortality.

Listen through the silence that is continuously present in this awesome forest of life. Listen through the love from the 'Heart' that is perpetually open, and perpetually free from all the conditioning of this conditional world. Come out of the dream. Come out of the illusion being served by the walking dead. Come out of hell. Lazarus, come out. This awakening is the greatest of all miracles. It is immediately present for you, the 'Me' that you are. Immortality.

All it takes is one glimpse of the unimaginable to bring about the total change to the state of one's being. For one glimpse is sufficient for one to lay down one's life in absolute service to 'It'.

> *A golden crystal for an instant pace*
> *On dappled waters, mystic blue;*
> *And then as yellow stems to hold a place*
> *Where early daffodils once grew,*
> *'Tis gone, no more 'tis seen,*
> *But yet to feel a magic true*
> *When sudden thoughts perch on the distant blue*
> *And shivers through the being.*

> *Summer, 1966*

Chapter 23

THE SLAYING OF THE MASTER

Woman is love and man is love with something to do, according to the teaching of the spiritual master. This something to do in man has resulted in the world as it has evolved in its present state. In other words the world is the outward projection of action piled upon action, the moving away from the centre that is love, the moving out of the Garden of Eden, so to speak, into the abyss of illusion.

In my own experience I can see this to be true. In my life as a busy man I gained worldly excellence while my love, neglected, vanished. There always seems to be something to be doing, from building skyscrapers to selling illusionary concepts to digging more graves. One can see this in the remnants of the old monasteries in Ireland, with their round turrets of stone protruding upwards to the sky, as expressed by an eighteenth century poet, in a poem that was aptly named, 'The Midnight Court'. Here it was illustrated how the men left the womenfolk forsaken as they placed themselves out of reach of love, as love expressed by woman and man copulating, in search of the depths inside those monastery walls. A young man in a dream entered the court in the forest that was presided over by women and was placed on trial on behalf of all the men who had taken to monastery life through wayward beliefs and left woman without man.

Here we are today in a world of science and technology, the current monastic expression, in service to the 'quick fix' with little space or time for natural love, so it appears. As was past so is present, this karmic recurrence of paradise lost, paradise lost again so it seems.

All that is said by the Australian master is true in my

experience. This moment of love, this moment of God, is being fullest expressed in the love between man and woman. As so it is seen, and the projection of mankind has changed it to sex. Yes man, I need to come to stillness within to transcend this worldly affair, even if it means a silent retreat behind those monastic walls, so the birdsong again can connect with my heart. For before I can come to know Goddess in woman I must first know God in myself as man. And all the mastering of tantra is useless without first acknowledging that.

Courtship may change its mask, either the dragging by hair from the cave or the pearls and diamonds and candlelight dinners or the sweetest eloquence of godly expression, but this does not mean there is any change in intent. The madman's insatiable desire to taste woman in all of her bodily forms can even possess the gods, for here too is the human condition the master. Man-gods, beware of the 'She' for now is the time, her time. The distant pulse of her heartbeat is tingling the veins of every woman of love and each moment grows nearer and nearer to the body incarnate from the far distant depths within. The two thousand year reign of the world demon on earth is now facing its end, for 'It' is awakening in woman. Her Goddess within is her true essence and 'She' is no longer being subordinated by the self-guided gods in the self-image of man. Of all the forms of abuse that woman has unwittingly received there is none more foul than that administered to her when blinded by forced light at the hand of the gods who claim their sanctuary on 'It' the most sacred. Masters of Tantra, is this your last dance? Yet it is as it is, and as this master himself has said, "Even gallstones must have their day".

The rainforests in Australia are spectacularly abundant in so many forms of life and through the intensity of such one lady stepped forward and offered me her hand. We walked and we talked, we cognised and embraced, and we sat silently together as one. But all women through the Australian master were deemed by him to be his, and particularly the one by my side. Yet she had chosen a place that seemed to be clear from the shadow of him who was crowning himself as Lord of the Dance. Then in the seminar of 'Beauty and the Beast' the sword was placed in my hand as the green-eyed monster foamed and screamed at me, challenging my courage to slay him. He clearly wanted this woman by my side and set out to remove me. All his intent and all his accumulative force he directed my way. I found the answer coming through me in stillness. Who am I but the student listening to silence where all is being heard, who am I to take up this sword against this giver of light? My name is not Michael, as that he metaphorically uses when shouting at me, yet it is I whom he calls to, I am the one. Then I am passing right through him. In stillness and silence with no movement of matter, no matter displaced but the matter that should, in the flash of Arjuna it is done.

Then everything changed and it changed for him too. The lion now aflame is released from the cage, and the beast reluctantly fades into the flooding of silence from whence it had come. It is as it is, this service is done. And what does it mean, these woes of myself then postulating with the woes of this master? The lion is the heart and the cage is the particular personality, whether master or student of life. The flame is the guru. As the flame devours the cage so the light of the guru devours the person. Even the master can need the outside guru to set his cage alight, as I was now experiencing to my utter amazement. In the instant that all this seems to be happening, the real guru witnessing is in the one that is permanently seated within. Now I stand alone in the void with no distance between 'Me' and God. But I acknowledge him as I acknowledge the others who

guided my misguidance back to the source and the seat of
God within. And I acknowledge 'She' who was part of my
burning in my own lingering years in hell, for a thousand
lives of misgivings is balanced by this one moment's grace.

Polished armour done
The heroes stand in might
Fearless in the sun,
To shiver in the night.
*

Clashing steel rings out
Re-echoes in the distant hills
Death the brave ones shout
So death, its belly fills.
*

The earth shall drink her pour
Of souls upon her crust
When thirst calls out she'll capture more,
Flesh in armour merely dust.

Summer, 1966

Chapter 24

TRUTH AND THE GREAT TEST

My financial business in Dublin continued in limbo yet I could now almost feel the conclusion of it all. Everything with a beginning has an end, even the mystical forests. But there was more to it all than my own particular part. There is no balance to the world of business and finance, I discovered.

The market is not an objective, neutral trading place. It is merely a collection of self-interests directing their attention where it suits with each self-interest being driven by its own particular motive, that is usually based on profit. Its 'status' is the consequence of will-power, particularly power over other wills. I was seeking out a balance in the margins of that space where the industry exists and trying to capture the attention of those interests to solve my particular business dilemma. There can be no balancing in this. Indeed the entire world of finance seems to find its survival through the juggling of margins. If all investors were to set about withdrawing their funds there would obviously be an immediate collapse. But the world of banking relies on the laws of probability to save it from such, while the money worriers must hold to the belief their investments are safe. It is so the bubble is sustained, the reality of it all being too awesome to face.

In the microcosm of my business I did not have such assurance as there were parties breathing mass panic into the minds of my clients. As a result I was being bombarded with pressure from persons wishing to withdraw immediately, regardless of their original agreements of not needing returns before a set maturity date. My business needed to survive until the property I had given to it reached a favourable market, and the final contracts worked upon were completed. Then the clients in this particular basket would receive their returns plus the agreed interest and the promised dividend proportionately shared from any profits left after everything else had been paid. This was my only option at that point in time and I had to stay with this situation and keep it afloat until it would reach an acceptable conclusion.

The enemy pumped fear and panic into my trusting clients yet, in spite of it all, the business was not a stricken ship and continued to stay above water. Some would call it a test of nerves, particularly those playing the psychology game in their efforts to break me in their personal vendetta, this being their service to wealth. But the wealth of this world is not my God and it shall not be imposed on me to serve as such by anyone self-widowed from love. No piety or publicly declared holiness can disguise it, for I no longer look at the outer expression of the person, however dazzling it may appear. I look at the inner state where reality can be immediately seen.

The situation continued on a razor edge and each day I had no idea what the next might bring. I could not even see the probability of a worldly future for me personally. Any moment could be my last. Now all my efforts were directed at keeping the business alive in whatever way possible until a satisfactory conclusion could be reached. I urgently wished for such a conclusion yet I had to accept the wisdom of the spiritual master when he stated that nothing happens before its time. Oddly enough the status quo remained in the accounts even in the confusion at the final hour of panic from a particular client money would somehow become available to satisfy the immediate need.

Apart from my own basic needs I had little requirement of money for personal spending outside of the trips on my spiritual awakening. I managed to attend most of the master's seminars in Europe and, after spending a year in being with the moment, I found myself back in Australia for the second master session. This was much different from the first and yet in the depths of it all it was more of a continuum, as if we had never left that place. In the truth of it we never had left, for it is a mark in the timeless, as nearest that words can describe, or a place for docking in time travel. But such descriptions are an imagining, and this is beyond even that. There can be no returning from this state, for it is beyond mind, beyond description, beyond being and belief, beyond death. This is the immortality, where there is no person, no personality, no one and nothing to reincarnate, no coming back.

The level of stillness was so profoundly fine at this Australian gathering that at times it seemed as if we physically faded into the void and nothing needed to be reaffirmed. Even the few still carrying personal stuff discarded it themselves without loading it on the master. He was not physically well and his appearances were infrequent yet the entire camp was aglow in the light, even in the darkness of the nights the hue seemed to be shimmering and engulfing every form of life. It was a joy to behold, so many now glowing from within in their own light. This was part of the movement in the consciousness of all humankind. It was an awesome privilege to be in the midst of all that was happening, even being as one with the beautiful trees of this place. When the time for parting arrived there was no need for farewells for we were all moving out to the four corners of the earth within the one light. My corner was Ireland still. My own obligations remained to the world of financial chaos, as the seeds of the weeds that were planted through the corn stood awaiting the hand of the harvester.

Then truth put its test on me. When I arrived at Dublin airport on that November morning two policemen from the fraud squad were waiting to take me in for questioning relating to the widow's money. The statement of complaint she had made was clear and precise from a narrow point of view, but conveniently omitted the fuller story. I answered their questions directly without elaboration. They were trained and efficient policemen and I had confidence in their ability to fully check the complaint themselves. Furthermore, it was public knowledge, I thought, that I had made an agreement through the courts with this woman and her money was adequately secured in the property of our business.

Some months later they proceeded to ask me further but similar questions to verify that I had spoken truthfully. My answers satisfied them but I was later to discover that the policemen's task, as far as they were concerned, was in building a case on the grounds of the complaint, having me charged, convicted and put out of business. Neither was there any consideration for the innocent parties who would lose their investments as a result, even the widow herself, for this is not part of their job. I do not blame the policemen for I did not inform them as to the full extent of this woman's actions. It was up to them to ascertain from the chaos of my business ensuing her play in my affairs whether or not they deemed that I held fraudulent intent or undue recklessness in my dealings.

Indeed, it was more important to me to get my final business contracts concluded so I could balance the accounts in favour of all. I wanted to close the doors to that part of my life and move on to some area of service that would have nothing to do with finance. I had no more personal need of money for myself outside of bodily sustenance, after being five years in the light of a spiritual master. But in the midst of my efforts to render unto Caesar what was Caesar's I was now beginning to understand that this particular Caesar did not specifically want me to balance my accounts. Her apparent wish was to keep me in the trap she had made in order to keep me under her control. It now seemed that I was permanently encaged in the abyss, on a pendulum swinging from the light of a spiritual master to the darkness of this widow's expression endowed with solid gold crucifixes and stories of apparitions. This seemed to be the monster that I was experiencing, this two thousand year old blasphemer to life in the person of this woman still trying to mirror itself in the person of me.

She too had sat in the presence of the spiritual master five years previous when he first visited Dublin, so from somewhere within her she too was seeking the good, not the false good as in the worldly show to the surface of the foolish, but a real good in her own agonising lament. Strange as it may seem to the surface world of ourselves I know what it is within her, and that I love dearly.

We have lost our true nature to a superficial reality through the existential side of ourselves. The permitted parameters of societal thought keep us bound within the confines of a mentally-imposed world of duality. My problems had arisen within these confines as my particular immersion in the psychic rhythm of the anguishing world. I had been conditioned to believe in a heaven and a hell and in the one nailed to a cross who is supposed to have said that we must love our enemies. Yet the Catholic Church that schooled me in such doctrines actively promoted the alienation of protestants. Through my mind as a child I could plainly see this appaling ignorance as the adults about me blindly served this blasphemy to all that is life and to all that is love.

Heaven is now, is truth, and hell is the world of illusion. For how long must we live in futility opposing the moment of truth as we wastefully defend our own particular pain? For how long must we revel in our sad, sad stories from dead mouths to dead ears? For how long must we be the fools of darkness? For how long, I ask.

Where are the lights for Charlie's heart that is heavy with grief? What is the matter with this woman who has so violently plundered his forest? Why has she got such a peculiar stare? His mother tells him "She has it since she was a girl of sixteen, when her father took her on the train to Dublin and left her some place for over a month. Before that, as according to the story being told, she was a plump and happy young girl but when she came back she was skin and bone. Your father would know more about this, for he grew up with the people of these parts and I can only tell you what others have said". This was all the information he could get from his mother and Charlie's father was reluctant to bring up the ghosts of the past. What is done is done and speaking of the past is like rekindling a fire from its own ashes, there cannot be truth in that.

Charlie wondered about her dark secret within, the occasional gossip about she bearing a child outside wedlock, was it some terrible sin that can only be committed by adults that is still causing such disturbance in her. Why should such violation be happening to the innocent stream and the trees? Once all the trees have been burned for firewood in one winter, then all will be gone forever, but yet nobody seems to take notice of the terrible calamity befalling the life of the forest. "Why is everyone seemingly bewitched by her wilful intent and why is she so violent with me", he asks. "Each time she sees me she immediately flies into a rage". How extraordinary it all appears to the questioning child trying to understand the dark ignorance of the world that is spinning about him like a mad dog chasing its tail.

Spring is in the air
The lambs are dancing free of care
The Emerald Isle is green
The daffodils again in being
My silent love on other shores aglow
Still playful on her winter's snow
My love, Her love, all love unseen
By the ungainly sty
In man-god's covet eye
The bird-song telling so
Hail to you, my Goddess Queen
For ne'er we are apart
Here in the Centre-Heart.
The lambs pass on
As do the daffodils
And all of dancing thrills
Just as the melting snow
Lovers come, lovers go,
Existence so, Aham;
Yet Love that is
'I' always am.

Chapter 25

THE HEART OF THE DRUID

The Druids were the spiritual seers among the ancient Celts, the priests of that time before the arrival of Christianity superimposed its own definition on them as conjurers and sorcerers of darkness. They saw the one great spirit as the life-source of the trees, vegetation, animals, insects, fish of the rivers and seas, birds of the air and man. Their vision did not conjure the duality of virtue and vice as they lived and worshiped in their immediacy to the earth. Life and death was seen as an instant pulse even though the living of a life takes several years. Such, and more, is the 'Sight' among these great seers that has become lost through ignorance in the outward journey of time. Yet the heart of the Druid can never be lost for it is always immediate to the ones who are ready to see.

The dark winter passed and the daffodils quite suddenly re-appeared throughout the countryside. Now all sides of the motorway from Dublin airport blossomed in glistening yellow as a welcome to all entering this mystical isle. Ireland is the land of the Druids, the timeless Shamans in time. When Christianity imposed itself on their divine mark they evolved through the change, which was only one of outer expression, to take their part in this island of 'Saints and Scholars'. Nothing has changed within. All remains exactly the same. It is as it is, one voice, one word.

The fools on the face of the land continue to argue about politics. In ignorance to life they march to the sound of the drum of division and hate and it is transferred through the milk from the infected breast of the mother to the infant reborn to serve it. Such is the human condition, fools re-living a stagnant past, from ashes to ashes, re-playing the same tune over and over in their evanescent world. This is the reverie of madness being played by a public at large, while the light of the Druid and the light of the Saint as the light of the shimmering sun, continues, ignored.

Oh misguided bishop of Christian division, pull back from your wall of obstinate partition, transcend this ignorance and move within to the light of the Druid. The time is now and your two thousand year reign of darkness is done. Now is the age of transparency and you have no more dark alleys to hide your wilful, misguided intent. It is in this land, this land of patient awaiting, you have been given the stage for your final farcical dance. Now the sight of your blackness is apparent to all and no more need the children serve you, for God is Love, God is Light, and you are a pain in the arse.

Through one of your divisions the widow came forth carrying your cold candle in her love-forsaken hand. The howl of the 'She-wolf' is the howl from the essence of woman mercilessly bound in your chains while man still emanates love from his grave with the stamp of the Druid in his heart. Oh my dark Rosaleen, do not sigh, you are not forsaken for the West is about to awaken.

As suddenly as Spring arrived, it moved on, and the days grew closer to mid-Summer. I found myself again driving westward to an appointment with a family at the gateway to Connemara. This is an idyllic place of natural beauty at the foot of some mountains less than a mile from Lough Corrib. I lingered awhile by the river flowing through from the falls above to the lake below, listening to its sweetness of sound and watching the waters flowing over the stepping stones leading to the other side. By its banks four horse-chestnut trees of grandeur stand defying time, as people of each decade come and picnic in their shade, then leave, then forget, then die, and seldom hear a word from their story.

As before the leaves from the drooping lower branches touched the stream as if sipping its waters. Two young children, one American one Oriental, walk by hand in hand, sisters in life. The trees are unmoved, as they stood where they stand, whispering their secrets. They have witnessed changing times, the passing of the horses and coaches, the arrival of the automobile yet nothing has changed from where these horse-chestnuts stand. People are born. Young lovers are made. Each feels the love is unique to this moment only, and perfectly true, for it is always unique and true to life only in this moment.

Memories of past are but last year's horse-chestnut leaves. The trees are never in mourning for last year's seeds as they stand in their fullness emanating their vitality to all in their immediate surround. In true harmonious style they speak to us of life that is 'now'. 'Now' is the window of timelessness where the psychological world is transcended through absolute stillness within that is the sap of all life being whispered to those who are ready to hear.

Yes, life is truly in the moment, each moment alive, where there is no thinking mind clattering and clanging its problems, its theories, the hell-sounds of the living dead. Beautiful life is in being, as these trees are singing aloud to all who can comprehend. The souls of the living dead arise from the perpetual corpse to reshuffle their lost belongings, only to return, while life in all its glory and all its beauty, just is. Be still, and listen to the whispering wisdom of the trees, for this is the heart of the Druid. It is your heart, your life, your truth within. But do not believe me. You must taste the salmon of true knowledge for yourself, for your taste is my taste, and all taste is one. There is but one life. Yes, in myriad forms, all life is one.

When I drove back to the city of Dublin all the beauty of this place came with me. I had been re-charged. It shone forth from my centre reflecting on all whom I met and the trials and tribulations of living the life of the public momentarily dissolved. Yet one does not have to go to the beautiful gateway of Connemara to receive it, for in all corners of Ireland such beauty abounds. Such is the essence in the reflection of life that is truly within, where your own Druid eternally abides. This you can discover when the shackles of blind living are broken and when all the ghosts are left with nowhere to go but back through the sullen shadows of mindful maya, back into the abyss. These shadows are but our numerous foolish attachments that have become the walls creating our prison of hell, the hell of our very own making and masking an evanescent world of reverie. These mental abstractions, these dreamtime impostors to life, are immediately vanished when the Druid within is awakened, as mine has been through the calling from the master outside that is but the echo of 'Me'. Is your Druid still in deep sleep?

Charlie's is unquestionably silenced. The trees of his boyhood are chopped to the ground and his magical stream is a valley of mud apparently caused by the woman with a peculiar stare. She has twisted her leg while trying to flee from one of her bulls gone wild in a pen as she tried to cut off its horns. Perhaps it is the spirit of the trees through the leprechauns magical powers getting their own back on her, he is thinking, as he sews a button back onto his sleeve. But then, as the needle instantly prods him, he is immediately told from somewhere within, this is not the temperament of the trees. This is not what they were saying to him in their silent wonder during his magical years.

In an instant flash back to his earlier childhood, it shivers

through his being, this knowledge from deep within,
whether here or gone, that he is at one with their story being
told.

Fix your mind on 'Me' alone
Let your thoughts dwell in 'Me'
You will hereafter live in 'Me' alone
Of this there is no doubt.

Bhagavad Gita XII 8

Chapter 26

CHOOSE FREEDOM, THE GODDESS ARRIVES FROM THE WEST

Another Summer had arrived with the message of stillness. The time for the Australian master's seminars in England and Holland was again approaching. Yet my attendance was not coming to life within me. There was something else in the air and I could feel from deep within that I was calling it up. The persistence of the widow's shadow on my heel as part of myself needed to be openly exposed and challenged. All that had gone adrift in the business affairs that had smotheringly surrounded me needed to be openly addressed. As a solitary figure there was nothing more I could personally do. Each lingering attempt I made to right the situation was appearing as only a temporary appeasement.

I had, to date, spent five years in the presence of the spiritual master and I was opened to accepting whatever must come in this story of life. Then Catherine arrived, this beautiful woman of light from the west coast of America, to spend one month in Dublin in the stillness of what was to become known to me as dharma dialogues. While sitting in a Dublin cafe, lost to myself in the dark and forlorn clouds of the financial dilemma that were flooding me out of this life, her unimpeded message 'Choose Freedom', reached to my heart when I first noticed her poster that read,

'In truth, your inherent nature is clear awareness. In this awareness one discovers a love that is not dependent on particular

circumstances or objects, and that is the most abiding form of happiness. You need not acquire anything to realise this. You need only subtract beliefs which obscure your living as this radiant presence, as love itself. This is what is known as freedom, and it is immediately accessible to you, even as you read these words'.

Is it not more than mere coincidence that I should have been guided to her poster at that particular time? This wondrous woman had travelled thousands of miles to rekindle the sweet message of the ancients buried beneath the monastic ruins and fairyforts of this mystical land. She was here to reaffirm the truth of my heart at that moment buried to the depths of desolation from the forces amassing against me as the ghost of myself.

Those Druids of Ireland awakening who had become aware of her presence gathered to her for each evening's sitting in Temple Bar throughout the mid-summer month. I was but one among them as the voice from the silence whispered its message of love to me. This love is the God immediate, that is life, that is truth, that is death, in the dignity of all that is being.

I had the privilege to walk with some of her companions on the ancient pathways of 'Saints and Scholars' in the tranquil Wicklow mountains and to breathe in the freshness of the less frequented lakes and streams. Their stillness within and their deep silent wisdom was love incarnate to me as we walked quietly together in acknowledgement of the wonder of life on that particular day. Catherine in person visited my home in County Clare and made sacred the place of my birth. The secret treasure was re-opened by 'She' through her presence and the sweetness of life revitalised my spirit in preparation for what was to come.

In silence I had called it up, for it was the time to render unto Caesar all that was Caesar's so that the worldly illusion could no longer validate itself by imposing its claim upon me. Catherine, with her gentle and loving friends, had met me and blessed me, for my final accounting. They came, they stayed for the mid-summer month, then they departed after filling this place with their gentleness and love. I sat replenished in silent waiting.

Then the morning arrived. It was the twelfth day of July, a day of disturbance in the Irish calendar. This is the day that men dressed up in the colours of King William of Orange take to the streets of the North in fevered parading, as the Battle of the Boyne re-winds itself through the divisive vibrations of religious determinists. The men and women of Roman allegiance get on with their washing and mending and try to forget their Catholic King James who still runs as fear through their veins in the corridors of time. Year after year it continues its flow from this blood-thirsty scene some three hundred years past with no one of sanity about to call an official close to this battle of kings for the British crown. This is the pageant of the twelfth of July as part of the Irish disturbance.

On the previous day I had travelled from Clare to Galway, then on to Dublin to attend my business. On Friday morning, the morning of the twelfth, they called to my father's house. There were three plain-clothed policemen looking to make a spectacular arrest. Unfortunately for them, their timing was out, but they did get an unexpected taste of the early morning sunrise in County Clare, with the dew on the grass and little pockets of mist by the hedgerows. The heavenly chorus of the birds welcoming the break of day surely would have been music most mystical to their ears and a change from the noisy city.

Now the man in charge, who was acting on behalf of the widow's complaint, was obliged to phone me as we had previously agreed and I made an arrangement to meet with them that evening in Dublin. I called to my friend James for reaffirmation of what I was about to allow to happen. Strangely, as I later drove through Dublin, another friend from the house of James unexpectedly pulled up beside me at a set of traffic lights in his left hand drive Italian car. He talked with me about life and letting go of negativity as we drove side by side from one set of lights to another through the city traffic. The teacher, who had set both these men's inner flame alight, whom I had never personally encountered but whose books and teachings I had attentively read, was now clearly connecting to the light within me through this coincidental meeting as I journeyed on, alone, into the jaws of the greatest test of my life up to that point in time. I met with the waiting policemen at the appointed meeting place, outside a hotel on the Lucan Road, at the appointed time of six-thirty that evening and they arrested me in the name of the widow. I was taken to the Bridewell Police Station, stripped of my personal belongings and locked in a cell to await the sitting of the late night court.

Now the eighteenth century poem, describing a young man being put on trial on behalf of the monastic men of Ireland for failing in their manly duties to make love to the womenfolk became a reality to me. I was locked in that cell awaiting my own 'Midnight Court' for failing to be a lover to the worldly widow obsessed by desire to possess me. This was her punishment from the fire of her passion and this is the truth of the situation, if the truth could only be heard.

It was a traumatic three hour wait for the court appearance. I was allowed a phone call and I did manage to get a message to my family and to a solicitor friend who managed to arrange for a criminal lawyer to defend me at that late hour. Then it was a long and silent wait as I sat alone on the concrete floor of the cell. Stillness is the way and all that I had received from the Australian master and the most recent presence of Catherine and her gentle friends was alive within me and had become part of my being. This was a three hour meditation. Although my body and mind was in shock, yet deep within, nothing had changed. Tears appeared intermittently, not just for my own particular state but for the state of everyone in relation to it, my dear father and daughters, my sisters and brother, my wild and free nieces and nephews, even this poor misfortunate widow who had been prepared to go this far, in her suffering from whatever darkness she was harbouring within. No, if I were to live a thousand years I could not love the darkness in that woman, or any woman possessed by it. Nor could I bow to it in any form again or allow my own greed to blind me as it had done.

Such I now fully realise, for this dark and forlorn cell was paradise compared to the bedroom of the luxury hotel she had once imprisoned me in and coerced me into bowing to her darkened desire. Yes, for that I was guilty, although I did not physically have sex with her as she demanded, but I did allow myself to enter that room and her bed. Now this moment locked in this cell, sitting alone on this concrete floor, I recognised the truth. This karma was done. Strange as it may seem, my heart was released through tears of joy.

I was moved to the holding cell beneath the court and waited to make my appearance. It was a living hell with graffiti covering practically every square inch of the dark and dirty walls, with one corner walled off to serve as a toilet. Man's inhumanity to man presented itself in this lingering medieval expression in a world too busy to notice. Yet amidst all the graffiti in those holding cells in the Bridewell I saw a pearl of great wonder written on one wall. It danced out to greet me as I read,

'They came
With sword in hand
Greed glistening in their eyes
And with Holy Book
To support their lies.
They came'.

Is this what I was being told? This cell, this courtroom,
was her current sword in hand to be used in her greed to
possess me, or destroy me with her holy book of support, I
having refused to dance to her particular tune. Now I was
the official villain, or at least about to be branded so by the
law that for now had become her law. I sat on a concrete
slab in silent waiting for what was to come.

It was close to midnight when they came and brought
me up from the basement cell to the courtroom. The
policemen reading out the charges against me requested
that I be detained in prison until the day of the actual trial as
I was a person familiar with travelling and was likely to
abscond. I spoke on my own behalf that I had come
voluntarily to face these charges placed against me and that
I had made myself available at all times to the policemen in
question. It was late at night and the judge commanded that
I be detained in prison for a week, according to the law of
the land, and he set bail at one hundred thousand pounds.
I was taken to Mountjoy prison after the midnight hour of
that Friday, the twelfth of July, by the two policemen who
had taken part in my arrest. On the way out of the
courtroom to the police car one of them spoke of the early
morning beauty of County Clare. Yes, these men also have
hearts. It was a long day for them, from early morning
witnessing the sunrise over the hills of County Tipperary
across the river Shannon from my father's house in County
Clare, to the midnight hour where their day's work was

completed as they deposited me inside the prison gates.

There were others in the waiting room being registered when I arrived and one young woman being detained insisted that I take the remainder of her potato chips for sustenance. The two policemen bid me good night and went home to their families. These people sitting with me in the waiting room on our way to the cells were my family now. There was one frightened man from Belfast in handcuffs. He had come to Dublin for that day to keep himself clear of the particular troubles on the streets of the North, but his moment of temporary freedom from tension spilled over in exuberance to land him in imprisonment at this side of the border of man's division.

There were other young men from the street scene of Dublin suffering from heroin addiction, but unlike the one from Belfast they were familiar with the run of the place. There were two young women, one of whom had given me my late night supper. Then after some time we were called out individually. As I entered another room I was told to stop and all my personal possessions were taken, placed in a bag and sealed. Then I was walked down a steel stairway and led to a larger room. Here I was told to take off my clothes. It was then that the prison officer noticed my cuff-links. These were of gold and were one of the gifts from the widow before she showed wilful intent. I had worn them on this day of my arrest as they had become the symbol of handcuffs and this was the most appropriate time to wear them. Now I handed them over with all my clothes. I walked naked through the passageway, all of my world behind me, with nothing left but this body. I washed in a shower, the only one I was given for the week, and dressed in prison clothes.

It was a most traumatic time in my life, but I have nothing to loose, nothing to cling to, for nothing is mine. It is as it is and life is good in all of its wonder, even the trauma of this terrible experience. I was led through to the inner prison, to what became known as Base, with three others. We were given four plastic covered mattresses to put on the floor and sleep on after being taken to the cell that was used for the newcomers. I lay there in stillness in the darkness, my ears filled with the sounds of electric motors pounding next door, and listened to the sighs of the other three men as they shuffled in their troubled sleep. This was the greatest trauma unfolding itself, each lingering moment an eternity of pitiful pain, our hearts heavy and our beings unified in numbness. Just before dawn my ears tuned into a louder yet familiar sound. It was water, water gushing down, the heavens had opened outside. I raised to my feet and managed to reach up to the tiny treble-barred window. I put out my hand and the rain, the sweet rain from the heavens, washed and caressed my palm. I wept with joy.

Yes, life is good in all of its wonder and whatever it brings I am to accept in the love of all that exists. I thank the Absolute for testing this spiritual awakening and allowing me this privilege of sharing it with you. For the trials and tribulations of this existence are but the flip side of its pleasures, and in this sensory world both are one and the same. But do not believe me, for believing is not knowing. It is through open heart and stillness of mind that the wisdom of life is freely available, as your gift, your inheritance, especially for you, in your immediate form, now, at this moment in time, through your own immediate experience. Our stories through sensory perception may seem to differ in the living experiences of life, yet from the heart centre of our being, I have found that all is one and the same.

This is the story of my personal death. I danced to the sound of the trumpet through the halls of the castles of worldly delight spun by the widow's entourage. The music stopped as reality dawned and I landed on the concrete floor of Mountjoy prison. Now the sweet sound of nature's rain cleansed all from this mind.

Hell is not in a life hereafter
As we wishfully try to surmise
When swallowing the words of some preacher
While listening through fear to such sighs.
As life slips into existence
That is measured from Earth to the Moon
And the millions of stars reflecting
As the nightingale's sweetest tune
Or even the daffodil's dancing
To passionate lovers romancing
Or the fragrance from blossoms in May
From the corpse of winter's decay
So too is Hell this immediate
If truth of it all I allow
The good the bad the nice and the ugly
Are all in this moment of Now.

Chapter 27

THE NAKED TRUTH

When we are born we arrive naked, totally naked. I do not mean just in the flesh, which is of no consequence at that time, but naked within. We cannot know this through imagination, in knowing as being in that state, but we can enter it when we reach absolute stillness.

Some people may be able to recall it under hypnosis, but they usually do so as a past experience which is secondary knowledge. When one enters it through stillness there is no past memory to recall, for it is now, as this moment is. In truth there is only the 'now' where all of existence, past present and future, actually is. The mind cannot get hold of this for it is like trying to measure infinity, or trying to know the size of the desert by measuring one grain of sand. It is the gnosis that is beyond mental knowledge, beyond worldly wisdom, beyond intellect. This 'beyond' is within, in the unfathomable depths of one's being. In order to be it one must be totally naked within, with no garment, no thought, yet fully awake and alert.

Reason and meditation are but instruments to help one remove the clothing and when everything has been removed then they have done their jobs. This is the process of letting go, letting go of all one's attachments, emotional and mental, and all one's beliefs. These are the shackles and chains coated in fear that bind one to the hard granite wall of the ignorance in living. And this is the re-discovery, the re-entering to the reality of one's being once the illusion of the evanescent world has been transcended. This is not a theory, or a particular point of view, it is a fact beyond word that can only be known through the silence within.

The closest I have physically come to reflect how it is within me since the moment of death in Australia is that moment of outer reflection when I walked through the passageway in Mountjoy prison with all of my worldly garments given up. In the womb I am yet as one in this glorious sanctuary and when I am born I come out of the infinitesimal depths of this oneness into this world of existence that gradually becomes the 'other'. As time pushes me out of the infant state further into this existence I begin to loose contact with the original knowledge of oneness, the knowledge of 'Me'. I soon become the body of flesh, blood, bones and sinews and I give it a soul and hang it on the sky-hook of the ignorant world. So it continues until the body, through wheezing and puking, draws its last breath when again it is suddenly seen. In a flash it comes back to 'Me', while hell's time-bound intruder burns on to the next unsuspecting body of matter.

It was now over five years since Mary had spoken, "Cleanse yourself as you come onto Me". This cleansing is to become as naked again. To let go of all my shackles and chains of putrid evanescent existence in which the vital energy is wastefully spilled when I falsely take this body of flesh, this spacesuit of time, to be the real 'Me' and put it opposing all others. In truth there is only One, as it was in the beginning is now and ever shall be, a beginning without beginning, an end without end.

When we look at the story of Charlie, his truth is the mystical forest with the early morning sun glistening through the cobwebs awesomely shaped between the branches. Here, where the sun, the cobwebs, the branches are all in the expression of One the mystery of life became known to him. It was through the combination of all three that truth appeared to flash for a moment through his consciousness of mind. Then his forest was physically destroyed by the outward expression of the terrible pain in the heart of that poor wretched woman, pain that had become an embodiment of her isolation from all that is love.

But in life nothing is truly isolated. It is a river endlessly flowing. And the torment of the woman with the peculiar stare is the legacy she received from the absurdity borne by her father from a previous time of false morality imposing itself on her as an innocent child. She cries out in her pain by tearing the heart from the forest as the embryo had been torn from the unprotected purity of her womb by the ignorance of man. Is this not the ignorance of the world endlessly forcing its grief on the mystical forest of life?

When I truly look into myself is this what I am doing? Is this my sad, sad story, my personal condition of grief by the hand of myself, and endlessly imposed upon others? Do I stand as the bearer of grief with my own peculiar stare? Or do I stand as the child, open in heart, to receive the mystical sight of my true nature? The great master has spoken, now two thousand years hence the message remains, "Come unto 'Me' and I will give you rest". Do I really have to stay ignorant of this even beyond my final breath? I acknowledge you Mary for blowing the dust from my eyes so I could be a true seeker. Now I have chosen freedom and I have been tasting it truly, even as my physical body is locked in an overcrowded cell inside prison walls. As Jesus has said, 'The truth shall set you free'. In my experience this is the freedom, the real freedom, regardless of the place or the state or the chains that are placed on the transient body. Freedom is not confined to the realm of time.

In the busy world of business there is usually not enough time for freedom as we are feverishly busy keeping up with the wants of ourselves. In a prison cell time usually stands still, as everyone is made conscious of time, while personal wants are unable to be pursued. While I am inside if I could really pause to notice the state of myself on the outside and when I am outside if I could do likewise as to really see my pitiful state inside then I may, perhaps, see that one is merely the reflection of the other. This living scene is a comedy of errors.

During the long days there was nothing to read in the prison and it was proving impossible to get permission to go to the library. The prison officers who barely coped with their demanding workload would not make the time to allow me access. Then one man lent me a book about life and culture in England during the last century and before. Towards its end I discovered an extract from 'Ananda' I think it was called, written by Florence Nightingale. Here amazingly it was again, even in the cold inner blackness of the prison, the voice of 'She' in the written word of this remarkable woman flowing through time and space of outer existence directly back into the stillness of my being. She spoke about death in that passage, not the death her body was about to enter, but the real death within her that had occurred many years previously and had given her freedom, the same freedom I speak of that is life immortal within. My real sister in life had paid me a visit. Closer than flesh, she lives in my heart.

Could it be clearer than that, this river of truth, never changing, ever present, flowing through the barriers of our defined limitations and showing us that all is in One? Her love, my love, her truth, my truth, her freedom, my freedom, that is the freedom of 'Me'. I have found that there is only one 'Me', dear reader, deep within you. Know this, for this is the seat of immortality. Here is the key to all that needs to be known. But do not believe me. Please take it and see if it fits in your lock.

Chapter 28

HELL EXPERIENCED, THE EQUILIBRIUM
REGAINED

I have two daughters, both positive young women to life and each has her own individual space. They are very much different in outer expression and give one another extraordinary room as they acknowledge is necessary through their experience. Being the recipient of their ongoing attention is my own place of learning.

When they entered adolescence they utilised the two islands of Ireland and Great Britain in order to co-exist with their need for space from each other. On one occasion when the older was returning from England, the younger departed for France on a boat that set sail one hour before her sister arrived. As the horizon took one it gave back the other to me their father, still confused by the learning I was receiving from these young women. Now they seem to have outgrown that stage of opposing expression. They have become more cordial and more understanding in their mutual acceptance of their distinctive differences.

My name was called in the prison yard and I was told I had visitors, my two daughters together with James from the Source. We met, and how awesome it was to receive, such power, such energy in the love flooding from these two supercharged young women of life, as they sat side by side across the man-made divide between me and them. For the first time in my own experience these beautiful daughters were totally together as one. This seeming calamity that had befallen me had now brought them to this oneness in their singular pain, as they stood firm and refused to allow me to loose myself to the prison world. Was this not a silver lining in the cloud of my anguish?

My daughters were seated before me in freedom and this was the greatest gift of the creation to me at that moment. Their energies had combined and what an awesome experience it was to me receiving such power of love. We were fully together as one. The younger read me a poem she had especially composed to read to the father now taken from her and locked behind bars;

> ' When you are freed from the clasp of Mountjoy
> Quiet sands lie in wait of your presence
> Upon their cool calming of soul
> Restoration of thine purest essence
> In cleansing of salted sea waters
> Of life returning your being
> The soothing of warmth thro' the sun
> Thro' love of what sight is seeing;
> When you hold space from the jaws of gardai
> Thro' your feathers the wind will give height
> From your truth may you glide like a Dove
> To bring all life back to the light;
> Together we'll walk to the light;
> Together we'll fly o'er the trees;
> Together we'll run thro' the fields;
> Together;
> When You are free.'

Yes indeed freedom is precious, even to the body. Yet before the body is imprisoned the mind is already encaged. This is the outer expressing the inner with the mind taking on the body. In my own experience my mind had been bound up in pursuit of life-assurance commissions and worldly acclaim that led to my entanglement in the web of the widow. But now I was free. I had descended to hell to cut loose these chains, not just the hell of the prison, but the hell in which I compromised my true essence, and now it was done, this karma was being resolved.

Yes, dear daughter, I am free for together we have walked to the light, and again we will walk through the fields. But are you free dear daughter, free of your attachment to me? It is not just the outer expression of this freedom I speak of, that is always a mask, a cover to what goes beneath, but true freedom, the kind of freedom that can only be realised through the state of formless attention. From this state there is no desire, no wanting, no need to endlessly try to preserve the image of me as your partial father, an item that belongs to you, that is an outer addition of whatever is squatting within. Must I be an item of possession dear daughter? Is this too not the story of the widow, as she endeavoured to possess me through the force of her wealth? Is this how it actually is when we honestly look at our personal relationships? I am that I am and if I am to be imprisoned or executed, can you allow that? Can you break through these chains that are binding you to your hell, as I had been bound to mine? Can you come out of your shell to hear? Can you allow another daughter to enter my life, one perhaps not even yet born? Can you free 'Me' from this prison, dear daughter, in washing the blood from your hands of the innocence you are psychologically slaying? Can you free yourself to be love in fullness to another in patient waiting for your love? Can you fly from this familiar perch out into the unknown with your loving heart to give to him in waiting? Can you allow yourself to know freedom and what it really is to be free?

It is not just you, dear daughter, I address with this fact

for it is the inner scourge in most of us clinging to our own personal items of love. We start with our immediate, our parent, our child, our pet, our lover as we place our need upon the other and in expectancy we live. Then when this bond is eventually loosened or severed we search for another to fill in the vacuum of pain through the loss so we can impose what we assume to be love on another similarly imposing and assuming. Is it not so? Is this not how it continues, this human condition, as blasphemy to love forever dodging the truth while love in itself is open and free? Can it be heard? Can it really be heard through our shells of consuming desires wilfully ignoring 'Me' that is truly our beauty within? My love for you is too great to allow you even for one moment to be deceived by yourself.

When these two wonderful young women, my pillars of light, departed from me I returned to my cell and the message in word from Florence Nightingale, a daughter in spirit, who had come through the locked doors of place and time to be my comfort and reassurance.

Such is the wonder of life, in all its mystery, in all its beauty. We must keep open to receive it, this life, this love, this truth. All of hell itself cannot stand against it, for this is the light of love that is shining through all our hearts. It knows no bounds for it transcends time, it transcends death, this nightingale song always gushing forth, rapturously singing through the darkness as it steps from timeless to timeless yet never leaving the 'Light'.

Chapter 29

WHO ARE THE REAL PRISONERS?

In one moment of silence in the prison cell a young man laying on the lower bunk across from me said,

"God I would hate to die in this dump".

The young man laying in the bunk above, in sharp Dublin wit replied,

"What difference. When you die you die. Okay. So if the grim reaper came right now and said your number was up, so what? You ask for temporary release? Okay. So he grants you temporary release. You get up and walk outside the gates of the jail onto the street. Then bang! You are dead. Inside or outside of this dump, what difference does it make? When you are dead you are dead".

Then the silence returned. Most of the men I shared the space with had a great respect for the silence. There was the odd one or two disturbed by their obsessions but they got little response to idle chatter. Almost everything spoken was meaningful to life and particularly meaningful to the moment.

I was in the remand section of the prison that was at most times overcrowded and the prisoners were continuously being moved through. After the first night I was moved to a four-man cell. There were six of us sharing and, as I was the last one in, for two more nights I slept on the floor. As others moved out I was offered a bunk and the ones moving in had to wait for their turn. Each one respected each other's space.

However small it commanded and received respect. These were good people. They were in pain. They had problems. Some of them had killed. But deep down I found these people to be genuinely good. They accepted their lot as best they could in the difficult situation of their lives.

On one occasion I overheard a conversation between a group in the exercise yard. They were talking about someone who was in for murder and the conversation between them went;

"The last fella' he killed he bleedin' well choked him to death with his bare hands".

"Jasus, if he keeps that up we'll be callin' him the strangler".

"But he's dead sound, ya know wha' I mean".

"Bleedin' right he's dead sound, you could trust him with your life".

Such was the loyalty and comradeship of these genuinely warm people locked away from a society not willing to care, for theirs was the alternative lifestyle to the frozen norm. Indeed for many of these inmates it was the only life they knew and they served it well in the only way known to them.

Here I witnessed great intellect and great willingness going to waste. The righteous in society turn away and are quick with the lip to condemn. In appaling ignorance the righteous do not know that these prisoners, no matter what they have done, are merely the physical expression of the unacceptable side of themselves. As such, these prisoners are honest, amazingly honest, as to what they are and to what they do, whatever it is and however they have to do it. How sad it is that the congested blundering of the system of things in relation to business and commerce cannot give itself time to stop and listen to the problems that these imprisoned people are carrying as the flip side of itself. It is easier to live with the lie of closing the uncaring eye and locking them away. While we continue to put the blame on the other we can never come near to knowing ourselves and all the piety and personal sacrifices in the entire world will not save us from hell. For we are already there. This is a fact. This is the stark naked truth. As long as we serve places for blame and for punishment of the 'other' we are all hellbound, politicians, vicars and priests, housekeepers and all, the lot, as blind leading the blind. Yes, we are hellbound in the shackles of our appaling ignorance and willfulness as we look the other way and cower from this truth. It only takes one to stop serving it and to break free, to give light to the eyes of the few ready and waiting to see.

Some people living on the streets came to Mountjoy to rest. Their free ticket is given once they create a disturbance. Others are here because of their livelihoods, such as dealing in drugs or fishing for salmon. The drug situation is a great sadness to humanity and most of the young men on remand are addicts themselves. Yet there is still great talent within them. These could be the real leaders where it really counts, on the streets of existence. They know the problem for they are the problem and the solution to any problem is always within it. Instead of punishing them they should be exonerated from their terrible experience and encouraged to seek the remedy, for their knowledge is vast and more true to the situation than most.

We should not forget that drug addiction is but another side of ourselves. Yet we cling to the lie as we polish our shoes for attendance at church and beat up our spouses of self-reflection behind closet doors. Someone must pay, as society dictates. Should it be just the street pusher? Perhaps we should be giving more to rehabilitation?

And what about the salmon fishermen? Let us look at their crime. It was about eleven in the morning when two of them from County Donegal were put into our cell. Apparently they had been using illegal nets to harvest the salmon outside of season and were sentenced to one week in prison or a fine of five hundred pounds. It would take a lot more than a week in their business apparently to earn that money so the week in prison was the obvious choice. They had been transported from a courthouse in Donegal by special police van that morning and arriving in our cell was the grand conclusion of their five hour journey. They still carried the freshness of the open Atlantic Ocean on their countenance and the dancing of the waves was in their voices as they spoke.

As I sat listening to their story it was as a play happening before me. Their friends had been caught last year, they told us, and had opted for the week in Mountjoy as well. As things turned out there was no room in the prison for their friends and, after being detained for less than an hour, they were given free passage on the express bus back to Donegal. When the bus pulled into a west midlands hotel for its mid-journey half-hour stop they were given a free lunch which was included in the ticket. Then, when they were just about to leave the two policemen who had transported them across Ireland to Mountjoy prison that morning pulled in to the same hotel with their van and their escort on their way back home. The fishermen were back in Donegal before them.

The two fishermen telling us this story also expected to be out in an hour. They have to use the illegal nets, they told us, as fishermen from other countries with massive equipment were cleaning out the fishing grounds without giving anything back. They are obliged to go for the salmon in the forbidden season that lasts for about six weeks in order to pay the mortgages on their boats, before they could buy food for their families and tobacco for themselves. This was their story among other tales of happenings and storms at sea. True to their expectations, they were gone within the hour.

The afternoon sun edged its light through the bars as silence returned to the cell. I can only imagine their adventures and their ongoing stories of glee as they travelled back to their beautiful county of mountains of peat and of sea. The others and I sit quietly, 'doing time', after savouring their richness of heart.

Chapter 30

YOUR BODY IS YOUR SPACESUIT

One week is as one moment, as is one year, as is one lifetime. Know this, and the fear of death cannot bind you. We enter, we exit, as in the same moment. Strange as it may seem yet that's how it is. We lose contact with this knowing as we slip into our minds, the fallen angels in time, spellbound.

The reality we perceive is actually the dream. We have moved out of our true self into matter. It is thick, it is dense, it is turgid. We bang and clatter off one another, bewitched and bewildered until our last breath, only to know then, it is as our first. We rationalise away from the truth as we divide, subdivide and split the atom. And we think we are coming to knowing the Big Bang. Are we not foolishly naive in all our assumptions and opinions relative to our conditioning that we poke at each other? It is like poking the fire with a wooden stick. Are not all our opinions burnt out in time? In one's own experience it can be observed that unyielding convictions inevitably dissolve through the fire of awareness. My cluster of opinions and rigid beliefs, whatever they are, is my present state of ignorance awaiting to dissolve in this fire. This is as inevitable as the wooden poker being left in the flame and disappearing through the ashes. Yet we seem to continue ignoring this certitude by replacing our old opinions and beliefs with the new, for burning again, nonetheless. In such blindness all conflict occurs.

In the long periods of silence I experienced the prison

cell as the shell immediately outside the prison of this body. In the body I am stuck in time. In the cell I am stuck in a specific space and doing time. Both are limited but only in relation to my attachment to either. Does spending a lifetime in just one spot truly make a difference? I must ask the sycamore tree. It is now over forty years since I planted it at the side of the garden, not even a moment ago, it seems.

Some times as I sat silently in the cell it was as if I was still there in the garden of my childhood. In those early years there were moments when I would pull out the weeds and enter a silent place beyond my childhood imagery, somewhere between the physical task at hand and the dreaming. It was that pause I was connecting with now in my prison cell. That is the moment between stillness and movement when there is neither thought nor imaginings, like the space between the stars in a pitch black night sky. It is always present, never changing, directly behind this sensory world. This is the door to the eternal where we enter and exit time. But we get lost in our attachment to our bodies, these spacesuits of matter, as we work on remedies to preserve them as long as we possibly can. Matter is then all that matters in my forgetfulness of the omniscience and omnipresence of 'Life' that I am.

To see the body as a spacesuit is not to deny the truth of its existence. The body is intimately connected with the mind and it is only through the body at each moment that one is conscious of life. The level of consciousness in each body is according to its lights. When the light in the body is that of cosmic consciousness then it is seen that the body is as a spacesuit in time. This can only be fully understood in the experiencing of it in your body where 'being life' actually is each moment of 'now'. This is the state of 'Being', the formless state, beyond the limitations of matter and mind. It is the state where there is no attachment.

We believe that we are bodies having consciousness. This is but a partial truth. 'I' am consciousness having a body. The body is only a movement in the vast ocean of consciousness of all that 'I' am. The observer to this is more than the 'I', beyond the vastness of consciousness. Bodily existence is merely a state of mind. The body itself comes into form out of the matrix of consciousness that is the earth, to which it dissolves back into again when its term is done. The ocean of consciousness that 'I' am is infinite and eternal while the body is but a momentary occurrence in time. Stillness is the way to this realisation when the body and mind become fully aligned and the participant observer melts into the one eternal witness within. This is pure awareness. But you must not believe it. Seek the source of consciousness to discover this for yourself.

I could now appreciate the torment of the widow burning out my worldly trail as a blessing. It gave me no place of temporary rest and it obliged me to shed my attachments. Everything is let go as I sit in this cell. I can no longer be a slave to matter with its endless demand of wants, a bottomless pit destined to graveyard before it even begins. Nothing with beginning and ending has permanence. Facing the circumstances of one's life in this moment is actually facing 'Truth' for one's immediate circumstances are the exact reflection of the level of consciousness within.

'Truth' can only be known in my immediate situation, this I have come to realise through my experience. 'Truth' and God are one and the same. This is expressed to me through 'Me' in my particular circumstances. In the quietness of the cell I could see that the widow in her anger, her confusion, and her misplaced love, as such I was receiving, was my God immediate in my awakening to the truth of myself. Strange as it is 'Truth' entered my consciousness through the form of 'woman'. Before awakening to the light of It's presence I had been locked in the subtle bind of a conditioned, patriarchal mind. God was an imagined figure outside of myself. In my experience the Goddess is the release from this bind that had to occur before the equilibrium could be recovered. The equilibrium is the point of 'aloneness', the eye of the needle, the balance to be reached before the notional duality can be dissolved.

This is the oneness I speak of where the torment of the widow and the grace of the spiritual master are one and the same to I the recipient. This is seen when my state is in equilibrium. It is through this realisation that one enters the state of 'Love', the state of 'Being'. In the state of 'Being' all conditioning dissolves. I remind you not to believe me, for 'Truth' can only be known from the place of absolute stillness within you, where 'Life' actually is.

We, the masses, have placed truth outside of ourselves through our moral principles relative to our changing societal needs. The truth we adhere to may be true for now, relative to our beliefs, but its shifting nature cannot be the perennial 'Truth'. We need to explore deeper than this to discover the changeless. 'Life', as I experience it, is the life I am in this body. To me this is a fundamental truth. In your experience the only place 'Life' truly is, in the 'being' of life, is in your own body. All life perceived outside of your body are forms of life, but are never 'Life' in the 'being' of life as you are within. In existence, in human consciousness, there is man and woman. The masses are the reflection of the human condition. I, as part of the masses, am the conditional self abdicating the seat of 'Life' to the external. In my own experience I became lost to 'Life' as I chased the illusions of transitory happiness in my external, conditional world. This is the world of duality, of happiness and sadness, good and bad, life and death, one endlessly cancelling the other. The first duality I perceive in existence is of me and you the rest of the world. The duality I am aware of as man, in the 'being' of life in my human form, is that of man and woman.

How did this duality occur? Let us observe the male principle that has been the dominant factor in this world of our own creation since time as we know it began. Then let us observe the female principle throughout this history of time. We need to come to a clearer place in which we can truly see the ridiculous nature of our conditioned minds and the limitations we place on ourselves. Let us see through awareness each gesture we make, each word we speak, each thought that arises from whence it all comes. Let us take courage to step through the thresholds of ignorance being guarded through our fears of what seems unknown.

Let us cry freedom from rigid beliefs and come to be empty within. From here let us look at the divine principle that is immediately behind the principles manifesting through form as male and female body. We need to perceive the inner suffering that is deeply rooted in the psyche of everyone born from the moment as an infant one enters this world. We need to examine the nature of this suffering so we may come to see beyond the strife that is present in all of us living the lie of the superficial reality to ourselves.

Let us discard our limited interpretation through the discursive, worldly, intellectual mind and allow clear intellect to function. Let us look from the place of emptiness within so we may re-discover the fathomless depths of 'I', the state of permanent bliss that is immediate to all once the blind that is mind is released.

In my experience entry into this realm is immediate, regardless of the circumstances of one's life or the foolishness of our philosophical reasoning as we try to convince ourselves that a long and laborious process of

preparation must be required. Relatively speaking this may
appear to be true for those of us attached to a relative world,
but it is not the absolute reality. Let us not be so deluded,
for 'It' is immediate. "Come unto 'Me' and I will give thee
rest". These are the words that were spoken. This coming
unto 'Me', that is 'I', can only occur in this moment of 'now',
right now, for this in my experience is the only moment of
existence. It is the only place where 'Life' actually is, where
'I' always am, infinitely shining through all sensory matter
perceived. The closer I am to the inner sanctum of 'Me' the
clearer the vision will be that all as perceived through the
sensory body and intercepted through the limitation of
conditional mind from this space is not even the shadow of
truth.

My own exploration has suggested much to me about
the male and female principle and the ultimate source of
conflict in the mind. Before 'I' enter this body, 'I' rise from
the depths of 'Me', that is neither male nor female. 'I' enter
the state of 'being' in the consciousness reflected through
matter that is then perceived through the senses. Thus
arises the sensory world. The human psyche is the vibration
of this matter perceived. Unfortunately it is like a musical
instrument that is out of tune and this is affecting the entire
orchestral piece. In other words the human psyche, that has
malfunctioned in time as perceived outside of itself, is
affecting the entire creation.

This malfunction occurred when the equilibrium
between the male and female principles was lost. This loss
of equilibrium is expressed in the subjugation of the female
principle, the custodian of love that permeates life on earth.
The essence of woman is the essence of love. In my
experience the male principle is the guardian of love, as is
the essence of man. When the male and female principles
are in absolute harmony they re-enter the one divine

principle. All three principles are manifest in every form of life in the creation. This is how it is at the beginning of time and this is the inner struggle of humanity to re-enter this state where the three principles manifest as the one and the creation has its beginning and ending. In my understanding this beginning and ending is the infinitesimal moment of 'now'.

The devastating subjugation of the female principle has come about through wilful force. It has been instilled in the human psyche by fear as expressed in a world made by man in the likeness of man. This is subjugating all natural life. It is vividly expressed in the history of the human condition that seems to confine reason between the narrow parameters of the patriarchal mind. This is the male projection of fear deeply embedded in the human psyche of all of us born, both man and woman, to be its bearer. What is it we fear? Simply the power of 'Love' that is the female principle on earth.

We have become lost to the belief that the physical form is the reality and so love on earth has become known as the force of sexual craving that is of the sensory body. This fear has led us to lose sight of our true nature. It has found its expression through the false beliefs of ourselves and spills into the matter perceived through the objectivism of the divine principle, that is truly our essence in being.

Fear is the root cause of all conflict in this world of male projection. Those of us dedicated to the creation of a world of peace, no matter how we may appear to succeed, will find all our efforts no more than temporary appeasement from this demon within. This will continue as long as we objectify love through our religious convictions and create a particular god, in accordance to our conflicting beliefs, that is seen as other than the 'Me' that you and I am.

We have created a duality through sexism having

extended ourselves out through the male principle into our current condition. Thus has arisen this world of man with its man-made beliefs and its man-made gods. This is the world that each of us is born to serve as the ongoing illusion outside of ourselves. Having subjugated the female principle of the creation we are out of balance, in a manner of speaking. In order to enter a clearer understanding of this, the balance must be restored. This is the equilibrium that I speak of being served. The Goddess is the female principle within the creation. The essence of 'She' must be fully embraced as it rises within us and this incurs a total dissolution of the male patriarchal side of ourselves, a total dissolution of all that is past that can only occur through balancing the other side of itself. It is so that the equilibrium is served as the psyche is returned to the centre where it instantly dissolves back into the nothingness. This is the ending of the world of duality.

The psychological revolution is about to explode on all humankind for the illumination is upon us whether we accept it or not. Let us break through these barriers of mind that have created a world of time in which the demon of fear resides in the illusory shadow of 'I', harbouring within the subtle confines of lust, anger, greed, in the vibration through the human psyche of past re-birthing itself. Let there be love, for 'Love' is the currency of the infinite good. Let us not forget that money is the currency of the temporal world and one cannot serve two masters no matter how eloquently we mentally reason through the rationality of mind. This is not to deny the necessities of life, for everything has its place in space and time that is but a passing occurrence. Am I not here to be the joy of life, as 'I' always am, beyond the narrow confines of this temporary spacesuit? But I must return to stillness within, with no thought arising, before this wonder of wonders can truly be known.

In the stillness within I realise that all mental concepts about a God and a Goddess are part of my conditioning. Yet everything has its place in the creation. My notional fatherly God was blasted by the notional 'She'. And who is 'She'? In my own experience from my early childhood she was first the Virgin Mary to whom I prayed in my raw innocence to make my body pure and my soul holy. As I reached adolescence 'She' was in every young woman I was eager to love. When I challenged Christian beliefs my mother made me aware that my body is the real tabernacle of God, as was the beautiful body of the girl I was passionately in love with at that time. This formed part of my conditioning where I came to see 'She' as the inner Goddess of love, of life, of truth, in the heart of every woman incarnate. Woman, when I look into your eyes I am looking at 'She', the Goddess that you truly are, within you. 'She' is the essence of love that is now permeating the consciousness of all humankind as it comes to the end of its patriarchal expression.

'She' serves 'Me' well. It is 'She' who has set me ablaze once the spark was ignited through Mary? Is it not the essence of 'She' through the widow's fury that has brought me to heel. I must be eternally grateful to the beautiful widow for together we have danced the dance of minds. How right it all is that she, the warrior of love's fury, should be my slayer. How great and precious the psychological death I encountered at the end of her sword. Now I know through my own experience that death has to occur before I can enter life. Thank you woman for setting me free. Yes, 'She' is my 'saviour' from myself, my slayer and my liberator, for I am 'man'.

Is it not so with each and everyone that 'Truth' is

immediate to you in the circumstances of your particular situation, whether it be a cesspit or a rosegarden? Or must we continue to lose ourselves in this false morality of division as we serve our self-made God that is not big enough or great enough to encompass all, thus creating the need for a heaven and a hell? Yet it is true, is it not, that we create this hell through our minds. Once created we proceed to live in it while harkening for the heaven conveniently postponed. We wantonly tumble from one sensory lust to the next in the shell of our spacesuits as we stumble over the other shells of ourselves on this shifting face of time. Is it these bodies, these spacesuits, that we actually expect to resurrect on a particular last day of judgement? Are we thus foolishly clinging to ourselves, or am I too still fast asleep and dreaming this madness? But no, I have awakened from this dream and am no longer bound by its chains.

In Mountjoy prison I have already met three who have momentarily tasted the truth. Even according to the parable, did not the one lost sheep found bring more joy than the ninty-nine safely at home. These men about me were much more than lost sheep. They may have sinned against society as I am accused of having done, some may even be a danger to their fellowman, yet there is a quality of wakefulness in many of them that seems to be absent in so many outside. We seem to be too busy serving our illusions and chasing our dreams in this raving cosmic convulsion called time rather than pausing for a moment to question. Is it a wonder that we seem to keep missing the truth?

The body calls for its fix. A shot in the arm that provides an immediate heaven quickly devoured, or fortification through abstinence now in the hope of devouring a whole heaven in a later existence. Is there really a difference? At least the one who takes the shot in the arm may have another day to realise his folly and his sorrowful state is immediate to see. The other expounds his theories and rattles the brains of his offsprings for generations to come, as we seem to be suffering for thousands of years. Why can we not see what we are serving? Or are we like sheep stampeding in mass and in terror of the sound of our own stampeding? It is all in one moment of time. We listen to the ten o'clock news describing a variety of happenings in a variety of places, yet it is always a similar story delivered in the high-pitched whining newscaster's voice. At least in the prison cell we were spared from listening to that, there was no viewing time and no opportunity for the ongoing pounding of the media to expand on the infection of our minds. There is time for reflection inside, having been given that freedom.

One day, one week, one year, is it not but one moment? Even all our yesterdays at this moment are now. The future that we spend all of our lives chasing, is there not a greater reality in the leprechaun's crock of gold at the end of the rainbow? Are we so tangled with the burden of the past and our life's effort to transport the past into the future, after chopping it and changing it to suit our attachments that we really have no time for the present, the actual moment right now, that is the only point of existence where 'Life' actually is?

But I must not let it bother me if I am not yet ready to wake up. If I cannot grasp it right now it is bound to hit me like a ton of bricks when I am drawing my last breath, at that moment of suddenly knowing I have missed it again. Yet I go on chasing the mirage of illusions. In commerce I call it expansion, in politics I call it democratic alignment, in economics I call it growth. In the world of insurance once I have delivered the injection of fear to the client I call it assurance and I immediately offer the cure. I have policies on heart failure, kidney failure, eye failure, loss of a limb and a myriad more to offer according to the depth of penetration that I the salesperson succeed in digging into my client with the shovel of dread. I am thus forever going outward into the mirage that has become the reality in my diminished vision. The further out I go the greater my hunger becomes. It feeds off the oceans of greed. The greater the protection I offer the greater the protection I need from the truth of myself, lest this bubble of illusion be burst.

When I was suddenly stopped in my tracks by the Australian master and I took my first ever pause, I was immediately flooded by the storms of fear. This man had challenged me to face into myself. But I had become the shooting star of the life-assurance industry. The forces of greed and fear had been my cascade. I had been unable to see this in the darkness of the macro expression in which I had blindly enslaved myself before I stepped into the light of the guru. Even meeting the guru was a chance encounter as I had no preconceived ideas about spiritual masters prior to my first meeting with Mary. Then I lied to myself that my heart was not yet fully open to receive. Yes I know, I thought, but I must first get this job at hand completed. Then tomorrow I will change. So it continued, one day, one year, one lifetime, while the only remedy is right now, in this very moment at hand.

Is there ever any other time this body is breathing, outside of 'now'? Yet I fail to look at this question preferring to continue in this mirage of relativity in seeking the remedy for shadows with shadows. I morally measure the causes of suffering as the 'wrong' and the mitigation of suffering as the 'right' yet such relative judgement serves only the illusion and maintains the ignorance. This is the human condition. Suffering and relief from suffering are only 'right' or 'good' when they dispel our ignorance of our true nature. Once dispelled, 'suffering' and 'right' no longer exist.

As I sat in silence in the prison cell in this world of relativity, while some fell into deep sleep, I witnessed the light flashing truth in some of those who remained awake. One in particular spoke briefly of the woman in his life describing the beauty of making love as they melted into each other as one. His words were of such warmth and such knowing and were of the absolute heart. The week I was spending in prison, although traumatically imposed, gradually flowered into a time of stillness and peace. Those who had needed drugs in their bodies to momentarily come to this place within now found stillness and freedom in silence.

Few words are spoken when the harmonious rhythm of life is allowed to flow freely. This can only be explained by what it is not. One has to enter it to know it and oddly as it may seem, the overcrowded prison cell provided such opportunity. Each man looked into himself and there was no pressing world distracting his view. One lifetime, one week, one moment, as one it is done. How long more must I cling to this spacesuit of time in my illusory world?

When the woman with the peculiar stare had destroyed the mystical forest, Charlie found himself slipping into a time where his growing attachment to his spacesuit, now entering adolescence, was taking over his freedom within. This is his entry to the forest of living, a place in which he may become lost for the rest of his life. Or perhaps his attention may be suddenly drawn to an early morning awakening in some other land in some other place and this may rescue him from himself.

Yes, how wastefully I serve my fleeting attachments

when I lose contact with 'Me' within. How wasteful I am when I lose contact with immortality as I painfully polish this fading spacesuit of time, lost to the wants of myself. Awakening from this mirage of the mind I realise that 'I' am the divine principal, beyond space and time, manifesting in this body.

To actualise this I must first divine myself. I know I am here to be the joy of life. But pleasure has become my foray. In all my efforts to find pleasure I discovered that I became subject to the whim of circumstances. Even when the fruit of my actions delivered the pleasurable I found such pleasure to be temporary. What is here today is gone tomorrow. It fades of its own accord when the seeking is spent or it is taken from me. This is the world I have served in my efforts to serve the wants of myself. I am sure it sounds familiar.

In my experience this is how it was until I was challenged by a spiritual master to divine myself. Then I discovered the primary pleasure is where 'I' always am. This is the perennial peace within. Nothing can take this from me. This is adulthood, being ready to embrace the pleasure of 'being' the primary pleasure of life. My youthful years had been an outward thrust chasing the secondary pleasures rising before me. All such pleasures are relative to my state of adolescence and serve only the illusion. Nonetheless, youth calls for action through the pleasures of 'doing' and it is so I gain through experience to eventually realise the primary pleasure of 'being' that I am.

This is how living my life unfolded for me. My experiences eventually brought about my state of adulthood, the state in 'being' the primary pleasure of life while secondary pleasures can freely come and go without I seeking or becoming attached to them. In this state I see the body exactly as it is where I am right now in space and time.

This is my spacesuit that I acknowledge and treat with the utmost respect. This is where 'I' am life eternal. I can 'know' what is not, what is I can only 'be'.

> *As fire is enveloped by smoke,*
> *As a mirror by dust,*
> *As an embryo by the womb,*
> *So is this covered by that.*

Bhagavad Gita III 38

Chapter 31

THE INVADER MASQUERADING AS LOVE

What is love? When someone says 'I love you', who is this 'I'? In my own experience of what is expressed I usually find this 'I' is a psychic demon. Does it love me? Or does it want to possess me to feed the empty gut of its own insatiable hunger? It feels that it loves me as long as it can get the attention it emotionally craves. Its main concern is to plant and develop a similarly recognisable emotion in me for it. It seeks to create a mirror to see its own face, for that is about all it is usually willing to acknowledge. Am I making this up? Is it true when you check it out in your own experience? All one needs to do is to listen from that place of silent listening when the words 'I love you' are spoken. But it takes enormous courage to actually face up to the truth. In facing the truth that is the end of the lie.

The impostor to truth has created religions and ceremonies around itself in justification of its presence as it stares out through the eyes of the misfortunates possessed. Do I see it when I look in the mirror? In this image of image do I connect with who or what is doing the looking? Am I aware of it as I speak to the one I love? Does it not live off relationships through mental disturbance, even served by psychiatrists, this vortex of ignorance self-perpetuating itself through the changing expressions of worldly communication? How do we challenge it? It has hijacked love and blasphemed it in the emotion of its wretched self..

Love is not a feeling nor a servant of feelings. Neither is it a sensation as what usually occurs between new lovers meeting. Both the feelings and sensations interpreted as love are the monster's domain. You know how it is. The magic is sparked through the sensations and then the feelings arise. You can feel the hunger of it within as you set out to embrace the object that sparked the sensation. You are madly in love. Another bedding, another wedding, another cooling off then another arising from the insatiable gut towards another object of fodder. I am not being pessimistic. This is merely an illustration of the skeleton behind the actions which we pursue in the name of love, a skeleton that most of our habitual behaviour supports. If I should really listen to my lover and listen to myself as a detached observer, it will surely dawn on me once I am totally honest about what is to be seen. Is it really my pain I am serving, my fear of losing what I have or not getting what I want? Is this how it is when I say I love you? Am I really serving this? Only I can honestly tell.

What are the media, the newsreels, the advertisements, the agony columns serving? Is it not all a pumping of feelings and sensations in feeding the insatiable gut? This is the hysteria that has gripped the world. Its strangle-hold is a suffocation to the essence of love. We hunger for gossip. And we feel we are doing it in the name of love! No, this is not love, and here we are merely touching the skin of the monster. But at least when I start being true to myself I can see it is not this. In my own particular experience, the widow has placed herself in front of me and has clearly shown me what love is not. She is my teacher, as is the enlightened master in this story of expression. Everything and everyone are my teachers when I allow my ears and my eyes to open. Yes, this woman has been pounding me continuously until I have no baggage left, apart from this body this spacesuit. And it is only a matter of time before this too must be discarded. Where am I then? Where is this putrid monster within as I leave this spacesuit behind? Is this what is carried to another body? Is this what is reincarnated? Is this for the cleansing house called purgatory? Or is this the perpetual hell, this ignorance, this madness, this human condition? Can I hear it answer? Or must I again turn away for it may be too close to the truth.

In my own experience once I stopped serving this monster the freedom was immediately there. But I had to face into the wall of fear as the demon in all of its might set out to destroy me, as this self of myself must be destroyed before the truth can be known. This is not a ground for feeble decision. Once I embark on the truth then I must be prepared to die, to die to everything, absolutely everything, especially to myself. Then all the challenges will immediately appear. They are all of my own creation and consist of the chains I have placed on myself in my service to the monster within. Then the burning is sure to commence. It can take a moment, an hour, a year, but it will continue until all of those chains of bondage are dissolved. For me it took three years, and the burning continues. Yet all through that time of incredible burning the freedom was there and there is nothing more sweet in all of the creation than that. This is the seat of love, as I truly discovered, as it became known. I thank Mary for being the bearer of the arrow through pure sensation that pierced open this heart.

Once I was truly ready to receive truth and love came from many directions. The light from the East, the enlightening man from Australia, Catherine with her angelic friends from the west coast of America and the widow in all of her fury from the west coast of Ireland as my mirror showing me what it is not. It came in abundance as I passed through the death of myself to the heart that is open to receive.

When woman and man truly come together in love, is it not 'Love' that is served? In this brilliant light, all the cloaks of piety that are worn by the other to disguise its wilful intent may fool the foolish but it cannot fool the heart of the enlightened. Willfulness is the monster, is it not so? When I usually look at love is it not through my own particular pain I am looking? My lover does not satisfy me in my own personal craving for satisfaction, or maybe my lover does everything humanly possible to please me and soon I get bored with that. Is this how it is? Are we not trying with more trying to cover this horrible craving within? Is this what we hear when we partake in the usual conversations?

"What shall we do this evening my love?"

"I think you would like to go to a movie my dear".

"No, no. I think you would like to go ice-skating my love".

"No, we will go to a movie my dear, for I know you would prefer to go to a movie".

"It is a nice evening for ice-skating my love, and you have not been for some time".

"But you are not happy with ice-skating my dear, I could tell by your face the last time we went".

Is this how it is? And we sometimes ask a psychiatrist to untangle this web of the willfulness that uses the other side of its mask. How difficult it is to be true to the situation when we are serving the monster within. Behind all the farcical play of living, behind the appeasement of this demon there is the stillness, the absolute stillness of divine will silently observing. In this stillness the entire creation is endlessly served. This is love. My first awareness of this in the body is when I am pushed from the womb and receive the air that is freely given to these infant lungs. This first giving to this body at birth, is it not the first taste of love freely flowing back into this spacesuit of time? As I mature in years and gradually lose contact with the immediate through the personal willfulness that is this demon, this human condition easing itself into my being, I then try to impose it on others. This is the 'psychological me' in its selfish assertion and the only love it can perceive is the wretched shadow of itself. Have you noticed how birds of a feather tend to flock together? Is this not how it is on this outer skin of sensual craving in the willfulness of all that I think? But only I can answer this truthfully to myself.

No one can give a true definition of love, for love cannot be defined. One can only 'be' love. But when we are open to hear then we can surely understand what it is not. We can refuse to foster this psychological invader masquerading as love. Here and now we can choose this freedom.

I am man. My immediate love is woman before me. Woman's immediate love is man. In my experience this is how the creation is. But I externalised my own self-importance and super-imposed my man-made world upon the wonder of nature as it is, the cost being my love. Woman suffers. Yet through all her suffering she still loves man. The all-prevailing power of love that is the female principle of the creation knows no bounds. To see the truth of myself as man of the world I must allow my awareness to shine on every facet of this patriarchal mind that stands between 'Me' and the love that I am. The love that I am is the primary pleasure of life. Having externalised love through my senses I abdicated my seat of guardianship by placing the image of woman, my love, as an object of secondary pleasure to be ravished and plundered. This is the plundering that causes suffering in woman. In her heart every woman wishes man to know and acknowledge her in love as 'Love'. She is the custodian of 'Love', the womb of all life in the creation. The sexual expression of love is a returning back in through the senses into being as one in the making of love. This is the melting into the oneness that the prisoner spoke of when his heart re-connected with the stillness as the sun cast its evening shadows through the stillness of the cell we shared. This is man allowing the male principle to be permeated with the female principle thus re-discovering his 'divinity'. Let there be 'Love' and see for yourself.

So when I say I love you, am I serving the wilful or am I the will? Only I can truthfully tell. What is love? Love is. When I truly love, there is no I, there is only love. But do not believe me. Beliefs serve the conditioned. 'Truth' is the servant of 'Love'.

> *No wonder 'It' remains unseen,*
> *Through haste in running wild*
> *Away from Love, away from Truth,*
> *Away from Being, our very root,*
> *While chasing shadow-self defiled.*
> *And Love that's pure, by self is soiled*
> *For fleeting pleasures flesh and mind*
> *With clinging soul in hell confined*
> *And nought but pain at end we find.*

Chapter 32

FROM DARKNESS TO LIGHT

A week in prison is an eternity. I was being held on remand until the police could find sufficient evidence to make a case against me. They had my files, my address books, a list of my clients and the statements of allegations from the widow. She had used the solicitors, the civil courts and now she was using the law of the land.

On the evening of my sixth day in confinement I was moved up from Base to a two-man cell in an older section of the prison. It was in a filthy state with rubbish piled high behind the door and mice almost as big as my hand living in empty milk cartons. I sat awake for most of the night staying with the calm as best I could. I had read Florence Nightingale's extract so many times to hold my sanity, I now almost knew it by heart. My next court appearance was to be in the morning. My father had met the conditions of bail but there still may be further objections. For my part all I could do was to sit in silence and wait.

The morning arrived and I was taken back out through the system where I was told to hand in all my prison clothing. Then, minus the shower, I was taken to the next room where my own clothes awaited me. It was strange getting back into a suit with a shirt and tie and the widow's cuff-links. I was ushered back into the holding cell with the others who were about to attend court that morning. We had also been given our personal belongings and these included my mobile phone. I felt rather unusual sitting there behind locked doors with that phone in my pocket.

Eventually we were taken out to the front yard and loaded into a mobile prison truck. We were locked into separate cubicles and then driven through the streets of Dublin to the cells beneath the courthouse. As the truck rounded a sharp bend I was thrown against the door and it flew open dropping me into the centre isle. The guard was not too perturbed as he helped me back in and locked it again. When we reached the closed yard behind the courts we were taken down to the cells in which I had first been held a week previously on that traumatic opening to the entire ordeal. Here the waiting continued. It was a tense situation. Some walked like caged lions around the inner parameters of the cell. Why should I be different? I got up and joined them. I walked seven steps over then about turn and seven steps back. So I continued for a couple of miles within a space of less than twenty feet. I could feel the tension that I had actually been unaware of beginning to leave the body.

Eventually my name was called and I was taken up some stairs to the crowded courtroom. I could see my father and daughters waiting. My case was called and my father took the stand to offer the security required for bail. His integrity and directness brought the members of the court to attentive stillness, particularly the judge, who acknowledged and commented in word that the symbolic presence of this man was not only refreshing to his soul but an inspiration to all. This seventy ninth year of life was the first occasion my father had ever been inside a courtroom. On this day he came to bail his son out from prison. That was to be the first severing from the web of the wilful widow. My father embraced me and his silent agony of a week was released. For me it was the moment of coming back to a life that I had never experienced before yet deep within nothing had changed. It is as it is. We are born, we live, and we die. Each moment of this life is part of our own creation and everything must be faced and acknowledged whether pleasing or painful, to allow this transcendence to freedom to occur. Life is not the pain that we spend most of our lives trying to avoid and, in so doing, become imprisoned by fear? In my experience this is how the world of willfulness is created. Let us look at it openly.

I start out by creating a worldly image of myself. I become a successful business man, according to its standards, yet I enter the web of its deceit. I give my life's blood supporting this image and I worry like hell when it is about to be challenged. Is not the integrity of the legal system wasted in its service to it? Even the legal firms become dependent upon it as lawsuit and counter-lawsuit feed them financially. All the time we are running away from the truth as we seem perpetually bound in our illusions. When someone arrives on the scene to awaken us, like Socrates or Jesus, what do we do? We administer them poison or we crucify them. Is it not bizarre? And then we build our churches and our statues in their image and we worship that in the name of truth? Who are we fooling?

This world is moving into a new age of consciousness. These are wonderful times. The bonds of our ignorance are being released and the doors to our dark vaults within where personal secrets abide are being blown off their hinges. The ugly and distorted nakedness is exposed. Are you going to be caught sleeping still trying to hide yours, as you desperately defend your dark room within that has now got no doors or walls? To you still refusing through blind fear to awaken, you may soon be outnumbered. How about that? This fresh wave of consciousness is touching all and particularly your own light within. The more we refuse to acknowledge this truth the more psychologically distorted we become. We will continue to need the psychiatrist, the faithhealer, the priest to manage our priestly conscience and the numerous others to cotton-up our wounded egos in our struggle to uphold our own self-abuse. Is this how it truly is? Or am I making it up?

We seem to have trapped ourselves in the dream of this human condition and its tale of woe as we hide from the fear of our shadows. We believe it to be the true reality even though we may hear the message of truth. We are still too involved in the illusion and our efforts to bring it to a pleasing conclusion, rather than paying real attention as to what is being heard. This is the madness. The guru, being the immediate circumstances of my life, demands me to wake up and to stop the crazy struggling for conclusions. Nothing concludes. It may change in shape or form but it does not conclude. Yet I have to see my dream as a dream before I can wake up to realise the falsehood and immense sorrow of the human state in which I have imprisoned myself.

In the dream I took love to be particular, even to the foolishness of expectation. On waking up I find that 'I' am love itself. It took all that I had experienced to awaken me from the illusion, 'becoming' a champion in life-assurance, 'becoming' the victim of the widow's obsession, 'becoming' so carried away with the rising tide of the financial illusion and then meeting a man of master consciousness who challenged me to the point of slaying him. But in truth I was slaying myself for all that I had 'become' I was seeing in him, he being the mirror of all that I was. I had personally sought to 'become' many things only to realise that we 'become' nothing, only illusions. When I sought to listen, when I was still, when I did not seek to 'become', then I saw truth.

As I walked from the Court of Justice that morning, accompanied by my father and daughters, and as we crossed the bridge over the river Liffey to the other side where the car awaited to take us home to Clare, to the birdsong, the early morning mists, the majesty of the trees, and all that is heaven to behold, I gratefully acknowledged the re-awakening brought about to all of us immediately involved. How privileged I am receiving this suffering that brought me to the light of awareness. This is right suffering, it is the passion of 'Love'.

Could I have possibly asked to be spared from any of it? If so, then what a terrible price may have been paid in the missing of this realisation.

Chapter 33

THE ANGELIC REALM

Now seven weeks of waiting were spent in silent reflection before the third court appearance. Those seven weeks were spent giving birth to this story for relay to you.

When the appointed day once more arrived there was a great calm in the family. We rose before six in the morning to set out on the journey across Ireland to Dublin. It was a beautiful September of Indian summer, with the early morning dew sparkling on the grass and the rising sun edging over the hills of deepest blue silhouetted the horizon. The white mists on the lowlands were visible through the trees now giving sanctuary to the birds in full chorus of welcome. This was their moment of blessing the magic, the great natural harmony in the timeless rhythm of life.

All of this fair land breathes in and breathes out and the great universal antibodies extract the poison of man's ignorance. The time has arrived for the truth. Men's world and women's dressed up within as men's, is now coming to its end. Man is rare in this world of millions of men and women who are ninety per cent men. We have the mediocre, a world of consumers chewing their way into the core of the great mother earth. The magnificent life in the trees is being slowly extinguished to feed the insatiable hunger of this plague, this curse on mankind. Yes, man is rare. But man is here, in the 'I', the universal 'I'. "I am the way, the life and the truth". Are these not the words that were spoken by the noble man to the multitudes? The truth is in 'I' but never in the multitudes. The multitudes are the illusion. And 'She' is here, for 'I', the universal 'I' in her heart is calling her up.

How awesome it is this time we are now experiencing. And 'She' is not coming from the East, as one might expect. 'She' is here, having come out through the West, from the farthest reaches of the plundering masculine expression that has dominated and ravished the natural harmony of earth for thousands of years. Is it now over? Is its day now done as the waters of 'She' are rising to purge the wizard of darkness out of existence together with all his dark queens? Is not the head of this serpent, obese from the fruit, about to be crushed by 'Her' heel? Is this not the 'Holy Grail', this illuminous light, as the sun re-appearing from behind the dark cloud of two thousand year's reign?

Those women who have become as the men in this final convulsion of the human condition to date, are they not the sacrificial lambs on behalf of all womankind? This is not an issue between men and women I speak of, but the patriarchal implant in all of us that has been placed through the use of brute force. This force is contrary to love. Love in harmony with the love of the creation expresses itself as giving and not in taking. Force takes, however subtle, and this is experienced by woman now hardened within through aggression. This aggression, that is part of the human condition, denies to us our true nature.

It has come to this in our western world, all of it necessary perhaps for each has its own particular part in the dance, the theatre of human expression. This two thousand odd years of altars and vestments is only a flicker in time, the brief pause given by man's abdication to ignorance to play out its part. This part being played is the hell of ourselves still eating the fruit of false knowledge in this world of demonic exertion as we live in vain hope awaiting a flicker of light through the darkness. 'She' is the one, in service to love, about to crush the head of this ignorance being served by the multitudes lost and bewildered to this bubble of mayhem. Is it not so the equilibrium is served, as the creation itself breathes in and breathes out?

We drove for two hours in beautiful silence. Words are too slow, laborious and limiting to match the infinite speed of nature expressing herself. One dark thought entered my mind and a tiny bird dived from the sky in front of the car, its life immediately extinguished. I took this as an instant warning from within. Now that I know truth I must be vigilant and guard against dwelling in my mind for the consequences will be shared by those around me. Responsibility comes with the privilege of knowing. I thank you Mary for being there to utter those words, 'Cleanse yourself as you come unto Me', for even one blemish, one stain denies access to this sacred realm.

It was a beautiful sunny morning as we drove through patches of low fog. There were no obstacles in our way and we arrived in Dublin in good time. We entered the courtroom, my father, my daughters and I, and my name was the first to be called. The policeman appearing asked the court for more time to develop his case and five weeks and six days were given. The action took less than ten minutes but the waiting continued. It now remains to be seen whether or not the charges being brought against me would be substantiated in the following court appearances.

My journey up to this point in time had taken more than five years for me to transcend this pitiful state and to take my final bow to the transient world. During that time I have struggled to make space for the accounts of the business and my personal domain to come to a final balance. But the demon's reluctance to let me go has shown itself in all the situations that occurred, from gunmen being engaged by someone unknown to take the life from this body, to my arrest under instruction of the widow. This latter event cost me the final opportunity, my hope, to amicably conclude all my business affairs. But whatever it financially costs, then so be it, as nothing more can be done. It is now solving itself, for the demon within has been slain. The widow must deal with her own, for this is how it must be, as so it appears in this story of life.

My father and daughters walked close by my side as we left the grounds of the Court and crossed over the bridge on the Liffey to immediately depart the congestion of grief expressed in that place. We returned to Clare as we had come, at peace with the midday sun and the beauty of life, as one family awakened to the omnipresence of love. All happens as it happens, pleasures and pains, glorifications and calamities. It is as it is. Why should I be horrified by the various plays of the repetitive human state? Unless of course, I am still attached to my own particular conclusion.

When I am truly the participant observer, detached from subject and object, I am pregnant with power. The mind is seen as a spreadsheet in time and the memory is recognised as a static reflex of past experience that dominates behaviour, it sticks the false notions of me and mine and I myself to this natural body. I realise that I am not just this person of joy or of woe and the one that set out as the seeker of wisdom has entered its own dissolution in the seeking. I am being dissolved by 'Me' who had imagined myself, through my own peculiar stare, to be the person with a particular personality and cause for existence that was particular to myself. Whereas in truth 'I' am beyond space and time and in contact with such only at this point of here and now in this body. All the problems in the experience of this body are all in relation to the person and the personality

I have come to serve as my psychological self. When the problem becomes great enough then I will either physically die under the strain of trying to support the image of my own particular making, or I will have to go beyond by letting go of it all, and dying within. Through my personal death I am freed from my own false belief that the psychological world is the reality. I too had been spending this life as its slave. It was known to this mind on the day I set out to be its European champion in selling financial concepts of assurance that each act has its consequences and every action has an equal and opposite reaction. All the sales hype of the Australian marketing expert spinning out the illusion inevitably led to the arrival of the Australian spiritual master.

I built the bonfire of myself. The intruder to life within the skin of this spacesuit fashioned itself on the ways of the world through the dazzling glitter of informative knowledge. When it was big enough and ready to blaze it was ignited by the Logos, as spoken through Mary, and what a burning it was. Let its flame extend to a raging inferno out through the black forests of living in blindness that is damming and damning the river of life. Let it bring light to all who are ready and willing to open within to the 'Sight'.

My journey was not planned. None of it was intentional. It was a letting go of all the supports of an image that allowed all to occur as it occurred, in space and time. It brought about the inner death of the intruder attaching itself to the psychic strings where this false personality manifests itself. The light from within that is always aglow, as is the sun, shines out in its own brilliance, once the intruder, the dark cloud, had been dissolved. But do not believe me, for believing is not true experiencing. This truth is your truth that is already yours from within, once you come to the absolute stillness of your being. It is through absolute stillness that you can understand that your immediate situation, whatever it is, is the truth of life speaking its volumes to you.

And what about the wild man who lives on the mountain with his sister who has a peculiar stare? What will be their fate? What will be yours? Will it not be according to the dark secret of the personality you support while denying your own true nature? Why am I here? Am I not here to enjoy and to be each moment the joy of life in this harmonious rhythm of being? Is it not as simple as that? It is the wilful within that has caused me to imagine myself to be the person I have become, whether twisted in pain in the midst of momentary pleasures or apparently inspired as saintly healer. Each is a contrasting measure of the same, the willfulness that causes restriction to sight. Is living as such not a terminal case?

Are there really angels? You know the kind, those portrayed in the remarkable paintings of the renaissance. Is this what we really believe? Are we still locked up in the imaginings of a now distant past, of a time that served the limitations of thought between the defined parallels of evolution as marked in the story up until then? I wonder where those images came from? Did someone actually see some of those angels floating around in space with their magnificent wings and proceed to paint an image of them. There were no cameras in those times to take an instant shot. Even if a camera were to catch the image of one of those angels right now would it really make a difference, more than the difference it made to you and I when man went for a walk on the moon?

When I am on my holidays on the sunny beaches, ski slopes, or wherever, enjoying every moment fully to each moment appearing, then I return to what I term my normal life of wishful thinking. I blindly step on the magnificent butterfly while on my hurried way, then I stop to look at the snapshots and think what a wonderful time I had in those couple of short weeks when I was fully present to each moment. But now, alas, out of it again. Can I hear it? Perhaps not, as I sit and stare at the icons, the snapshots of my holidays. I wonder why the others who had not been with me cannot see the joy I had when experiencing it. Indeed am I in the same joy as I look at the snapshots or am I just in the memory of it? What is memory in relation to life, to actual life as it is? Is there a distinction between making love in 'being love' and being in the memory as the mental impression of it? When man and woman are making love, both of them fully in the service to 'Love', it is the nearest in bodily sensation to the absolute state. Where do I usually abide as I bide my time for the next fleeting taste of the cherry? When tasting it am I in my mind equating the taste to some distant taste of the past? Where is the intelligence in this? Where has the wisdom gone? All it takes is an instant glimpse of the absolute reality to dissolve for ever all this living in memory.

Do I ever wonder why there is no historical trace of whatever greatness in understanding occurred to the intelligence on this planet, or of this planet, some thousands of short years ago? Or am I still in the short history span of yesterday? Is this my life, my ongoing preoccupation, striving with the tuneless tune of pulling sackfuls of yesterdays perpetually towards tomorrow? Will I always be just one day ahead as each day I add another yesterday to my overweight sack?

Do I notice the cat, I mean really notice the cat, as it purrs and purrs in the fullness of being? What about the birds, singing profusely for no apparent reason? Can I hear it? I mean really, really hear it, without any distance between?

Or do I hear it as, 'Oh yeah, how nice, the cat purring, the birds singing, but that does not serve my mortgage'. Well then, what does serve my mortgage?

To discover what does let us first look at the word itself. When we break it in two the first part, 'mort', in the French language means 'death', and 'gage' apparently is used in the English language as a slang word for some addictive drug. Am I drugging myself to death through debt? Is this what I am really serving? Let us not be critical of the concept of mortgage as such, as it is but part of our current expression of forced existence imposed by all on the beauty that is. The mechanics of the huge machine serve the world as a whole but I may be lost in the mechanics, a cog so to speak, in my own particular groove that I am conditioned to serve with only time out to notice the sunrise during a fleeting holiday. In the course of my life I may be spending most of my time in the forests of living confusion apart from the few occasional weeks when bathing in the river of joy. That is, of course, if I manage somehow to stay connected to the beauty during those few occasional weeks otherwise all of my life, the holiday times and all, may be lost to the confusion of living. Is it from this limitation that I continue to accept my condition, as I doodle over my now one-dimensional holiday snapshots?

Yes, I can look at the photos of those succulent dishes but I cannot taste them or smell them, or hear their crunchy sound. I cannot even touch them for now I have entered imaginings. My eyes are blinded, as is my mind's eye, to serving the memory of a static moment in a now static past. Do I ever wonder where the great intelligence of whole civilisations has disappeared? In my wondering do I stop and allow all movement to cease to amazingly discover, perhaps, that it may not have disappeared at all, rather I myself may have disappeared from 'It'?

There is a mythological tale of a savage hound that ate everything in its path and instilled the world with fear until one day it swallowed the infant son of Chu. This act brought it to the end of itself for Chu, being the fiercest warrior of all, instantly challenged the mighty hound. She thrust her right arm down its throat and out its behind whereupon she grabbed its tail and, swiftly pulling it inwards in one swift action, she turned it inside-out. Immediately her son was spotted, among everything else that had been swallowed by the savage creature that day, now openly exposed for the trembling world to see. Is this what I am doing, I the individual that I serve as myself, in swallowing everything in my path to feed this hungry bellow of 'I-know-not-what'? Must I too be turned inside-out to come to the end of it? Perhaps it is so, as so it seems, when I devour all the knowledge there is, relative to all that I think I am, in my own particular insatiable hunger. Until perchance, I see myself swallowing and find myself facing the fiercest warrior of all, one sure to turn me inside-out and bring me to the end of myself. Where then will be my imaginings as all my decaying inners dangle outside of my shell exposed to my exterior imagery world?

And that very special lover of my dreams when strolling by may suddenly exclaim, 'My God I never knew it had eaten that! And that! And had swallowed that as well?' But no, this should not happen to me. I will play it safe and be wary of what I eat and say. Mine will be a nice existence. I will preserve my talent and tuck it away, neatly and safely. Another wasted space is it not? Will 'playing it safe' lead to the door of discovery, the angelic realm as such? I must be prepared to open myself somewhat beyond my cosy beliefs of permanence for yet another wrinkle-free moment of passing. I must not get caught up exclusively in modern scientific discovery or western heaven or eastern higher self or whatever may offer a place to hide behind in fear of facing the truth of my transient self. This self lives in its singular forest of living confusion surrounding the beautiful river of the omnipresence and omniscience of 'Me'.

And where is our friend Charlie now? Let us look at his story and consider whether or not it is really any different to yours or mine when we have the courage to enter within. The last I heard he was pushing his way into adolescence and had forgone the magical essence of the trees that spoke so intimately to him in his earlier childhood days when he played alone with the mystery of nature sweetly caressing his being.

The nightmare of his childhood, the woman with the peculiar stare and her land-grabbing brother who shares her pain, have still not finished reclaiming the land. They seek to adapt it to their shifting suitings from the natural forest it was when it shared its magic with Charlie as a child. Now it is neither here nor there, field nor forest. The beauty of its previous magic is now buried beneath the anguish of the woman and Charlie. This taste of beauty, alas tarnished with her pain, now mingled in his, is perhaps Charlie's first experience of the madness of living the lie of this world. One day some beautiful young woman, perchance, will discover the key he has hidden to the treasure within as she takes him to her breast in the natural embrace of love. Both of them may come together as one in service to 'It'. Can I see it unfold, this river of life, as it flows through the dark forests of living from matter to ether to matter again? If not, then I am doomed to read it again and again as ignorance reborn for such is reincarnation, until my vision eventually clears.

This is the journey to nowhere. It is finished before it begins, as it always was it always will be for all the ones who can see. The rest of us flurry about trying to get it together as we bury ourselves in our own self importance. We serve our bellies of hunger as our bodies from childhood grow bigger and we come to believe, as ourselves we deceive, that this body is 'Me' and we hope it will last forever. Have you not noticed that it is always somebody else who dies and never myself. Intellectually I know that my time will come, but is it not always in the future? Yet when it occurs it can only be in the moment, this moment of now. This is the truth as I experience it. We scurry along, pushing everything on to tomorrow in these bodies of time. We journey from timeless to timeless until perchance the illumination occurs and I am frizzled back in through my senses.

As I step within its light I am beyond the limits of the body. I leave my attachments to the spacesuit behind. There is no need of it as there is no need for anything clinging to past, now extinct through enlightenment. My eternally ever-changing relative state enters the light of the never-changing eternal abode and it happens through 'Me', the 'Me' that is you now reading. There is but one 'Me', dear seeker of truth and within your heart 'It' abides. We as ourselves have slipped out of 'Me' into a world of our own particular making where we abandon our innocence, as what occurs in the unfolding story of Charlie. For his story is our story, the story of life in this living confusion of slipping outside of ourselves.

Matter reaching out to matter is a matter of fact. Man has walked on the moon but there was no lively atmosphere there, no hustle and bustle of day to day living, no bars or nightclubs, nothing apparent to sensory desire, so he returned to his spacecraft of matter and gave up his moon-suit to the national museum. As the mustard seed assiduously extends itself to a tree, so the scientific experiment has extended itself to its current position. In all of this changing of shapes where is the immutable?

I build a great castle, my fortress for ever, and gradually the ivy silently creeps over it after my body of bodies returns to dust having gone through the reprocessing of food for the worms. It is a hell of a job this existing in existence where everything has to be continuously repaired according to liking. I take to a new spouse, or somebody else's with the greatest of zest. I read about it all in the papers, grasping at another moment's fleeting glimpse of happiness while chasing again my illusory dream. This time it is going to work against the greatest of odds and then we amazingly shit on each others table-cloths! As if we have never done it before. Who has taken the alarm-clock? I need to wake up! So let us enter the moment, get ourselves into the rhythm of life and be fully present to experience the joy of each moment passing. Let us enter the story of the play as it being part of ourselves, as there is nothing separate, not even the illusion of we thinking there is.

Charlie is back in what remains of the forest. He is now seventeen and extremely confused. His schooling in the city has come to its end and he and all of his peers have been scattered back home now the final exams have been done. It has all been so sudden. Five years of schooling went so fast, as if it never took place. It is summer and everything is green. The wounds of the forest seem to have healed and all seems strangely normal as if its magic expression of yore was but a mid-summer's dream.

Charlie is now having problems coming to terms with the whole question of reality. Is there anything real, he ponders? Is it all but a dream? His childhood years, now centuries behind, and that magical place where three trees stood closely together all drooping with ivy that formed his magical tepee, is now less than a speck in his mind. The one tree still standing of the magical three now looks as if it has always been standing alone. It had been bought at the auction for firewood by a man who died from a sudden disease before he had time to cut it. It is larger than ever, this magnificent oak. Strange as it seems, some trees have their own way of protecting themselves. He reflects on the moment, now five years ago, when an old man had told him so.

Now Charlie is noticing that the older he gets the farther he moves away from all that freely made sense to him as a child. In those early days he accepted everything that he was told as being the absolute truth. Now the time has come where he must logically relinquish his natural acceptance of fairies and leprechauns as he edges into the adult beliefs that are rooting themselves in his rational, developing mind. Charlie is now entering the world of rational logic with its peculiar way of putting second things first. Scarcely anyone in worldly education has allowed the intellect to open to the realisation of who or what is doing the looking and thinking through all the theoretical objectivism of matter, as a matter of fact.

This is going to be a summer at home, his last opportunity to come to terms with whatever is true. He feels that when he goes to college in the fall of the year nothing will be left of his magical world. Already it is rapidly fading under the weight of worldly desires flooding his being. Even this moment at hand, in the ease of the long hot summer days, he is finding it difficult to pause. But pause he must in his effort to come into rhythm with the speed now pumping through the veins of his body and the dark shadows of worldly wants now entering his mind.

There is work to be done on the farm and his parents are pleased to have him at home among the houseful of others. Charlie is always willing to face into any task he is given without unduly complaining, as everything to him he takes as a challenge. Last week at the chapel he noticed Anne was home for the summer as well. She has grown into a beautiful young woman, as he became surprisingly aware of when she smiled his way for a moment. Now it is totally gone from him, those times some five years past, when she had a wild crush on him and he ran in acute embarrassment shrinking from the remarks of his peers. No, he is not running now, as he silently looks forward to chapel next Sunday. The thought of her shapely womanly figure close to his sends shivers up his spine. He gets on with the work at hand, mixing concrete to repair the pathway at the front of the house.

His mother is pleased with his presence and indulges herself in long and questioning conversations with him during the special tea-breaks they have together between mealtimes. This is their personal time out together. They both seem to know the fleeing swiftness of youth as the world of responsible manhood approaches to place itself on the shoulders of Charlie. Yet some of the magic remains. She gives approving attention to the miniature shelter of stone he builds out of sight of everyone but which her attentive eye has detected. He has built it beneath the laurel hedge as a gesture acknowledging the invisible friends of his childhood. His father would have no understanding of this and such does not matter to Charlie. His father's world is the world of seriousness, the world of adult responsibility where all attention is focused on work and that world is time enough to be entered.

This first week at home is a special week after having spent five years of his secondary schooling in the city. When he finished the final exams and spent that afternoon and evening celebrating with his friends they shared it with joy and sadness. The pressure was over yet their time together had ended. No one had paid much attention to this leading up to that day as all thoughts were consumed in preparing and completing exams. Their imminent separation exploded on them that evening and they all felt somewhat cheated, even Patrick, his rival with whom he had spent five years in physical contest to the point of being expelled on several occasions. Now even he was expressing feelings of warmth. It was a heart twisting moment as they broke up the revelry late in the evening battling against the emotional tear that would be a sign of weakness. Charlie had a final tussle with Patrick at the bus-stop and it felt unreal as they were both inclined to let the other win. Yes, that was the final goodbye. Only then did Charlie realise that Patrick had been as dear to him as all the others in the five years they spent together in fighting.

It is over, the speed, the shouting, the teachers, the tears and the joy. Now there is an extraordinary stillness at hand as he works at repairing the path by the hedge. Even the buzzing of five years of city noise has left his ears in less than one week, as if it was all just a dream. There is a new sound entering his awareness, the sound of the silence and he is beginning to find it even more deafening than the wild and exuberantly unrelenting sounds of his schooldays. This deafening silence, he now discovers, is immediately behind his mind of daydreams and mental thinking. It is something that has always appeared to be there but is especially obvious this week, now that his world of five years schooling has ended. It seems that everything else has just been a dream, or an image on a cinema screen and from this place of stillness he is the silent observer. Yet it all seems very consuming.

One morning in particular Charlie could not but notice the beauty about him. The sun blazed high in the sky, the birds sang and the bees hummed as he pauses in wonder after straightening his back to ease the muscles awakened by the manual working with concrete. The profusion of greens and the scent from the flowers and wild roses all weave their magic around him. This is the beauty and wonder he feels as all of its heart is flowing right through him to give him the knowledge that he is at one with all that is here to behold. This nature at work and nature at ease is the outer reflection of the ease he is feeling within. Then the voice of his mother calls, "The kettle is on, would you like some tea", in a rhythm that gently flows through the sounds of the air. Sitting with her, sharing the taste of the home-made butter on freshly baked bread, is the most succulent joy. There is a special moment of sharing the tasting, for now the pressure of not having time for life has temporally gone. Each day is long without the rushing to school or studying for exams in the ways of the man-made world.

This is the start of a long hazy summer as he gives all of himself back into the nature that nurtured him so as a child. He discovers he is now closely aware of the abundance of life in this blossoming of nature, even the attention to detail being expressed in the beautiful perfection in the wild flowers of the meadows with perfumes so faint, as he lingers in stillness to receive them. His heart misses a beat each time he thinks of the blooming of Anne, the beautiful young woman she is, still feeling a tingle of excitement towards him as he instantly noticed in her smile at the chapel. Through the joy of the week he eagerly awaits their next meeting.

Then his father is calling. There is serious work to be done with moving some cattle. No time to notice the call of the curlew as evening draws in, with this job of consuming importance at hand, or the sound of the blackbird flying low by the hedges as day turns to night. Even the beautiful sunset of purple and red, blazing the western sky, seems to go unnoticed by all but Charlie. The cattle are herded and their pastures are changed for the world of his father still appears to only have acknowledgement for work.

Yet through it all there is a tingling excitement in his veins, an anticipation of sorts, like being at the edge of a volcano. All he can do is silently await for whatever it is that is about to come over his horizon. The future of change is upon him and he is acutely aware that the time he is sharing with his family will be gone for ever once this summer ends. Each moment is precious as they return from the fields in the moonlight, his father, himself and the dogs. Few words are spoken, as he lingers with the burning awareness within, while savouring the sensation of Anne. The dogs rise a hare and with furious barking disappear out of sight, down into the valley, across open fields, through the shadows of trees and into the darkness of night. The silence again returns beyond the sound of his footsteps.

Soon they are home and supper is ready. Fresh lettuce, young beetroot, onions from the garden and slices of home-cured ham decorate the table with the freshness of life ready for tasting. All the family are present. The tales of the day from the ones back from town send the laughter so gay into the walls of the house to join with the previous re-echoes. Indeed each night is a joy without questioning why. Charlie takes to his pen and poetry and some times he finds himself wishing that it should never end. Deep in his heart though he knows that once he steps out of this magic to start in college at the end of this summer it will be gone forever. For such is the fleeting story of life that he suddenly discovered when saying goodbye to his friends after the final exams at school. Now he is aware that he is almost at the realisation of his dream of becoming a man.

On this particular night it is warm and heavy as the family retires to sleep. Charlie is feeling the weight of his blankets and soon he removes them all but one. Still he is too hot for comfort. He is aware of a strange energy in the air as he lies in wait for the increasing heat to reach its crescendo. Then the storm breaks, lightening explodes in the sky followed by a shattering banging of thunder that seems to consume the house.

Everyone is awakened and the younger sister is scared out of her wits as a second explosion occurs right over the roof. The heavens open and the rain comes furiously down. There is confusion in the home as the thunder and lightening continues for over an hour with the rain still increasing in volume. It is well past midnight and now everyone in the household are wide awake. Windows are closed and stillness pursued lest the nervous energy of the family become a magnet for the storm. Everyone is up and sharing the fear, except his father of course, who is content in getting on with his sleeping.

Charlie is gazing out his bedroom window enthralled by the strange magnificence of it all, each flashing ball lights up the night sky, until it gradually fades out over the distant hills. Then an uneasy calmness follows. The house settles back into sleep to the background noise of distant rumbling as the night storm moves on. But Charlie is actively awake. It has become impossible to sleep. All tiredness has vanished with the presence of a sharp energy that spurns him to write, as these are his best moments of expression. It is still raining outside, increasing in volume then easing again in a rhythm like breathing. He takes to his pen and his hand can hardly keep up with the speed of the words flooding through. Then he hears his mother's light being switched off. She is an avid reader and when she has an interesting book it can hold her attention until sunrise. Now there is silence. He returns to his pillow and eases into the darkness of night. Sleep re-enters his being in tune with a gentle thought of his bed being a boat on an ocean of soft rippling waters. There is none other but he on this ocean and all of the creation returns back into the vacuum of stillness that Charlie savours within.

The story continues as we enter the dream when the body re-awakens from its natural sleep. Yet as morning begins and turns into day, then evening followed by night, is there any change within for those who are the bearers of Light? Let all who are mentioned in the telling of this tale be touched by the magic of Heart. Who am I? Is 'It' still unknown? Godspeed to you on your journey beyond the dark corridors of worldly ignorance through the terrors of the inner self. Godspeed to you on your quest to discover the realm within. Godspeed to stillness.

Chapter 34

SATSANG

Catherine returned to Ireland to give nine evenings of dharma dialogues in Dublin. She arrived for the next climacteric of this story being told, although the climacteric of every expression of life is perpetually present when the present as usually perceived is turned outside-in. In all our reshaping and changing of the taste and the texture of these forms of life is not each moment the conclusion of each moment past? When it is seen that 'All is One' what can be there to conclude? Even in the relative world the falling of the seed from the tree is the ongoing process in the re-making of itself where life is perpetually present. The illumination is the clarity of vision so I can be in this presence of endless life.

This is 'satsang', an unfolding of the veils of darkness from our cyclical eyes. This Sanskrit expression as adopted by the American West means a coming together in oneness, as being in the company of saints, or in association with 'Truth'. This is known to those who have entered through the proverbial eye of the needle yet the tingling sensation of this inner knowledge is open to all of us swallowed in worldly affairs should we offer our intensity of time to the silence. This inner silence can even be present while the body is absorbed in action. There must be inner stillness to see what is infinitely beyond mind. We must relax our chronic possession with the ongoing clattering of thoughts. One needs to re-discover the perennial silence behind this noisy, cascading disturbance that we falsely assume to be our true nature. This I discovered through my own experience. The state of 'Being' is stillness. This stillness can be immediately discerned when the mind is empty and free yet it can only be fully realised when one is free of all attachments.

In the merriment and tribulations of the dance of life through this story unveiling, the earnest seeker of wisdom may come to acknowledge the awesomeness of the inner silence, the 'satsang' of one's being, that is in truth the essence of God forever as one within us. It is this oneness, this one without another, this universality of 'I', the one and only 'I' in the universality of all that there is, that is the eye of the needle, and the first transcendence beyond all our imposed limitations.

Catherine had offered me the privilege of meeting her arrival at Shannon Airport on the Sunday of whit-weekend. She was to spend one night in the house in Clare that was now at the focal point of the ongoing dilemma spinning about me. Here I had been silently sitting in the eye of the tornado for almost a year, each moment in the presence of 'now' in the stillness of being, as even one step outside the moment was presenting itself as a trip to immediate insanity. This was not by choice, for anything other than this had been denied to me by the circumstances of my life, that are but the reflection of this self of myself that had been brought to this state of frozen reality.

Many years previous I had earnestly called to life through the challenge from the spiritual master when I uttered those words from my heart asking 'Life' to take from me everything that was necessary in order to make me pure in this body. Then it was all so sudden, so swift, yet an eternity in the pain of the burning. I had asked in sincerity for the truth, not knowing when I asked that to be in the truth is to pass through the end of the world of myself. That is not to deny the world its place for all of this world at the sensory side of ourselves is also a part in the oneness. But to come to the knowledge of truth I had first to see and acknowledge the illusion. I had called to 'Life' to show me its light so I could place my tamasic finger in this mortal wound in my side. Was it not 'Life' responding through the hand of the widow that had inflicted this mortal wound to the worldly side of myself? Had I not, through worldly success, denied all that was love? In my denial of love I had abdicated my seat of integrity. The widow, in the fire of her passion, was obliged to seek manipulative ways in order to awaken me to this truth of myself. In the story unfolding is not the widow the deliverer of truth, the instrument of 'Life' in all of her fury? This is the awesome awakening. My passage through the death of this egotistical self came after being brought to my senses by the fire of the widow's passion, in essence, the Goddess of Love.

Everything in one's life is relative to the whole and as one moves closer to the point of reality then the finer parts of the whole relative to the truth of the entire situation unfolding become clearer. This is well illustrated by the coincidence some days before Catherine arrived. I received a phone call from the young woman from the east coast of Ireland whom I had first met at the funeral service of her husband, as recalled at the opening of this story. She was coming to Clare to be with me for the holiday weekend together with her children and the man now in her life, along with his sister and her family as well. This was the first time she had responded to an invitation I had previously given to her and it coincided with Catherine's arrival. The approaching weekend of assumed stillness with Catherine was now taking on its own course of direction. She was about to meet in person with the wife and children of the deceased brother of Mary whose funeral service had brought me in line with the immortal arrow of

'Truth'.

The beginning and ending are one and the same. It had been the arrow through the Logos, as the piercing word coming through Mary, that had first brought me to heel. My loveless personality of temporary worldly acclaim was brought to its end through the relentless force of the widow. Mary sparked the fire within me, the presence of the spiritual master provided the space and the fury of the widow provided the fuel for the flame. This is 'Life' responding and the hand of 'Love' being expressed.

'Satsang' through the remarkable nature of Catherine had commenced in me even before she arrived in person. Although I had not been back to Dublin for several months my legal council now required my regular attendance and these visits coincided with Catherine's calendar of dharma dialogues in the city. Each day of legal attendance consisted of intensive interrogation to unravel the complicated web of distortion that had become the tornado spinning itself about me. Afterwards I spent each evening sitting in silence with Catherine and all of those present. I sat in the illumination of 'She' through the shining countenance of 'woman' sitting in stillness before me. It was from this stillness that my circumstantial web began to unwind.

During this time I was still obligated to make my daily appearance to the local police station in County Clare. In the middle of the first week of attendance as I was being driven to the railway station by a good friend to catch the morning train from Dublin to Clare I was unexpectedly delayed when we had to change a wheel. As a result I missed the train and had to pass two hours in the station waiting for the next one. This did not cause me undue concern at the time, for everything is as it is, when we come to accept whatever situation that life places before us.

The later train was considerably empty and I sat in the

freshness of a non-smoking carriage. But then the unusual occurred. When the train pulled away from its first stop at Newbridge a nervous young man came into the near-empty carriage and sat on the seat across the centre aisle from where I was sitting. I could not help but notice him as I immediately became aware of his nervous energy, his roughly unshaven appearance, his lack of purpose in direction and the strong smell of stale tobacco from his clothes. It bore the appearance of an unexpected journey for him away from the familiar surrounds of the drug comforts of his native Dublin, as could be plainly read from the jittery unease in his body. After a few minutes I also noticed, through the corner of my eye, his apprehensive staring at me as I sat silently reading a book. Then he did a very curious thing and the wonder arose as to why this man was sitting across from me in a non-smoking carriage? He placed a stubbed cigarette on the table in front of him quite obviously in desperate need of a smoke. Yet all he needed to do was to move a few carriages down and he would be in a smoking compartment. I let it pass as the text of the book that I was reading was absorbing more of my attention.

Later when the train pulled into Portarlington another man got on board, also a smoker from the smell of his clothes, and sat in the seat directly facing the first man. They remained for a little while as though they were strangers and I found it more than peculiar that both of them, smokers as such, should not only be sitting in a non-smoking carriage but sitting together when most of the seats in the carriage were empty. This second man, unlike the first, was silently calm and assertive when he boarded the train. He had deliberately sought out the seat facing the other and while placing his carrier bag directly in the rack above him had intentionally not looked my way. Unwilling to acknowledge these ominous signs I continued to read, refusing to acknowledge the intuitive side of myself.

After a few minutes the first one started to open conversation with the other as though they were strangers, although it became obvious to me they were not. Their texture of speaking when they mentioned the 'Joy' and some names of inmates in that prison personally known to each of them gave them away. Still their words of exchange were brief for the second man seemed eager to sit in silence as he stared out the window in an unassuming manner while making a conscious effort to not give me any particular attention. But I could instinctively feel through his deliberate control in not looking directly my way that he was, nonetheless, acutely focused on my movements. It was as though he was psyching out the level of receptivity about my presence. Was this my own imagination taking over the scene? I pondered as I continued to doubt the ominous signs being given.

A story that Catherine had once told came into my mind about the ignorance of a man who had expected his god to save him from drowning when his house and his village were flooded. The waters continued to rise and he was forced to seek refuge on his roof. Then a rescue party came by in a boat but he refused their offer of assistance as he had placed trust that his god would save him. Yet the flooding continued and he was eventually obliged to climb onto the chimney where he waited in shivering hope. A helicopter came by and a basket on a rope was dropped towards him to save him. Again he refused telling them that he had placed all of his trust in his lord. The rains continued to fall and eventually swallowing the chimney itself and the wretched man was drowned. When his spirit turned up at the gates of his heaven he cried out to his god, "Did I not fully believe in you? Did I not place all of my hope in you? How could you have forsaken me so?" "I did not forsake you," spoke the voice of his god in reply, "Did I not send you a boat and a helicopter?"

I sat silently amused in myself as I recalled this tale and the train pulled out of Portlaoise station. Then I noticed the second man looking intently at me as I caught his reflection in the window. If I should continue my reading without giving due consideration to my instincts I would be as the foolish man in the story. I began to suspect that this man was a hired killer and I determined that I would have to test the situation to discern the intuitive from the imaginative. If what I suspected was true it was probable that the first man had spotted me at the station in Dublin when I was waiting for this second train and had passed on the message of my whereabouts. It would then have been his task to travel with me to identify me to the assassin. It is a fact that such people deliberately scout railway stations as spotters.

As the train approached the next station, Templemore, I closed the book and put it into the green canvas carrier bag I had on the table in front of me. I began to take note of how I appeared to the eyes of this stranger. The presence of such a bag was much out of place with the business suit, shirt and tie I was wearing. As the train slowed down I gave the appearance in body that I was about to get off. In response the second man also moved, folded his paper and placed himself in preparation to leave. When the train came to a halt I did not stir and neither did he.

Was it becoming like Catherine's story of the foolish man still refusing to acknowledge the obvious signs of eminent danger? Nonetheless, I felt that I still needed to give the situation the benefit of the doubt in my mind. I took out my book and continued to read but I kept my right hand resting on the open zip of the bag. The situation continued unchanged until the train came to a complete stop at the next station, Thurles. This time I gave no indication that I was likely to move. Both men were relaxed and not stirring. It was obvious that neither were planning on getting out at this stop. To clarify the situation once and for all I suddenly got up and walked off the train at the rear of the carriage. The platform was relatively busy with passengers getting off and others boarding for Limerick as I briskly walked back the length of two carriages. Then I stopped and swiftly turned in the manner that I had been trained as a youth in military fashion. He was on the platform behind me, having alighted from the other end of the carriage but instead of walking towards the station exit he was walking in my direction. From the look of dismay on his face I could see that he had nowhere left to disguise his intent. I stood and faced him with my carrier bag resting on my folded arm and we both looked, in amazement, directly into each others gaze. I had no idea or thought in my mind as we stood for that moment alert and poised, in total connection with each other through our eyes. Both of us instinctively knew a choice was being given by this turn of events. The play between us could end there and then with either one of us dead, or we could abort from this confrontation and depart our different ways instead. The moment had become a frozen pause with neither of us willing to make the next move. The signal that the train doors were about to close was given and I took it as the cue to break the deadlock. I stepped back on board without taking my eyes from his and he stepped back and rested his shoulder against the station wall. He half looking away, yet held me in the side of his vision.

I could see how professional he was as he knew he had no reasonable alternative but to give up the chase. I could also see how clear he was with his task. He had been called out at short notice to carry out this assassination. He was assertively still in his mind and free from all emotional attachment. I saw the open amazement in his eyes that he had been met with similar alertness, in similar clarity of mind. There was neither fear nor emotion present to mar our mutual acceptance of the moment through the silence of all that was spoken between us. All his movements were with an ease and a swiftness that were fully aligned. The space between us was spotlessly clear with an unspoken understanding of life and death while the people about us were unaware of the scene as they hurried along in their personal worlds.

The train continued its journey to Limerick and I was now seated some carriages back from the first man still on board. But this one was under the suppression of fear and posed no threat. When we eventually arrived in Limerick I walked up the platform directly behind him. If there happened to be others waiting I felt this was my safest position. He spotted an elderly woman and asked her for a light. I stood beside him and waited until a person close to her obliged. Then he scurried around the corner and joined the bus queue for Ennis. There was no point in taking this any further, even though it was obvious that he was the one who had spotted me at the train station in Dublin and had travelled to Limerick with the singular task of pointing me out to the assassin. I was thankful to be still alive and it was not their fault that my situation was as it was. They were merely acting out the type of living that they had chosen to live and it was the circumstances of my own life that had brought us together.

I was amazed at the calmness and ease in my body throughout the entire experience. But we must not be deceived by the surface signs of our actionable selves. When I later met and spoke with my father I found that my voice had dropped several octaves. In the world of cause and effect all is causal and effectual it seems, even when we foolishly think it is not, especially at those moments of astute assertiveness when we are most likely to miss the finer discerning message being stated.

At the following meeting with my legal council I felt obligated to inform them of this occurrence for someone outside of myself needed to be aware of the danger still imminent. Nothing else could be done for the moment. I interpret these events as the second remarkable coincidence of open expression during this time of 'satsang' with Catherine. During my previous two encounters with killers I was riddled with fear. On this one, the third, all that occurred, occurred in stillness. There was no panic, no emotion, no fear whatsoever in this moment of clarity and precision. I had been physically presented with the object of my previous fear, the hired assassin, and had discovered the beauty in the oneness of essence in his eyes. There was no distance between us, no personal me conjuring the other as an object of concern and there was no emotion in him as he moved with open exactitude.

In that moment we were as two actors on the stage of life's performance, separate, but together in the oneness of the scene. This, I can say, is 'satsang' as I know it expressed through the stillness of being. In the intensity of the moment when faced by this hired killer I found that our mutual connection with the oneness allowed the communion of 'Truth' to happen between us. It seemed as though the occurrence was embraced with divine precision. But do not believe me or indeed anyone else on such matters. It can only be known in the truth of oneself, where life actually is, and everything other that this is but a reflection. Whatever I am I must meet in the world that is but the manifestation of myself about me.

During the following meeting with my legal council, the District Attorney's office placed a request through my solicitors for another adjournment of the approaching date for the court hearing. I did not deny their request although it was by now a year since my arrest and everything they needed to know about me and all these affairs they already knew. In any case the matter was settled before I arrived in Court. On the following morning, Friday the thirteenth, four extra months were given to the state to prepare their case and my ongoing bail obligation of reporting daily to my local police station was reduced to once per week. It began to appear that all concerned was placing the matter in the hands of time for dissolution. The circumstances were beginning to be seen as they were and not through the distortion of convenient interpretation.

Man must live by possibilities alone. This to one's own self is true. No matter how certain we may seem to be with our securities of exteriorisation we can never be sure that we will be here in the next moment to enjoy them, or indeed to avail from them the solution for yesterday's problems. The token gesture of acknowledgement from the state in reducing my obligation of reporting to my local police station from daily to once per week had given me an unexpected freedom. This allowed me time to attend four day seminars with the Australian master who was visiting England shortly after Catherine's departure from Dublin. Then the third coincidence occurred. When I was about to board the plane I had occasion to phone my friend who had come to my assistance that night on the Wicklow mountains when I had been in terror of losing my life. This is the friend who had sought out assistance from someone he knew who might try to make contact with the hired killers who were intent on killing me. This someone he knew, whom I had never met, had given me good advise through him. Now he was attending this man's funeral as I phoned him on my way to the spiritual master. The man had himself been shot dead by an assassin a few days previous. It is a terrible sadness and a terrible waste.

Is it not so in the chronic madness of the world that we foolishly spend all of our moments churning our yesterdays gone waiting in hope for the expectant tomorrow? In the foolishness of all the rushing and seeking of solutions nothing can change as each tomorrow slips by into another yesterday locked up in the madness. We must step outside of our usual selves, outside of the incessant mayhem, as the detached observer and look from that place of silent looking without making movement or comment. This, apparently, takes extraordinary courage, but it is the only way out. Otherwise one is obliged to stay in the perpetual churning of the lunacy that most of us take to be the norm in this system of living that we seem to be continuously wrapping around our world-weary eyes.

In facing the truth of the situation it is knowledgeable to see that we live by possibilities alone. It can only be in the stillness that we might connect with the opportunities at hand. These are not the apparent worldly opportunities that can never be other than the problems they are for each 'opportunity' has its root in the problem being fed. When one openly looks at the state of one's life this can be seen. In the external world of deceiving ourselves everything is relative. We endlessly stumble from cause to effect and then the effect is the cause of the next one arising. In this perplexity of living there is no opportunity and what momentarily appears as such is merely another illusion. It is so that we seem to be endlessly serving our problems.

The opportunity I speak of is immediate to all who are ready to let go of everything, absolutely everything, that one clings to in worldly support of oneself. You can feel it within, this deathly grip of holding, of clinging to one's image, one's wealth, opinions, convictions, one's religious beliefs, all bound up in the pitiful personality that one sees as oneself. We rob and we plunder, we torture, we maim, all in the name of progress. We polish our image and conveniently distance it from the front face of the truth in the system of things that is the reflection of our contemptible selves about us. In the perpetual spinning of this darkness there are no opportunities for the corpses we are, in the turmoil of our sensory world deluding ourselves from our own putrid stench. This is the actuality we are faced with. That is, of course, if one has the courage to face up to the truth of oneself. We are born, we live, and we die, without asking the reason why. It is as if the societal illusion has an automated production of bodies endlessly serving itself. For the rare few who dare to challenge the system of things by asking a pertinent question, Who am I?, numerous religious convictions spring up in service to the illusion. It is as if an inbuilt mechanism, a release valve as such, has been programmed into the system. Even if we see the falseness in our rigid beliefs we hurry to adopt some others rather than face the actual truth. This net of deception we serve is as the gladiatorial net thrown over this wondrous earth. The mind that is mad is getting madder and madder through this exteriorisation of self in this western scientific world of measurement. The quality of life as such is being dragged through the hollow nets of quantity yet quantity is in the realm of limitation while quality is the essence of 'Being'.

Looking back I can see that eerie night in Galway city when I, the child-man laying on my bed, awoke to that putrid presence forcing itself upon my body. Did I not see it then pushing its psychic hell into this blood of life, drinking its fill from the quality of youthful innocence? Was this not my first realisation when the foul breath of the demon entered this body? Even though the innocence had uttered those words for it to be gone yet it managed to take part possession, raping its quality and quantifying it becoming part of the masses endlessly spilling onto the crowded streets of lust, of greed, of insatiable hunger. The demon had entered, had arose from within the depths of the psyche, and all but extinguished the light. I entered this forest of living as part of this human condition and so I continued in this wretched hell of myself lost to the illusion until the Logos, the God-sound of divine intervention, entered this tomb of darkness. It is so the re-awakening occurred.

As I passed through the spiritual master I realised I had passed through myself. The demon was myself as is every self sucking from the blood of life. Having crossed over the threshold, having passed through the psychological and emotional death of myself, I was freed from the pits of the abyss. But do not trust me in what I am saying for what I am saying cannot be said. This understanding of truth can only be made known to you in your experience.

'Satsang', meditation, communication, prayer meetings, masters, mystical experience, all have their place in space and time. Yet behind it all is this absolute communion in 'Me', this 'Me' that you are, eternally are. In this communion within, the answers to all our questions can be instantly known. But do not believe me or anyone else who may be telling their story. Are we not here to experience the truth for ourselves? Let 'It' be so. Let your truth be served.

By devotion he knows 'Me' in truth,
What and who 'I' am;
Then having known 'Me' in truth,
He forthwith enters into 'Me'.

Bhagavad Gita XVIII 55